# MODERN AMERICAN HISTORY ★ A Garland Series

Edited by
FRANK FREIDEL
Harvard University

# CHANGING IDEAS ABOUT WOMEN IN
# THE UNITED STATES, 1776–1825

## Janet Wilson James

Garland Publishing, Inc.
New York & London ★ 1981

**Library of Congress Cataloging in Publication Data**

James, Janet Wilson, 1918–
 Changing ideas about women in the United States, 1776–1825.

 (Modern American history)
 Thesis (Ph.D.)—Harvard University, 1954.
 Bibliography: p.
 1. Women—United States—Public opinion—History.
2. Public opinion—United States—History.   I. Title.
II. Series.
HQ1418.J35   1982     305.4′2′0973     80-8474
ISBN 0-8240-4858-X                      AACR2

All volumes in this series are printed on acid-free,
250-year-life paper.
Printed in the United States of America

# C O N T E N T S

INTRODUCTION: RECOLLECTIONS OF A VETERAN IN WOMEN'S HISTORY

The work that follows, completed in 1954, will be
familiar to many scholars who have borrowed the dissertation copy on interlibrary loan. I am grateful to Garland
Publishing for making it available in print. Studies published since the explosion of interest in women's history
in the late 1960s have added new information and new dimen-
sions to our understanding, throwing the limitations of
this older work into relief. Yet it is still authoritative
as an account of a body of opinion about women's nature and
role that found favor with the American reading public
during the first half-century after independence. It also
constitutes a connecting link in the historiography of the
field, as one of the few examples of women's history
scholarship from the generation preceding the present one,
when feminism was at a low ebb and social history emerging
from its formative stage.

The study is reproduced in its original form, with the
addition of this introductory essay and an index. The essay
is an attempt to describe informally the environment in
which the book was conceived and written and may have some
intrinsic value for those interested in the field of women's
history.

It may be of interest to begin with to know how a
doctoral candidate came to work in women's history in those
unpropitious years.  In 1945 probably nowhere but at
Harvard would she have been steered into such a topic, and
nowhere else would its viability as a contribution to
knowledge and a springboard into the profession have been
taken for granted.  Arthur M. Schlesinger's students were
all aware of his long-standing interest in women's history.
Within the profession he had pioneered in the definition
and synthesis of social history, and women's role had been
one of the New Viewpoints in American History he had proposed in an influential book of 1922.  He had few women
students: only four among his seventy-two Ph.D.s.  It was
therefore no surprise to anybody when I headed in that
direction.

Privately I had doubts, a real urge to find out about
women in the past competing with an uneasy feeling that the
subject was out of the mainstream, not one a man would have
chosen, and therefore second-class.  But Schlesinger's professional eminence and the weight of his personality allowed
little doubt as to the wisdom of the undertaking.  It was
decided that I would investigate the antebellum era, building upon Elisabeth Dexter, Mary Benson, and Julia Spruill's
work on women in early America.[1]

---

1 Dexter, Colonial Women of Affairs (Boston, 1924); Benson,
  Women in Eighteenth-Century America: A Study of Opinion

After only a week or two of reading, my misgivings evaporated. The literature in the field was very scanty, and I could see that I had embarked on an exciting voyage of discovery. In my pre-teens I had consumed narratives about polar explorers and compiled a scrapbook, inspired by reading in the newspapers in 1930 about the Arctic discovery of the remains of the lost Andrée expedition of 1897. At age eleven there had appeared to be little opportunity for a girl in exploring. At twenty-six, a voyage into the history of women seemed likely not only to produce a dissertation and that important first book but to continue for a scholarly lifetime.

Thus I plunged, in the then approved manner, innocent of preconceptions, hypotheses, or models, into the sea of printed sources. But the grand survey of ideas about women, as I framed the title in the limited vocabulary then current, was never written. After two years of research I returned with masses of material and many questions to Dexter, Benson, and Spruill. But I had moved from descriptive social history into a tentative sort of intellectual history, and the explanations I needed weren't there. My efforts to find them gradually turned into this study of opinion before 1825, sufficient for a dissertation but too slight for a book in the market of 1954.

---

and Social Usage (New York, 1935); Spruill, Women's Life and Work in the Southern Colonies (Chapel Hill, 1938).

The rest of that decade went into family concerns. Bringing up a son and a daughter merged into the creation, during the 1960s, of a reference work, Notable American Women, 1607-1950 -- edited with my husband -- and the development of the Arthur and Elizabeth Schlesinger Library on the History of Women in America, as its third director. In 1971 I began teaching American social history and women's history at Boston College. Thinking again about research of my own, I confronted the boxes of notes on antebellum women and my old hopes. But social history, social science, and the feminist impulse were writing new programs. The time for my survey, based largely on prescriptive writings, had passed. In the end I abandoned my relic and joined the new generation.

As I made my way through the American Ladies' Magazine and Godey's Lady's Book, back during that first year of research, I discovered that the debate which I was tracking in the mid-nineteenth century was still going on in the middle of the twentieth. Philip Wylie's Generation of Vipers (1942), a wartime satire on our national materialism, lambasted the American mother as a greedy emotional parasite. Members of the armed forces participating in off-duty education programs were encouraged to discuss the question "Do You Want Your Wife to Work after the War?"; Elmo Roper conducted a survey for Fortune magazine in 1946

on the same issue. The next year the best-selling <u>Modern</u>
<u>Woman: The Lost Sex</u> warned that social health depended on
woman's fulfillment of her sexual role; this fitted the
postwar mood and was interesting to many as their introduction to Freud. Margery Wilson, a popular authority on
etiquette and charm, declared ambiguously that "a real
woman, wants to fill the need of a mate who exercises the
age-old authority in their relationship," even though
"many men . . . can't tell the difference between authority
and tyranny."[2]

That same year the American Academy of Political and
Social Science for the third time in the twentieth century
published a book-length research study on the sex, <u>Women's</u>
<u>Opportunities and Responsibilities</u>, "to assist the public
in forming an intelligent and accurate opinion." Its
editor, Louise M. Young, reflected that changes in the
status of women could not be "measured in terms of victor-
ies won or rights established. . . . " She pointed as an
example to the field of education, where women had equal
opportunity with men but were "denied all but the most
meager opportunities for social usefulness in the professional fields to which most education is directed."

---

2 "Do You Want Your Wife to Work after the War?" (Washington: War Department, 1944); Ferdinand Lundberg and
  Marynia Farnham, <u>Modern Woman: The Lost Sex</u> (New York,
  1947); Wilson, <u>How to Make the Most of Wife</u> (Philadelphia, 1947).

Freedom and equality, she said, were states of mind; their
realization for women was being impeded by cultural mores.[3]

Discovering such parallels between past and present
added zest to the pursuit of scholarship but complicated
one's life. In the forties most of us believed that our
rights had been won and those tiresome old issues laid to
rest. Women had joined the world of men and therefore were
equal. In my middle-class universe (the WASP one that we
who belonged to it still thought of as the norm), we tended
to assume that convention and the status quo were normalcy.
The kind of change that was to come with the affluent sixties lay beyond the ken of a generation battered by depres-
sion and a second world war. Social and sexual mores had
been stabilized. Blacks were still Negroes or even negroes,
their disabilities largely ignored by the white community.
A minority meant the losing side in a vote.

That was the day of the one-career family. The husband had the career, and the wife was the support force:
aide and adviser, household manager and director of the
family. Perhaps it seemed like equality because besides
having the vote we shared authority at home. In the postwar years most young wives of my generation were supplementing the benefits of the GI bill with their earnings to

---

3 Young, ed., Women's Opportunities and Responsibilities,
  American Academy of Political and Social Science,
  Annals, 251 (May, 1947), inside front cover, viii.

put their husbands through graduate school and looking
forward to the time when they could stop working and start
their families. One had the impression not so much that
they had consciously given up the development of their own
intellect and talents as that no one had given any thought
to the matter. Many academic wives, in that day before
public and private foundation grants, became expert research
assistants, editors, and typists, without recognition other
than often heartfelt tributes in husbands' prefaces.

In the women's colleges which had been my habitat
since the 1930s undergraduates seldom made long-term plans
for employment or self-support. Many got excellent leadership experience in student activities, which in later years
they put to use in volunteer community work. We tended to
be passive in class and had little intellectual dialogue
of our own. There was no such thing as a feminist on my
campus. A small core of radical opinion subsisted among
scholarship students living in cooperative dormitories.
The chief leaven in campus intellectual and political life,
they promoted such causes as pacifism, labor organization,
and the popular-front American Student Union. The women's
colleges routinely saluted distinguished women in the professions or public life with honorary degrees but were not
heard to worry about the small percentage of their alumnae
in these walks of life or occupying seats of power anywhere.
Power was not publicly mentioned any more than sex.

Subconsciously we felt that the price of success in the public as in the private world was feminine grace and accommodating ladylike behavior.

At most of the women's colleges, half or more of the faculty were women, including a generous number of scholar-professors, unforgettable teachers. If they produced major original work, like Mildred Campbell of Vassar, Nellie Neilson of Mount Holyoke, or Marjorie Nicolson of Smith, they were recognized in the profession -- even, in Nicolson's case, advanced to a major university post -- though they remained on the social sidelines at professional meetings. Most poured their energy into teaching and college affairs and seldom published; in explanation it was sometimes observed that they did not have supportive wives to keep house, help in research, and care for aged relatives. Little note was taken of the fact that men often did not publish much either. Women professors often shared living quarters; we did not discuss their sex life, assuming that they had none.

The small number of married women faculty had a special glamor; a pregnant professor, an astounding rarity, was the subject of warm and sympathetic student interest. Married women pursued academic life, however, under considerable handicap. The mores did not encourage mothers of small children to pursue a career; they experienced long delays in completing dissertations, degrees, and books, and

sometimes their courage flagged. Few dropped out permanently, but when they returned to employment it was usually
not to a place on the academic ladder. Holding subordinate
and untenured jobs in research, editing, and administration,
often part-time, they enjoyed the change from home, using
their talents, and supplementing the family income, and
took for granted, most of the time, the fact that they got
less recognition and pay than their work warranted.

Most professional women, in my observation, are feminists to some degree, whether or not they have a movement
to belong to. The ideology one developed in the forties
was highly practical, subservient to convention, and centered on the needs of women of the same class and color.
Family or literary role models could be predisposing influences. A tradition central in my mother's family was the
experience of her grandmother, a Congressman's widow who
had brought up five children in the 1870s and 1880s with
the aid of the postmastership in an Oregon frontier town.
As a child I had recognized a kindred spirit in Louisa
Alcott; in high school I responded to Jane Austen and Vera
Brittain. Testament of Youth (1933) was my introduction
to modern feminism, but I recovered this memory only when
rereading the book after its dramatization on TV in 1980.
Certainly I encountered no women's movement to associate with. In the thirties and forties moral crusades and

emotional appeals were under suspicion. The idealism of
World War I now appeared to have been naiveté, its rallying slogans an exercise in propaganda. Hitler and Musso-
lini's harangues had turned suspicion into alarm. The
aftermath of the prohibition crusade had been particularly
disillusioning for those who had believed that this reform,
so long associated with women and religion (read Protestantism) would be a cure for all society's ills. Women's suffrage had not realized its promise either.

Worst of all, the split in the ranks of the former
suffragists, and the ensuing bitter struggles between the
sponsors of the Equal Rights Amendment and the devoted
defenders of special protection for women workers, had left
feminism in the possession of the National Woman's Party,
thus discrediting it in the eyes of the other side. The
term and its concepts had taken on distasteful connotations
and were actually disavowed by women in public life who
were still deeply concerned with women's issues.[4] Many of
the former suffragists, too, had been exhausted by the red-
baiting attacks of the twenties on women active in the
pacifist, labor, and social welfare causes. And by the
forties even the younger suffrage veterans were advancing
in age.

Women intellectuals, adopting the currently popular

---

4 See, for instance, Susan Ware, Beyond Suffrage: Women in
the New Deal (Cambridge, 1981), 16.

economic interpretation of history, could even reject their crusading foremothers. Dorothy Canfield Fisher, whose parents had both been ardent feminists, in 1939 expressed mixed feelings in a reference to "the chip-on-the-shoulder attitude of the bold and free spirits in my mother's generation," whose work "to give women a fairer show in the activities of modern life," she said, had actually been unnecessary since economic forces would have brought about the same changes "without any help from feminists." Mary Beard, invited by the male president of Vassar to discuss her book On Understanding Women (1930) before a faculty meeting, was shocked by her reception. The "women teachers cried as if with one voice: 'The time has come to forget women! Now we are winning equality with men. We are becoming human beings.'"[5]

Two groups kept a remnant of feminism before the public in the long lull between the suffrage victory in 1919 and the gathering of new forces in the 1960s. The hard core of National Woman's Party veterans single-mindedly persisted in their advocacy of the Equal Rights Amendment, making few converts but keeping up their political connections. Another more fragmented group concentrated on promoting women's history, by writing and by

---

5 Fisher to Harry Emerson Fosdick, May 16, 1939, in Mary Beard Collection, Schlesinger Library; Ann J. Lane, Mary Ritter Beard: A Sourcebook (New York, 1977), 56.

building collections of historical materials.

Rosika Schwimmer appears to have taken the first steps toward the safeguarding of records. A refugee from Hungary with papers in her possession documenting feminist struggles in early twentieth-century Europe, Schwimmer gave Mary Beard the idea of a world center for women's archives.[6] Miriam Holden, a National Woman's Party adherent, collected printed works about women of all countries. By giving her papers to Radcliffe College, Maud Wood Park, who had directed the Congressional suffrage lobby in the last, ultimately victorious years, provided the foundation for today's Arthur and Elizabeth Schlesinger Library. Mary Beard played a part in the early history of both this repository and the Sophia Smith Collection at Smith College.

Women's history continued to find readers. The momentum of the suffrage movement carried over into the early thirties. Alice Ames Winter retired from the presidency of the General Federation of Women's Clubs to write The Heritage of Women (1927), a popular survey of western civilization bonded by a sense of women's kinship, past and present. National Woman's Party activist Inez Haynes Irwin produced the more strident Angels and Amazons for the National Council of Women's observance of the 1933 Chicago World's Fair.

---

6 Barbara K. Turoff, Mary Beard as Force in History (Dayton, Ohio, 1979), 52.

Biographies tapped a larger market. Katharine Anthony's psychobiographies of women had a recognized niche, Alma Lutz's devoted portraits of women's rights pioneers a smaller following. Major literary figures (Fuller, Stowe, Alcott) always attracted good professional writers and large readerships, and when by the late thirties the settlement house leaders were also lodged in the pantheon, the first biographies began to follow their autobiographies. Recent lives of Sojourner Truth and Harriet Tubman had won a little notice, but Sadie Daniel's black Women Builders (1931) remained in obscurity.

None of this literature was of much help in establishing a scholarly base. From where I stood, firmly in the Schlesinger social history tradition, I gradually distinguished three other areas of work which seemed to lead away from the pieties of suffrage toward fresh interpretation: literary historians' investigations of popular culture; Mary Beard, an intellectual movement in herself; and the post-World War I writings of British women historians and feminists.

Arthur M. Schlesinger had brought to Harvard in 1924 his striking new social history synthesis. He devoted his thirty years on the faculty to incorporating this new dimension into the history teaching of his day and to promoting new research extending its boundaries. Many college students learned something about women in courses on "social

and intellectual history" modeled after the one he taught
at Harvard and Radcliffe, or utilizing material in the
twelve-volume History of American Life which he edited
with Dixon Ryan Fox (1927-1948). But his efforts to promote research in women's history, an early priority, took
more time to bear fruit than he had expected at the time
suffrage was won; those two female Ph.D.s who did dissertations did not publish. In the end his contribution was
to set up research facilities at Radcliffe College, the
women's sector at Harvard. A research library and a
biographical dictionary were thus ready at hand when women's
history scholarship arrived in force at the end of the
sixties, a triumph he did not live to see.

It is revealing that the first threads, as he would
have called them, that he traced through his social history
fabric were immigrants and women, for probably the two
strongest influences in his life were his immigrant parent-
age and his feminist wife. At least by 1912, Elizabeth
Bancroft had introduced him to the women's suffrage cause.
He was a somewhat reluctant convert. Reporting to her
about this time on a New York City suffrage parade that he
had "stood patiently in the sun" to watch, he related that
"One of the banners read: 'Men bear arms, and women bear
men.' I couldn't help wondering how many of the marchers
had actually borne men. What a shame it is to expend such
immense energy on a cause that just pricks the surface of

the great social questions of our time."[7]  But by the time
the amendment was passed, women's rights had not only come
to be taken for granted in the Schlesinger household, but
Elizabeth's convictions and her reading and thought had
helped construct a new dimension in his historical thinking.

Schlesinger's essay in his New Viewpoints on "The Role
of Women in American History" remained the only scholarly
survey of the subject until 1971, when Mari Jo Buhle, Ann
Gordon, and Nancy Schrom's "Women in American Society"
appeared in Radical America and my "Historical Introduction"
in Notable American Women, 1607-1950.  Built on previous
work by Alice Morse Earle, Edith Abbott, Arthur W. Calhoun
and J. M. Taylor, in addition to the Stanton-Anthony History of Woman Suffrage and the Croly History of the Woman's
Club Movement, Schlesinger's essay touched upon the major
areas: the family, work, legal status, education, individual and group achievements in reform and in wartime.  The
History of American Life series, as he edited it, had more
space for women but little new aside from descriptive
material to put in, discriminating and carefully crafted
though the descriptions were.  The new material, on marriage and sexual morality, manners, high society and
fashion, the use of leisure time, children's upbringing and
child labor, merely expanded the largely middle-class image.

---

7 A. M. Schlesinger, In Retrospect: The History of a Historian (New York, 1963), 42.

Schlesinger's generation set great store by foreign visitors' travel accounts, which were thought at the time to provide value-free views of American society: his historical thinking about women was permanently blocked by travelers' remarks about American men's deference to the opposite sex. An occasional good insight appeared; one was what is called today the feminization of American culture. Women were most successfully integrated into the larger picture as the subjects and instigators of reform. Nothing really unpleasant was to be found on those pages; the chief binding agent was the confident Progressive optimism that remained at the core of Schlesinger's outlook throughout his life. The absence of a women's viewpoint left the picture somewhat lifeless and is conspicuous today; feminism with Schlesinger was more principle than feeling. Principle, however, could go a considerable distance: a powerful force in professional affairs, in 1931 he brought the women historians' Berkshire Conference into the deliberations of his American Historical Association committee on research needs and opportunities.

The few scattered pieces of historical scholarship about women in the interwar period thus could take for granted a social history framework. It was part of the background for Mary Benson, for the educational historian Thomas Woody, and for the sociologist Ernest Groves (The American Woman: The Feminine Side of a Masculine Civiliza-

tion, 1936). Julia Spruill had Schlesinger's counsel in
the preparation of her classic Women's Work in the Southern
Colonies. Schlesinger suggested the topic and directed
Elizabeth M. Bacon's 1944 Radcliffe dissertation, "The
Growth of Household Conveniences in the United States,
1865-1900."

By the time I came to graduate school, dissatisfaction
with this kind of social history was in the air. Some of
Schlesinger's students were looking for means toward more
explanation of causes and development. The next step seemed
to be digging deeper under the familiar surfaces for the
ideas propelling events. Intellectual history was beginning
to separate from social history; Mary Benson's Columbia
dissertation, Women in Eighteenth Century America: A Study
of Opinion and Social Usage (1935) had been an early move
in this direction.

Leading the way into intellectual history were the
literary scholars who, as Ralph Gabriel remarked in 1942,
had been drawn toward the study of ideas in American literature to compensate for its artistic deficiencies.[8] At
Harvard in the early forties we were imbued with Puritanism
and emerged from the American literature survey respectful
of theology and the power of religion over human behavior.
Puritanism was not of much help in explaining the Evangeli-

---

8 Review of Van Wyck Brooks, New England: Indian Summer in
American Historical Review (January 1942).

cal culture from which my early nineteenth century British
writers on women proved to have come; in my ignorance of
British history I floundered until David Owen suggested
Maurice J. Quinlan's Victorian Prelude (1941).

Professors of English also embraced popular culture,
as they shared in the search of the thirties for American
traditions and artifacts. Bernard De Voto's Americana
Deserta series, published by Knopf, included a collection
on The Genteel Female (1931) which presented the distinctive role of women writers and readers in nineteenth century
American culture. Douglas Branch's The Sentimental Years,
1836-1860 (1934) was a further introduction to the ethos
that Barbara Welter would later dub the cult of true womanhood. It took humor to appreciate this material, and the
English professors were lively and clever writers. Herbert
Ross Brown's Sentimental Novel in America, 1789-1860 (1941)
was positively addicting; his wry, slightly patronizing
parody of the female style still echoes in my pages.

Most Americans interested in their history in the
interwar years had read Charles and Mary Beard's Rise of
American Civilization (1927 and many later editions and
revisions). Mary Beard's passages on women as workers,
their status in the family, women's education, and their
"revolt against the masculine supremacy crystallized in the
common law" were brief but compelling, even in that vigorous

narrative. We know now that she was responsible for the striking cultural history dimension which combined with Charles Beard's economic interpretation to give the book its distinctive character and wide appeal.[9]

Mary Beard's Woman as Force in History (1946) came out soon after I started my dissertation. This flawed book turned off most readers since it was too detailed for the general public and too idiosyncratic and hortatory for the academic community. Ann Lane and others have recently published studies of Beard which provide all the biographical information we are likely to get. They also offer sympathetic insights into the life of a Progressive who in the increasingly troubled postsuffrage world pinned her ongoing hopes for woman as redeemer to a consciousness of her history.[10]

Mary Beard's angry break with the champions of the Equal Rights Amendment and their doctrinaire equalitarianism freed both her and us from the orthodox feminism of the suffrage movement and its view of history. The standard concept of women in subjection had served to explain their

---

9 See Turoff, Mary Beard, 2.

10 See the books by Lane and Turoff; Berenice A. Carroll, "Mary Beard's Woman as Force in History: A Critique," in Carroll, ed., Liberating Women's History (Urbana, 1976); Carl Degler, "Woman as Force in History," Daedalus 103 (Winter, 1974); and Gerda Lerner, "Autobiographical Notes," in The Majority Finds Its Past (New York, 1979).

wrongs for the nineteenth century, but it falsified their record in what she called long history. Denying oppression was going to the other extreme, but it fitted our perceptions of ourselves. This was emancipation: if women had always been active participants, we had a green light as women and as historians.

Beard's recent biographers have discussed at some length her connection with the efforts to establish a women's history archive at Radcliffe College in the mid-forties. President W. K. Jordan's correspondence with her, begun late in 1943, proceeded briskly through the following year, when she visited the college and gave $1000 and a selection of books from her own library. After the spring of 1945 the letters lapsed, leaving Beard with a sense of frustration and disappointment.

As we surmise what may have lain behind the surviving record, we should note that Mary Beard was dealing with two academic historians, Jordan, who doubled as Radcliffe's president and a professor of history at Harvard, and his colleague Arthur M. Schlesinger, a Radcliffe trustee and longtime member of the college council (executive committee). The plan Jordan outlined to Beard in his first letter, "to build . . . a strong research collection that would deal with the historical status and cultural contributions of women in this country . . . ," was close to Schlesinger's heart. It also appealed to both men as a

way to enlarge the functions and independent usefulness of
Radcliffe, which had no teaching responsibility. For Mary
Beard it revived the high hopes dashed by the recent failure of her proposed World Center for Women's Archives. Radcliffe, however, had more reputation than resources. Even
with the benefit of Mary Beard's enthusiasm and wide
acquaintance among prominent women of her generation,
Jordan's efforts to raise money for an archive failed, and
in 1945 he turned to more urgent matters such as financing
the new dormitories needed for Radcliffe's postwar expan-
sion. Without any formal break in relations, communication
ceased. Beard's bulging and ambiguous concept of women in
long history could not have been in step with Jordan's and
Schlesinger's formalized views of their discipline; it also
disregarded the practical wisdom of confining the collection
to American materials. Behind the scenes the two historians
acquired materials as opportunity offered and in 1950 managed
to open the Women's Archives on the coattails of an adult
education project which promised a good financial return.[11]

Mary Beard's interest in women's history went a long
way back in her life. She and Charles Beard are important
American links with the British socialist and labor

---

11 Lane, Mary Ritter Beard; J. W. James, "History and Women
   at Harvard: The Schlesinger Library," Harvard Library
   Bulletin 16 (1968); Mary Beard Papers, Schlesinger Library; and Council Minutes, Radcliffe College Archives.

movements, with which a variety of intellectuals, writers, and reformers were identified, including some leading feminists. Newly married and at Oxford in 1900 and 1901, the Beards had thrown themselves into workers' education and women's suffrage, and absorbed the ideals of the cooperative movement. Mary Beard's introduction to the history of women apparently came from Edward Carpenter, an exponent of cooperative living also remembered as a sexual reformer. Before the Beards went home, she had written two articles about women's history for Young Oxford, the magazine of Ruskin Hall, the workers' college that her husband and another American had founded.

As my dissertation led me backwards into the English culture of the eighteenth and early nineteenth centuries, I discovered the British histories and historians of women and began to learn something about the scholarly and feminist backgrounds of this work. At the London School of Economics, established by the Fabian Socialist group, research on women and labor was encouraged by two historians from Girton College, Cambridge. Lilian Knowles and (later) Eileen Power brought with them the strong middle-class feminist tradition of Girton, which in the 1870s had been the opening wedge of the women's campaign to enter the old universities. Knowles taught Alice Clark, whose landmark Working Life of Women in the Seventeenth Century (1919) was the intellectual highpoint of my dissertation reading.

Knowles and Power guided Ivy Pinchbeck's study of early
women industrial workers. (Clark's and Pinchbeck's research
was underwritten by Charlotte Shaw, wife of the dramatist
and a major benefactor of the Fabian group.) Eileen Power's
studies of women in the middle ages, published in the 1920s,
gave me the assurance that women's history could equal the
best.

The English women associated with the struggle for
higher education and with the leadership of Millicent Fawcett also produced good amateur historians in Ray Strachey
(linked through her mother with American feminism) and Ida
O'Malley, whose Women in Subjection: A Study of the Lives
of English Women Before 1832 (1933) brought the subject more
to life than anything I had read in modern history. The
Fawcett Library in London survives as this group's effort
to preserve the historical record.

The biggest star in the British firmament, of course,
was Virginia Woolf, whom most of us had met in college reading in the thirties. A Room of One's Own (1927) and the
sensitive sketches of obscure women in the English literary
past published in her two Common Readers gave me a permanent
interest in the female author.

Looking back now upon this study, contemplating this
mouse brought forth by my mountainous labors, I realize how
much it belongs to the complacent, consensus-minded 1950s,
when most of it was written. Then the feminist theory of

the past had been discredited and nothing new was ready to
replace it. We middle-class women with "outside interests"
were looking for proof that family and "career" combina-
tions could be had without anything so unladylike as a
fight. I could even declare that woman's role was not an
issue in the Anne Hutchinson case and find Mary Wollstonecraft's rhetoric overblown. Since then, a new feminism
has set off a mass investigation of women's history. The
college courses in women's studies that Mary Beard tried
to get started are available to a younger generation of
students. New books arrive in my mailbox all the time,
and I open them eagerly.

This book, now belatedly published, was one of the
numerous attempts being made twenty or thirty years ago to
add an intellectual history dimension to American social
history. Such a study dealing with women, relating attitudes to the intellectual and social milieu (even that
limited milieu inhabited by people who wrote books), was
then something new. A decade or so later Anne Scott would
lead the way into the collections of family correspondence
that has since enabled other historians of the same period
-- Nancy Cott, Mary Beth Norton, Linda Kerber -- to round
out the story with women's experience in their own private
voices.

Working in that eighteenth and early nineteenth century climate of opinion, I found the English ideal of the

decorative and virtuous lady, the radical feminist thought
of the Enlightenment, and the moral reformism of the religious revival known in America as the Second Great Awakening and in England as the Evangelical movement; I tried to
show how the process of change occurred. My focus on
religion indicated a line of inquiry that would be increasingly valuable in social history and women's history.
Exploring the British sources of American thought was a
venture in comparative history, which remains an approach
still little used. Women's history has only begun.


Boston College, 1981                    Janet James

# PREFACE

Ever since Eve was formed from Adam's rib the female
sex has been a favorite bone of contention. Experts and
plain citizens in every society have debated the Woman Question, analyzed the mind and temper of womankind, and prescribed the size and shape of woman's sphere. One age,
having worked out a formula to fit its own needs, gives way
to the next, and a new generation of citizens, smiling at
the backwardness of their forebears, sets out to revise the
old mores and contrive new ones.

Thirty years ago most Americans thought they had solved
the problem for all time. A century of agitation for"woman's
rights" had culminated in the achievement of political equality with men. Women had access to education on equal terms.
A new freedom of manners was sweeping away the hampering
conventions of social life. With the minds and energies of
half the nation unfettered, the men and women of 1920 looked
forward confidently to an era of harmonious and constructive
effort.

Today at mid-century we take "emancipation" for granted.
The third generation of girls to enjoy complete formal education is passing through college. Many of them will enter
business, the arts, or the professions, where it has become
commonplace for women to earn their own living and even to

win distinction. For thirty years the women's vote has been figuring in the calculations of candidates for public office. "Woman's sphere," that cramping phrase once so dear to writers on the subject, has become a mild joke, surely a sign of its obsolescence.

Yet a certain dissatisfaction with the American woman's lot lurks in the back of the public mind. During 1947 uneasy readers flocked to buy a book exposing the plight of Modern Woman: the Lost Sex; in 1953 they were anxiously exploring two angry volumes on The Second Sex. A pair of articles inquiring "Why Mothers Fail" provoked four hundred Atlantic Monthly readers in 1947 to address its editors with their opinions on the subject. A prominent woman anthropologist, writing in 1953 for a symposium on Women Today, Their Conflicts, Their Frustrations, Their Fulfillments, estimated that a quarter of American women, and these the best educated, were unhappy with their place in the world. Evidently "emancipation" was not to be the end of woman's difficulties; it seems increasingly apparent, in fact, that it merely introduced a new phase of an ancient problem.

Chapter One

COLONIAL THEORY AND PRACTICE

# Chapter One
## COLONIAL THEORY AND PRACTICE

The Woman Question came to America with its founding
fathers and pioneer mothers. The families who settled in
New England and the Southern colonies in the earliest migra-
tions brought to their new homes the ideas about society and
woman's place prevailing in the England they left behind.

These were not passive assumptions, inherited from by-
gone days without thought or question, for the subject was
very much alive in the dawning seventeenth century. It was
a time of turmoil in men's minds. The new learning of the
Renaissance, the Protestant reformers' challenge to the old
religion, the vistas of wealth and prestige opening up on
every hand -- these had stirred people to fresh thinking on
all topics. Nearly every emigrant, whether he was heading for
a Bay colony village or a Virginia farm, belonged to the rising
middle class in England. He and his relatives and friends
were ambitious, self-respecting, hard-working folk, anxious
to manage their affairs properly so as to get ahead in the
world. A stable family life was essential if a man were to
prosper. These people therefore had often consulted the manuals on domestic relations which could be found in profusion
in the book stalls, or listened attentively to a Sunday sermon

5

on the duties of husbands and wives.[1] In the New World one
had few books and less time to read them. The church, however, especially among the Puritans, took pains to inculcate
principles of family management, and prominent clergymen like
Cotton Mather, who kept in close touch with current thinking
in England, would sometimes publish their teachings on the
subject.

Emancipation was no issue among these seventeenth-century
Englishmen. Men and women alike accepted the theory that subjection of the weaker sex was foreordained. This subordination was supposed to have been a fixed part of the social order
in every known civilization. The concept had been embedded in
the English common law for centuries past. A girl's property
passed upon her marriage into her husband's ownership and management; henceforth she had no independent legal existence.
As an English manual on The Lawes Resolutions of Women's
Rights explained it in 1632,

> When a small brooke or little river in-
> corporateth with . . . the Thames, the poor
> rivulet looseth her name; it is carried and
> recarried with the new associate; it beareth
> no sway; it possesseth nothing during cover-
> ture. A woman as soon as she is married, is
> called covert; in Latine nupta, that is,
> "veiled"; as it were, clouded and overshadowed;
> she hath lost her streame. I may more truly,

---

1 Louis B. Wright, Middle-Class Culture in Elizabethan England
(Chapel Hill, 1935), chs. 5, 7; Chilton Latham Powell, English Domestic Relations, 1487-1653 (New York, 1917), ch. 4.

farre away, say to a married woman, Her new
self is her superior; her companion, her master . . . .[2]

"The common laws here shaketh hand with divinitye," the
same writer observed, and correctly, for the teachings of the
Christian church had strongly reinforced the doctrine. Womankind was obviously inferior to man because Eve had been second
in the order of creation. Her complicity with the serpent had
completed her subjection, for had not an angry God, in meting
out punishment for the first sin, declared, "Thy desire shall
be to thy husband, and he shall rule over thee"? And the
Hebrews' God had not relented. Paul the apostle, preaching
his word, had stated categorically that "the head of the
woman is the man" and repeatedly warned wives to "submit yourselves unto your . . . husbands."[3]

In recent generations, however, the rigors of the subjection theory had been somewhat abated. The Protestant leaders,
readjusting Christian doctrine to the needs of a commercial
society, had done much to raise women's status. The rising
tradesman or yeoman needed a responsible, thrifty, energetic
helpmate. His authority as husband remained supreme -- the
testimony of the Scriptures on that point was incontrovertible -- but common sense dictated that the wife enjoy equality

---

2 Quoted in Julia Cherry Spruill, Women's Life and Work in the
Southern Colonies (Chapel Hill, 1938), 340.

3 Genesis 3:16; Colossians 3:18; Ephesians 5:22.

in the actual management of the household. Protestants from
the early sixteenth-century reformers to the ministers of
Puritan Massachusetts softened the Biblical emphasis on subjection and enjoined husband and wife to practice mutual
forbearance and sympathy.[4]

The subordination intended in the Bible, declared the
Rev. Samuel Willard of Boston, was "such as is to be managed
so by the Husband, as that his Wife may take delight in it,
and not account it a Slavery, but a Liberty and Priviledge
. . . ." He "ought not, under pretence of Authority, to forget that she is the nearest Companion that he hath in the
World, and is his second Self . . . ." It was his duty to
love his wife, to be patient with her, and to prove himself
worthy of his position by being a good provider and a wise
counselor. The wife, on the other hand, owed her husband
deference, but not slavish obedience. Both "respect and common Interest oblige her carefully to Consult him in every
matter of weight," but she could always debate "the Prudence
of the thing."[5]

The law still permitted a husband to beat his wife, but
the Puritans could not condemn this practice too strongly.
The learned Cotton Mather dealt with this problem in 1692,

---

4 Wright, Middle-Class Culture, ch. 7; Powell, English
Domestic Relations, 114-116, 126-128.

5 Samuel Willard, A Compleat Body of Divinity (Boston, 1726),
610-612.

in his Ornaments for the Daughters of Zion, A Discourse Which
Directs the Female-Sex How to . . . Obtain Both Temporal and
Eternal Blessedness. Mather advised the victim to read to
her husband "the Emphatical Words of the Blessed Ancients in
the Church of God, Loudly Thundering against this Inhumani-
ty . . . ." His colleague the Rev. Benjamin Wadsworth,
author of a handbook on The Well-Ordered Family, took a
more practical approach: "Such Husbands carry it more like
bruits, than what becomes men: they deserve sharp reproof,
and severe punishment too."[6]

The Puritan lawgivers also raised women's standing in the
spiritual realm. Some of the early church fathers, impressed
by the weight of original sin, had consigned all women to per-
dition as frail inheritors of Eve's disgrace -- all except
those who denied the flesh in a life of celibate devotion.
This idea, popular throughout the Middle Ages, still survived
in the seventeenth century.[7] To Protestants, and especially
the Puritan left wing of the movement, it seemed harsh doctrine
indeed. Cotton Mather had no use for the "many Licentious

---

6 Mather, Ornaments for the Daughters of Zion (Cambridge, 1692),
  87; Wadsworth, The Well-Ordered Family (Boston, 1712), 37.

7 Powell, English Domestic Relations, 147ff. For medieval
  attitudes toward women see Eileen Power, "The Position of
  Women," The Legacy of the Middle Ages (Oxford, 1926);
  G. R. Owst, Literature and Pulpit in Medieval England
  (Cambridge, 1933); and Alice A. Hentsch, De la Littérature
  Didactique du Moyen Age S'Addressant Spécialement aux
  Femmes (Cahors, 1903).

Writers, [who] have handled that Theme, Femina nulla bona,
No Woman is Good!" On the contrary, he assured pious feminine
readers "that you are among, The Excellent in the Earth."[8]
The notion that women could not be saved so disturbed Judge
Samuel Sewall of Boston that he sat down and wrote a tract
to disprove it. Pointing out that God had specified only
subjection and the travail of childbirth as punishment for
the first sin, Sewall argued that women had access to Heaven
equally with men.[9] His pamphlet was confidently entitled in
Hebrew, "Talitha Cumi" [Young Woman Arise].

---

[8] Mather, Ornaments for the Daughters of Zion, 43. Mather
explained his reasoning in detail. It was true that "a
Woman had the Disgrace to Go First in that horrid and Woful
Transgression of our first Parents, which has been the
Parent of all our misery . . . ." Nevertheless "a Woman
had the Glory of bringing into the World that Second Adam,
who is the Father, of all our Happiness . . . ," and
though he was far from regarding the Virgin Mary in the
same light as the "Popish Idolaters," yet he believed "we
may safely account the Female Sex herein more than a little
Dignify'd." In making Adam assume his share of responsibility for the trouble in Eden Mather was following standard
Protestant practice. Protestants liked to point out also
that Jesus had performed his first miracle at a marriage,
and that at the resurrection he had appeared first to women.
    Mather, however, did think it necessary to give women
a special warning to be on their guard against heresy.
"Tis noted of Seducers, that, like their Father the Divel
[sic], the Old, the First Seducer, they have a Special Design upon the Weaker Sex, who are most Easily Gained themselves, and then fit Instruments for the gaining of their
Husbands, to such Errors, as cause them to Loose [sic]
their Souls at last . . . . Indeed," he added, "a Poison
do's never insinuate so quickly, or operate so strongly,
as when Womens Milk is the Vehicle, which tis given in."
Ornaments, 4, 44, 48.

[9] Mary Sumner Benson, Women in Eighteenth-Century America
(New York, 1935), 120-121.

The idea that celibacy was the only passport to eternal life seemed even more preposterous. "It was a great abuse," Mather complained, "which the Ancients who doted upon Virgin-ity, put upon those words of the Apostle, . . . . Those that are in the Flesh, cannot please God; when they supposed all Married Persons to be Those intended. A Vertuous Wife is one that pleaseth God, as much as if she were cloistered up in the strictest and closest Nunnery . . . ."[10] To Protestant Christ-tians wedlock was the truly holy state, where man and woman together did the world's work "in all honesty, vertue and god-liness."[11] Thus religious authority lent its blessing to the practical demands of life in a new colony. Frontier living so depended on the home for comforts, companionship, and live-lihood that young men took wives without delay, and with the scarcity of women in the new settlements a girl could have her choice of suitors.[12]

---

10 Ornaments for the Daughters of Zion, 77.

11 Thomas Becon, The Boke of Matrimony (c. 1562), quoted in Powell, English Domestic Relations, 127. See also Wright, Middle-Class Culture, 203.

12 In New England religious pressure further spurred the young man into matrimony. The Puritans regarded the family as the basic unit of the social order and their chief in-strument for enforcing God's laws. Massachusetts and Con-necticut, fearful of the "sin and iniquity, which ordinar-ily are the companions and consequences of a solitary life," required young bachelors to settle themselves in some well-ordered family where a paternal eye could supervise their conduct -- no doubt a strong incentive to establishing a home of one's own. See Edmund S. Morgan, The Puritan Fam-ily (Boston, 1944), 84-86. The quotation just above, from the Essex County (Mass.) court records of 1672, is on pp. 85-86.

Concerned though they were that woman enjoy equal status in the home and in the eyes of God, seventeenth-century Englishmen had no notion of educating her like a man. A century before, to be sure, in Tudor England, the humanistic spirit of the Renaissance had produced a generous enthusiasm for women's education. Such prodigies of learning as Sir Thomas More's daughter Margaret Roper, Lady Jane Grey, and the great Elizabeth herself had seemed to vindicate for all time the power of woman's intellect. Their superb training, however, had been merely an aristocratic luxury, a fashionable indulgence of certain brilliant noblewomen. It had established no permanent tradition of higher education even for girls of the upper class.[13]

Even in Elizabeth's time, as Europe became embattled in religious warfare, the humanistic spirit had withered before the hot blast of militant Protestantism. Under the Stuarts, as England moved into this new climate of opinion, royalists and intransigent Puritans alike came to consider the flowering of mortal mind a poor object in comparison with the safety of the eternal soul. The pursuit of knowledge became a search for spiritual illumination. For educational practice, and especially where women were concerned, this meant a strong emphasis on the teaching of conduct, to the detriment of polite learning.

---

[13] Myra Reynolds, The Learned Lady in England, 1650-1760 (Boston, 1920), 16, 23, 28; Dorothy Gardiner, English Girlhood at School (London, 1929), 185.

In the England of the 1630's, both Cavalier and Puritan
distrusted erudition in women. In educating their children,
they trained their sons in the ancient languages and litera-
tures; it was enough for their daughters to know their own
tongue sufficiently well to master the Bible, the catechism,
and the prayer book, perhaps in addition a little French.
Gentlemen of the King's party sent their daughters to boarding schools, where they read French romances and learned
music, dancing, and certain elegant domestic arts.  Puritan
girls stayed at home and were thoroughly instructed in housekeeping and piety.

In the frontier surroundings of colonial life, all education inevitably deteriorated, and that of girls, being
least essential in the economy of that day, suffered most.
Women's strenuous household tasks, requiring the complete processing of food and clothing for large families, could be
little aided by education and left no leisure for enjoying
its benefits.  Luxury schooling in the ornamental arts and
graces disappeared, except for the daughters of well-to-do
Southern planters who might be taught by private tutors or
sent to England for instruction in boarding establishments or
the homes of Cavalier relatives.  Some girls mastered the elementary branches in neighborhood schools in the South or the
dame-schools of New York and New England.[14]  But in these

14 Spruill, Women's Life, 185-187; Alice Morse Earle, Colonial
Days in Old New York (New York, 1896), 35; Earle, Child
Life (New York, 1899), 97.

early years a large majority of colonial women, probably between sixty and seventy per cent, were illiterate.[15]

Instruction in domestic skills was by no means so neglected. The Puritans set their little girls to heavy plain
sewing before they were six, being eager to keep them from
the sin of idleness as well as to raise capable wives. And
many children, even those of the best social standing, were
apprenticed out in other families at about the age of twelve
or sent to live for long periods in the homes of relatives or
friends to be further instructed in housekeeping.[16]

For the average girl proficiency in "all the Affairs of
Housewifry" would suffice. Cotton Mather, however, writing
in 1692 when the rigors of pioneer days had largely passed,
had more ambitious plans for the really industrious maiden.
Not content with "a good skill at her Needle, . . . [and] in
the Kitchen," she should also, he felt, familiarize herself
with "Arithmetick and Accomptantship, . . . and such other
Arts relating to Business, as may Enable her to do the Man
whom she may hereafter have, Good and not Evil all the days
of her Life." If she had any time to spare after this, she
might "learn Musick and Language," taking care, however, not
to become "proud of her Skill." When she became a mother,

---

15 Spruill, Women's Life, 187; Samuel Eliot Morison, The Puritan Pronaos (New York, 1936), 80.

16 Morgan, Puritan Family, 37-38. This practice dated back to
medieval times.

Mather expected her to be able to give her children their early lessons, first "to make 'em Expert in some Orthodox Catechisms," after which she should "have 'em Learn to Read and Write, as fast as ever they can take it . . . ."[17]

This was the kind of education which Cotton Mather, a loving and conscientious father, gave his own daughters. He planned to have the older ones also acquire some extra skill, such as a knowledge of medicines and "chirurgery" or "any other employment to which their own inclinations may the most lead them." This would enable them to be useful to others and if necessary to support themselves.[18]

Mather seems never to have considered educating his daughters in the subjects his son studied at Harvard College. He evidently did not disapprove of learned women on principle, for he admired the "Ingenious Writings" of accomplished ladies of the past and was proud that "the New-English part of the American Strand" could boast an authoress or two. Decency and law might forbid women to be warriors, he remarked, but they "have with much Praise done the part of Scholars in the World . . . ."[19]

Perhaps Mather's own daughters did not inherit his

---

17 Ornaments for the Daughters of Zion, 74, 94-95.

18 Elizabeth Bancroft Schlesinger, "Cotton Mather and his Children," William and Mary Quarterly, 3d ser. X (April, 1953), 186; Benson, Women in Eighteenth-Century America, 111-112.

19 Ornaments, 5-6.

intellectual gifts. Fond fathers with girls who showed a
strong interest in learning often encouraged their studies
at home. The Rev. Benjamin Colman, pastor of Boston's Brattle
Street Church, doted upon his bookish daughter Jane and permitted her to browse at will in his library. Jane shared her
father's penchant for composing verse; the poetical para-
phrases of the Bible which she submitted to him at seventeen
prompted Colman to admit that "With the advantages of my liberal Education at School & College, I have no reason to think
but that your Genius in Writing would have excell'd mine."[20]

Other colonial gentlemen, to be sure, would have questioned the wisdom of Colman's course. Nor would they so
readily have granted the possibility that women's minds could
stand on a par with their own. John Winthrop stated the conservative opinion firmly in 1645 in the case of Ann Hopkins,
"a godly young woman, and of special parts," the wife of his
brother governor, Edward Hopkins of Connecticut. Mistress

---

20 Clayton Harding Chapman, "Benjamin Colman's Daughters," New
England Quarterly, XXVI (June, 1953), 169-192; Benson,
Women in Eighteenth-Century America, 116-117. A woman with
family responsibilities, however, could rarely afford the
luxury of study. Busy Esther Burr, daughter of the theo-
logian Jonathan Edwards and wife of the president of
Princeton College, was faintly exasperated in 1755 when
her husband suggested that she take lessons with the French
master boarding in their house. "Mr. Burr has had a mind
that I should lern," she confided to her diary, "but I
have no time -- The married woman has somthing [sic] else
to care about besides lerning French tho' if I had time I
should be very fond of lerning . . . ." Josephine Fisher,
"The Journal of Esther Burr," New England Quarterly, III
(April, 1930), 299.

Hopkins went insane, and Winthrop saw clearly that this was

> by occasion of her giving herself wholly
> to reading and writing, and had written
> many books. Her husband. being very loving
> and tender of her, was loath to grieve her,
> but he saw his errour, when it was too late.
> For if she had attended her household af-
> fairs, and such things as belong to women,
> and not gone out of her way and calling to
> meddle in such things as are proper for
> men, whose minds are stronger, &c. she had
> kept her wits, and might have improved them
> usefully and honourably in the place God
> had set her.[21]

Such a hunger for learning was so rare among females,
however, that there was little occasion to argue over the
propriety of it. Indeed few persons of either sex in the
seventeenth century had the inclination or the need to go beyond the rudiments. It took intelligence and common sense
to make one's way in the world, but little formal schooling.
A boy learned a trade from his father or a neighbor as a
child around the home -- farming or carpentering or rope-
making, for instance -- as his sister was mastering the complicated arts of housekeeping under her mother's eye. Both
were ready to leave home at an age when modern boys and girls
are still in high school. In their lesiure time men or women
might read a little in the Bible, but by and large they got
their information about this world and their notions about
the next not from the printed word but from listening to
sermons or talking with fellow-townsmen. More advanced study

21 John Winthrop, The History of New England from 1630 to 1649,
James Savage, ed. (Boston, 1826), II, 216.

was a privilege of the well-to-do, who might patronize schools
or employ tutors to educate sons and daughters according to
the taste and means of the individual family. In the middle
classes book learning was reserved for gifted boys who were
destined for a profession. In the lower ranks men and women
were equally illiterate. The average citizen in England or
America did not regard education as a matter of great moment
for either sex.

The term "career" had not yet been invented in the seventeenth century, but the women of that day were by no means
confined to a wholly domestic existence. Despite the heavy
work of running a pioneer household a woman could often enjoy
the satisfaction of contributing to the family income or ex-
ercising special talents in business or other fields. As the
colonial towns grew, there was an almost inexhaustible demand
for goods and services; at the same time, most businesses in
these days before the advent of industrialism were small, un-
complicated enterprises, and manufacturing chiefly handicrafts
easily carried on in or near the home. This was the age of
the artisan, and a woman's lack of formal education did not
hinder her success as storekeeper or artificer. A wife picked
up business experience and technical skill helping her husband
in his shop; if she had taken Cotton Mather's advice and learned

bookkeeping, so much the better.  If she were left a widow,
nothing was more natural than for her to carry on the business.
The community needed her products or her services; she had
her family to support, and idleness or dependence on relatives
was not to be thought of in a new country where there was
always more work to do than hands to do it.  More often than
not the widow remarried; to abandon a prosperous enterprise
with an established reputation would be throwing money away,
so she usually kept it going under her new name.[22]

In New York and Boston, and the smaller towns as well,
"she-merchants" sold everything from dry-goods and groceries
to china, furniture, and hardware.  Women commonly conducted
taverns and coffee-houses.  Others were carpenters and cabi-
net-makers, braziers, soapmakers, cutlers, and ropemakers,
often doing the work themselves, and it was not unknown for a
female to run a blacksmith shop.  The more hardy of these occupations had been inherited from deceased husbands, but their
widows seem to have taken over such masculine work quite
matter-of-factly.

On the semiprofessional level women were equally active,
and for the same reasons: a short-handed country could not
disdain womanpower, and in colonial times these occupations
required little education.  Nurses and midwives had more

---

22 Elisabeth Anthony Dexter, Colonial Women of Affairs (Boston,
    1931), 182-192.

patients than they could take care of, while other women did
a flourishing business concocting popular nostrums for various human ills. The school-dame, rehearsing the toddlers
in their abc's, began to be a familiar figure in the colonies
in the latter part of the seventeenth century, and women frequently taught in the common schools as well.[23]

A number made a striking success as printers and newspaper
publishers. The first of them, the widow Dinah Nuthead, took
over her husband's press in Maryland in 1695. Mrs. Nuthead
became official printer to the province government, though
she must have hired a journeyman printer to do the work since
she was not sufficiently educated herself to sign her name.
In the next century Anne Franklin, relict of the brother
James to whom Benjamin Franklin was apprenticed as a youth in
Boston, continued her husband's printing business for nearly
thirty years after his death and in the closing years of her
life published a newspaper as well. Mrs. Franklin was as-
sisted by her two daughters, who were "correct and quick com-
positors at case," having been trained by their father.[24]

Women of the upper class were often called upon to manage
large property interests. Mrs. John Davenport, wife of the
minister in New Haven, handled the extensive affairs of

---

23 Ibid., chs. 4, 5.

24 Ibid., 166ff. The description (by Isaiah Thomas) of the
Franklin girls' skill is quoted on p. 168.

Governor John Winthrop, Jr., during his absence in England
in the 1650's, seeing to the planting of his fields, the
selling of his beaver-pelts, and the operation of his iron-
works.[25]

This kind of talent, however, was most in demand in the
South. The outstanding woman of her day in the Southern
colonies was a large landholder and business agent named
Margaret Brent, one of the first adventurers into Maryland
and an associate of the Calvert proprietors.[26] Mistress
Brent has come down in history as something of a feminist.
In 1647 she appeared before the Maryland assembly and requested a seat in that body; when the delegates refused, "the s'd
Mrs Brent protested against all proceedings in this present
Assembly unlesse she may be present and have vote as afores'd."[27]
Actually she may, with some logic, have regarded the Maryland
government as a kind of public corporation, and far from demanding political rights[28] she may have sought membership in
the house merely to expedite her handling of the Calvert affairs.

Englishwomen of the aristocracy were accustomed to take

25 Ibid., 111-112; Earle, Colonial Dames and Goodwives (Boston, 1895), 52-55.

26 Spruill, Women's Life, 236-241.

27 Earle, Colonial Dames, 48. "Mrs." was a courtesy title
given to single women of middle age until early in the
nineteenth century.

28 Edward Channing, History of the United States (New York,
1905-1925), I, 267.

part in the management of their family estates, and the few
who happened to remain unmarried, like Margaret Brent, had
naturally more leisure for business concerns and a more ad-
vantageous legal position from which to conduct them. Across
the Atlantic, where in the South as well as the North there
was almost unlimited economic opportunity together with a
chronic shortage of manpower, any woman who could spare time
from her household for business was a valuable adjunct to
the community. A number of women, like Margaret and her sister Mary, received land grants, especially in the proprietary
colonies, emigrated with large retinues of servants, and
established plantations in something like feudal style. But
none was probably so successful as the energetic Mistress
Brent. Besides her farming, she owned and ran a mill which
brought her a good income.[29] Her name appears constantly in
the Maryland court records, usually in connection with suits
against her debtors (and winning her cases). Impressed by
her ability, many friends and relatives confided their affairs
to her management, under power of attorney. Besides these
important private trusts, the turn of events in Maryland gave
Margaret Brent a hand in deciding public policy at a critical
moment. Yet at no time during her career, except for the episode in the assembly, does any issue seem to have been made
of her sex.

---

29 Spruill, Women's Life, 306.

When Leonard Calvert, the proprietor's brother, died in 1647, Mistress Brent was executor of his estate. The colony was in the midst of civil war, with the Baltimore regime threatened by an army gathering in Virginia and sustained only by a hungry and mutinous band of hired soldiers demanding rations and back pay. Finding Calvert's personal estate insufficient to meet the emergency, Margaret Brent obtained power of attorney from the assembly to act for Lord Baltimore as well and sold enough of his cattle to pay and feed the soldiers. Her prompt action averted further conflict and probably saved the Calvert family's heavy investment in America.

Far from appreciating Margaret's courageous action, Lord Baltimore, far away in England and ignorant of the real urgency of the crisis, reproached the assembly for the loss of his livestock. They rallied loyally to Margaret's defense, writing that "as for Mrs Brents undertaking and medling with your Lordships Estate here . . . we do Verily Believe and in Conscience report that it was better for the Collonys safety at that time in her hands than in any mans else in the whole Province," adding their opinion that "she rather deserved favour and thanks from your Honour for her so much Concurring to the Public Safety then to be liable to all those bitter invectives you have been pleased to express against her."[30]

---

30 Ibid., 240.

Considerations of broader policy, however, kept Lord Baltimore from restoring Margaret Brent to his patronage.  To
retain his colony under the Puritan Commonwealth he found it
expedient to withdraw his favor from prominent Catholic
families in Maryland, including the Brents.  They moved to
Virginia, and little is known of Margaret's later life.

Other women besides Margaret Brent were drawn into
public life in the seventeenth century at times of political
turmoil; several actively aided and abetted their husbands
in Bacon's Rebellion in 1676, one to such an extent that she
was specifically exempted from the general pardon passed by
the Virginia assembly at the end of the hostilities.[31]  Other
women also managed large plantations single-handed, usually
widows like Mrs. Elizabeth Digges, who so improved the estate
of her husband, a former governor of Virginia, that at her
death she owned more slaves than anyone else in the colony.[32]

The professions had traditionally excluded women, if
only because it was inconceivable that they could ever pursue
the long intellectual training required of a clergyman,
doctor, or lawyer.  Yet the Puritans in one famous case
permitted a woman to stand in the wings of the most learned

31 Ibid., 233-234.
32 Ibid., 305.

profession of all, the ministry -- until her flouting of
the church's authority became insufferable. One of the most
remarkable personalities of her century in America, Anne
Hutchinson precipitated an upheaval in the Massachusetts Bay
colony comparable in violence only to the witchcraft mania
of a generation later.[33] Yet throughout the crisis caused
by her aggressive airing of unorthodox religious views very
little issue seems to have been made of her overstepping the
boundaries of her sex.

"A woman of a ready wit and bold spirit,"[34] Mrs. Hutchinson began sometime during 1636 to hold private Thursday
meetings of her sex at her house in Boston to discuss the
preceding Sunday's sermon for the benefit of those who had
been unable to attend. Before long she was adding interpretation and comment of her own and criticizing the ministers.
The sessions attracted men also and soon became more popular
than public worship.[35]

Anne Hutchinson had a new answer to the awful question,
so momentous for the Calvinist, how to determine whether or
not a person was one of the elect, predestined by God to

---

33 Charles Francis Adams, Three Episodes of Massachusetts
   History (Boston, 1894), is the most detailed modern account of the Hutchinson case.

34 Winthrop, History, I, 200.

35 Samuel Eliot Morison, Builders of the Bay Colony (Boston,
   1930), 119.

salvation. She declared the only sure sign to be an in-
dwelling of the divine spirit within one (the "covenant of
grace"); that the mere leading of a godly life (the "covenant of works") could be no proof that a man's path tended
heavenward. Her preaching also galvanized local dislike of
the Reverend John Wilson, pastor of the Boston Church, a
somewhat harsh-natured man of rigidly orthodox convictions
for whom Mrs. Hutchinson had a strong antipathy. Presently
she rose in church at the beginning of Wilson's sermon and
walked out on him. Some of her disciples did likewise, while
others stayed in their pews and heckled the preacher.

Such insubordination and such doctrine dangerously threatened the power of the Massachusetts ruling class. The Puritan ministers and magistrates were familiar with the consequences of both from the history of a group of German fanatics
who had professed a similar brand of Calvinism under the
name of Antinomianism. If an individual believed God's grace
had visited him and secured his salvation, he might become
careless of his conduct; and if he were to be the sole judge
of the spiritual experience, he might well dispense with the
services of a learned ministry. That way lay anarchy and
the destruction of the religious Commonwealth which the
Winthrops and Dudleys, the Wilsons and Shepards, had come to
New England to establish, a state built upon God's law, not
as revealed to the man in the street, but as set forth in the
Bible, interpreted by a highly educated clergy, and enforced
by the civil government.

Mrs. Hutchinson's theology thus made a strong appeal to
the unlettered. "Come along with me," said one of her followers to Edward Johnson, the Puritan historian.

> I'le bring you to a Woman that Preaches
> better Gospell than any of your black-
> coates that have been at the Ninneversity
> [sic], a Woman of another kinde of spirit,
> who hath had many Revelations of things to
> come, and for my part, saith hee, I had
> rather hear such a one that speakes from
> the meere motion of the spirit, without
> any study at all, than any of your learned
> Scollers, although they may be fuller of
> Scripture.[36]

But the covenant-of-grace doctrine also attracted persons of
standing, including John Cotton, assistant pastor of the Boston church, and Sir Harry Vane, an attractive young aristo-
crat lately come out from England.  Vane, recently elected
governor of the colony, was a potential focus for political
discontent and especially dangerous to the Puritan oligarchy
because of his powerful royalist connections in England.  As
the Antinomian movement neared its height, almost the entire
Boston community flocked to Mrs. Hutchinson's standard.

With such powerful support, Anne Hutchinson may have
dreamed of establishing a new regime in Massachusetts.  She
certainly hoped to see Wilson ousted from the Boston church
and John Cotton in his place, with her brother-in-law John
Wheelwright as his assistant or "teacher."  She grew bolder
and more vehement in her attacks, castigating not only Wilson

---

36 Ibid., 120.

but also all the other ministers of the colony outside Boston "for not preaching a covenant of free grace, and that they had not the seal of the spirit."[37]

This time she went too far. The congregations outside the capital, never exposed to the Hutchinson spell, solidly backed their outraged pastors in a counterattack that drove these revolutionary elements out of the colony. By a clever stratagem Winthrop in the next election defeated Vane for governor, and Vane returned to England. Wheelwright, convicted of sedition for a rash statement in one of his sermons, was banished, fleeing to the northern wilds of New Hampshire. His brother ministers won Cotton over to their side. Mrs. Hutchinson, tried by the General Court, was sentenced to exile "as being a woman not fit for our society."[38] After a winter of imprisonment she went south to the free-thinking settlements in Rhode Island.

Anne Hutchinson hardly fitted the pattern of wifely submission to which her society subscribed. Yet the rulers of Massachusetts Bay, notoriously exacting in their dictation of personal conduct, let her prophesy unmolested until she had set the whole colony in an uproar. She was a valued midwife, kind and sympathetic, very popular among the Boston women, and esteemed by all for her vigorous intellect. To be sure,

---

37 Winthrop, History, I, 294.

38 Winthrop, quoted in Adams, Three Episodes, I, 508.

gossip had sized up her husband as "a man of very mild temper and weak parts, and wholly guided by his wife,"[39] but the Hutchinsons were people of means, middle-aged, Anne the exemplary mother of fourteen children and already a grandmother. At first the elders of the church actually approved her gatherings as further encouragement to godliness among their people. After all, history recorded many instances of female ministry: the Hebrews had had their prophetesses, the ancients their oracles and sibyls, the medieval church its saints. The apostle Paul had gratefully acknowledged women's help in his missionary labors. Even after Anne had flouted the authority of her pastor and aspersed the teachings of his colleagues they argued with her privately, trying to reconcile their theological differences. Failing in this, the ministers held a synod of the church to iron out the points at issue. This body publicly condemned Mrs. Hutchinson's assemblies and her followers' disrespectful treatment of their minister.

Nevertheless it was not until the dissidents had defiantly persevered in their tactics over a period of months, and the controversy had developed serious political aspects, that the full rigors of the law were visited on them. Even then, Anne Hutchinson might have escaped her sentence of banishment had she not become so entranced with the sound of

---

39 Ibid., 381.

her own voice as to indulge in a detailed description of her
revelations from God, a blasphemous claim from which the
Puritan oligarchy recoiled with horror. In the rain of
abuse that poured down upon Anne as her church cast her out,
the minister of the Salem church cried, "You have stept out
of your place. You have rather been a husband than a wife
. . . ."[40] No doubt the congregation agreed, but this transgression seemed relatively unimportant when weighed in the
balance with Mrs. Hutchinson's spiritual power and the contagion of her erroneous opinions.

Within little more than a generation after the Hutchinson affair the whole tone of Puritan society had begun to
change. Gone was the austerity of the early days, when the
whole community had concentrated its energies on physical
survival and spiritual salvation. By the 1660's the coast
towns had established a thriving trade with the outside
world; by the '90's the merchants of New England were well-
to-do; by the 1720's they had accumulated large fortunes.
In New York and Philadelphia, too, trade was swelling the
coffers of the merchant class, while farther south the big
planters ruled over tobacco empires of land and slaves. A
colonial aristocracy had come into being.

---

40 Ibid., 529.

On the fashionable streets of the big seaports and along the rivers of Virginia and the Carolinas these families began to assume a more luxurious standard of living. The signs of change were nowhere plainer than in women's lives. A rich planter or shipper could afford to pamper his wife and daughters. No longer essential to the family economy, freed from arduous household tasks, these upper-class women were set at leisure to pursue the pleasures and cultivate the graces that would serve as a badge of the family wealth and social position. The lady now made her official appearance on the American scene.

For instruction in the arts of leisure colonial ladies looked to England; a ship newly in from London would carry books and magazines, new dresses and shoes, ornaments of all kinds, and letters from friends describing the latest styles and amusements. Fashion was the dictator of the age, and one English visitor in Maryland was "almost inclined to believe that a new fashion is adopted earlier by the polished and affluent American, than by many opulent persons in the great metropolis."[41] The ladies vied with their London cousins in the richness of their hoop-petticoats, the low cut of the bodice, the fantastic height and decoration of the headdress. They too spent hours with dancing masters, learning not only the intricate patterns of the minuet but various arts and

41 William Eddis, quoted in Spruill, Women's Life, 92.

mannerisms of feminine grace like the proper use of the fan. They purchased or concocted the same beauty preparations and applied them with equal care.[42]

Such elaborate dress was the mark of a social age, and American ladies had constant opportunity to display their persons in public, at assemblies, balls, races, and (in the South at least) the theater, as well as in the streets and shops of the larger towns.[43] No doubt social life was gayest among the plantation aristocracy of the South. Puritan New England, though much relaxed, still frowned on pleasure-seeking. Nevertheless Cotton Mather as early as 1692 felt it necessary in his Ornaments for the Daughters of Zion to preach at great length against extravagance in dress. The ornaments Mather

---

42 Philip Fithian, tutor at "Nomini Hall," the seat of Councilor Robert Carter of Virginia, left the following description of a stylish young lady visiting nearby a few years before the Revolution. "She is a well set maid, of a proper Height, neither high nor low . . . . she sits very erect, places her feet with great propriety, her Hands she lays carelessly in her lap, & never moves them but when she has occasion to adjust some article of her dress, or to perform some exercise of the Fan . . . . When She has a Bonnet on & Walks, She is truly elegant; her carriage neat & graceful, & her Presence soft & beautiful -- Her hair is a dark Brown, which was crap'd up very high, & in it she had a Ribbon interwoven with an artificial Flower--At each of her ears dangled a brilliant Jewel; She was pinched up rather too near in a long pair of new fashioned Stays . . . . I imputed the Flush which was visible in her Face to her being swathed up Body & Soul & limbs together--She wore a light Chintz Gown, very fine, with a blue stamp, elegantly made, & which set well upon her--She wore a blue silk Quilt [petticoat]-- In one word Her Dress was rich & fashionable." Quoted in Spruill, Women's Life, 132.

43 See ibid., ch. 5.

approved of for females were spiritual ones, not the "Garish, Pompous, Flanting [sic] Modes" that he saw on the streets of Boston. Many a woman, he suspected, was spending "more Time in Dressing, than she do's in Praying. . . ." Mather's strictures on the use of cosmetics and the "haughty Carriages Learned in the Dancing-School" afford further evidence of the backsliding of Puritan womankind.[44] Quaker Philadelphia was no more sober, if we may judge from Benjamin Franklin's criticisms in the 1740's of the luxury and ambition for show which, he said, had become the ruling passion of the age.[45]

Cotton Mather was surely pessimistic when he fancied he saw "a Proud, Light, Vain, Giddy, Trifling Soul"[46] under every fashionable exterior. Yet the eighteenth-century lady

---

[44] Ornaments for the Daughters of Zion, 54, 58, 16, 44. Low necks were a special abomination in Mather's eyes. "For a Woman to expose unto Common View those parts of her Body, which there can be no good End or Use for the Exposing of," he sputtered, "is for her to expose her self unto the Vengeance of Heaven. . . . The Face is to be Naked because of what is to be Known by it; the Hands are to be Naked, because of what is to be Done by them. But for the Nakedness of the Back and Breasts, No Reason can be given; unless it be that a Woman may by showing a Fair-Skin Enkindle a Foul Fire in the Male Spectators; for which cause even Popish Writers have no less Righteously than severely Lashed them; and for Protestant Women to use them, is no less Inexcusable than it is Abominable. . . ." Besides being indecent low cut gowns were a menace to health, as was tight lacing, and both were further reprehensible because they prevented a woman from doing any work. Ornaments, 52-54.

[45] Franklin, Reflections on Courtship and Marriage (1746), reprinted in A Series of Letters on Courtship and Marriage (Springfield, 1796), 10.

[46] Ornaments, 54.

undoubtedly had lost both mental and moral stamina in acquiring her beauty and grace.  Her education, more expensive than her seventeenth-century forebears', was even less substantial; whether she was taught at home or attended one of the fashionable boarding or day schools which flourished in the colonial towns, she spent most of her time acquiring the ornamental accomplishments of music, dancing, and fancy needlework.  A North Carolina gentleman voiced the general attitude when he left provisions in his will for his children's education. The boys were to have a thorough classical training, but for his daughter it was enough that she be taught "to write and read & some feminine accomplishments which may render her agreeable. . . ."[47]

Both in the colonies and in England there were constant complaints of the effect of this sort of education upon the female character.  "By this method of management," Franklin observed, "they are polished to a superficial lustre," while "true good sense, and sound judgment, . . . are but little considered. . . ."  As a result girls reached marriageable age prepared to dazzle a man's eyes but too likely also to make him "a vain and capricious, an empty and insignificant companion."[48]

---

[47] John Baptista Ashe, quoted in Spruill, Women's Life, 207. Mrs. Spruill describes "The Schooling of Girls" in the South in ch. 5; custom in the Middle and Northern Colonial towns was very similar.

[48] Reflections on Courtship and Marriage, 2-3.

This age, however, like every other, had no shortage
of persons eager to undertake the task of elevating the
weaker sex.  Clergymen sermonizing on female manners and
morals, anxious fathers giving advice to their daughters,
novelists with a moral purpose, and essayists holding society up to satire -- all took their turn at writing such
books.  Most of them were English, though the colonists also
read a few French works in English translations and now and
then an American would try his hand at the genre.  Where
they wrote or when they wrote made little difference; from
the 1670's to the 1770's these gentlemen (and an occasional
lady) set forth the same ideas and standards with only minor
variations.

Englishwomen, it would seem, stood in greater need of
these exhortations than their American sisters.  Restoration
England, intoxicated with boom times and release from Puritan gloom, had plunged into what moralists regarded as a
"desperate state of vice and folly."[49]  In this fall from
grace the female sex had played a conspicuous part.  Women's
frantic pursuit of pleasure, their drinking and gambling,
their easy morals and manners and loose talk had alarmed sober
citizens who overlooked the fact that only a small percentage
of the sex -- mostly Londoners of the upper classes -- were

---

[49] The Spectator, No. 10, quoted in Jane H. Phillips, "Addison
and Steele and the Women of their Time" (unpublished undergraduate honors thesis, Smith College, 1938), 2.

guilty of these excesses. In the simpler provincial society of the colonies the ladies managed to adopt the new fashions without corrupting their morals. Card playing, for instance, was popular among both sexes, but women seldom gambled.[50] Nevertheless the English writers' injunctions to modesty and delicacy in behavior, to quiet and sober habits of life, could do no harm, and judicious fathers or husbands often selected these small volumes in Boston or Philadelphia bookshops as improving gifts for their womenfolk.

Nor was it only the ladies in the governor's or the planter's or the wealthy merchant's household who read this literature. Middle-class wives and daughters were still busy in the kitchen and the shop, but if the family fortunes took an upward turn they might well find themselves rising in society. With this eventuality in mind they too bought the advice books and studied the most approved models of conduct.

English gentlewomen had had the benefit of this kind of instruction as early as 1673, when an anonymous manual entitled The Ladies Calling was published in London. This heavily pious volume, which may have been the work of Richard Allestree, royalist preacher and principal of Eton, quickly became a classic. The early editions seldom reached the colonies, where women as yet felt no need to seek beyond their Bible and catechism or prayer book for moral guidance.

---

50 Spruill, Women's Life, 108.

The Puritan woman who read Cotton Mather's <u>Ornaments for the</u> <u>Daughters of Zion</u>, however, unknowingly received echoes of Allestree's advice at second hand. Selections from <u>The</u> <u>Ladies Calling</u>, again without credit, later appeared in <u>The</u> <u>Ladies Library</u>, an anthology of 1714 which was widely read in the colonies as well as at home. This compendium also included parts of other late-seventeenth-century works, notably <u>The Lady's-New-Year's-Gift, or, Advice to a Daughter</u>, by the Marquis of Halifax, statesman at the court of Charles II, and the <u>Traité de L'Éducation des Filles</u> of the French theorist François Fénelon, archbishop of Cambrai.[51]

These manuals supplied the market for the next half century. Utilitarian writers, however, were by no means the only ones to espouse the cause of female improvement. Literary artists made it a favorite theme. When Richard Steele in beginning the <u>Tatler</u> essays in 1709 announced that "The general purpose of this paper, is to expose the false arts of life, to pull off the disguises of cunning, vanity, and affectation, and to recommend a general simplicity in our dress, our discourse, and our behavior,"[52] he had the female sex particularly in mind. Steele and his colleague Joseph Addison

---

51 Benson, <u>Women in Eighteenth-Century America</u>, 16-23, describes this literature.

52 Quoted in George Sherburn, "The Restoration and Eighteenth Century (1660-1789)," <u>A Literary History of England</u>, Albert C. Baugh, ed. (New York, 1948), 873.

took frequent occasion to poke fun at feminine foibles.
Their deft portraits of the giddy coquette, the spendthrift
wife, and other types deviating from the quiet and sensible
norm hit home with readers on both sides of the Atlantic.[53]

The Tatler and Spectator had a legion of imitators, including young Benjamin Franklin, whose first literary effort
was an essay series contributed anonymously to his brother's
Boston newspaper in 1722.  Franklin, then sixteen, wrote in
the guise of a voluble New England widow, Mrs. Silence Dogood,
and followed his English models in generously attributing
female faults to the attitudes of the dominant sex.[54]  Twenty
years later he came forward again as woman's champion.  In
his Reflections on Courtship and Marriage Franklin took the
affirmative side in an argument over whether women were fit
to be rational companions for "a man of sense and judgment."
The Reflections became the first of his works to be reprinted
abroad.[55]

---

53 Benson, Women in Eighteenth-Century America, 34-39.

54 Mrs. Dogood, noting that women were most often accused of
idleness, ignorance, and folly, inquired tartly, "Are not
the Men to blame for their Folly in maintaining us in
Idleness?  Who is there that can be handsomely supported
in Affluence, Ease and Pleasure by another, that will chuse
rather to earn his Bread by the Sweat of his own Brows?"
The other two charges she threw back at the men "for not
allowing women the Advantages of Education."  "The Dogood
Papers," The Writings of Benjamin Franklin, Albert H.
Smyth, ed. (New York, 1907), II, 15-16.

55 Reflections, 3; Carl Van Doren, Benjamin Franklin (New York,
1941), 152.  The book also went through four American editions in thirteen years.  Arthur M. Schlesinger, Learning
How to Behave (New York, 1946), 9.

Essays like these, graceful and urbane, yet chaste and practical, made ideal reading for ladies' leisure. Their popularity was unchallenged until the novels of Samuel Richardson appeared in the 1740's. This serious London printer had an uncanny insight into the feminine mind. Pamela and Clarissa Harlowe depicted the familiar scenes of domestic life, yet were full of romantic interest, being written in a letter form which allowed minute treatment of every harrowing twist and turn in the heroine's emotional adventures. But Richardson was not satisfied with merely entertaining his readers. He intended Pamela and Clarissa to serve as models of the female character, and developed his ideals of conduct even more explicitly in homilies incorporated into the narrative.[56]

These eighteenth century classics would be read and re-read for years to come. By the 1760's, however, the old manuals like The Ladies Calling and Halifax's Advice to a Daughter, for all the excellence of their content, had begun to seem somewhat archaic in style. There was a need for some up-to-date handbooks, and several new writers now replaced the old favorites.

One was a personage known as "the admirable Mrs. Chapone," a member of the coterie of Bluestocking ladies who dispensed intellectual fare to London society from their salons in the

---

56 Benson, Women in Eighteenth-Century America, 45-52.

third quarter of the century.  In the 1770's she produced
two books of advice to her sex which went through repeated
editions both in England and America and were still being
quoted sixty years later.  Equally popular was Dr. John
Gregory's A Father's Legacy to his Daughters, published in
1774, two years after Hester Chapone's Letters on the Improvement of the Mind and often coupled with it in a single volume
in later editions.

Gregory, who held the chair of medicine at Edinburgh
University, wrote in failing health to advise his motherless
daughters, and his book was published after his death.  Mrs.
Chapone directed her letters to a favorite niece.  Their
books therefore struck a personal note which was missing in
a third book of this later period, Sermons to Young Women,
by the Rev. James Fordyce.  This fashionable London preacher,
however, won great admiration for his elegance of style and
sentiment, and his collection of fourteen sermons was three
times reprinted in America before 1800.[57]

If questioned about his motive in writing, every author
from Lord Halifax to Dr. Gregory would have replied sincerely
that he wished to raise the standards of female character and

---

[57] Ibid., 58ff.  Gregory's book went through twenty-seven editions in America between 1775 and 1798, and magazines often
excerpted parts of it.  Mrs. Chapone's Letters were reprinted six times between 1783 and 1797.  Schlesinger, Learning How to Behave, 9.

conduct. The eighteenth century, however, was an intensely practical age, and not least in ethics and morals. It is hardly surprising, therefore, to find all these writers frankly centering their counsel on the young woman's major concern in life, the pursuit and the care and treatment of man.

Winning a husband was a girl's chief end, since, as everyone clearly recognized, marriage not only gave her status but was often her only means of support. An old maid, The Ladies Calling declared, was "the most calamitous Creature in Nature." Only one crumb of comfort could be held out to these unfortunates: if they would "addict themselves to the strictest Virtue and Piety, they would give the World some cause to believe 'twas not their necessity, but their choice which kept them unmarried. . . ." If on the other hand they kept up the chase, trying "to disguise their Age by all the Impostures and Gaieties of a youthful dress and behavior," they could only expect "scorn and censure."[58]

To escape this fate women bent every effort from an early age. Girls of twelve in Virginia and Maryland knowingly calculated their matrimonial chances[59] and took as much interest in dress and feminine adornment as their older sisters. The Spectator and other writers frequently scolded the sex for

---

58 The Ladies Calling (Oxford, 1677), 158-159. See also Gregory, A Father's Legacy to his Daughters (New York, 1775), 37-38.

59 Spruill, Women's Life, 139.

their love of finery and urged modesty in attire, pointing out that virtue was more lasting than beauty.  Regarding the latter, however, most females had observed with one Southern belle that though "Wisdom says it is a fading flower, . . . fading as it is, it attracts more admiration than wit, goodness, or anything else in the world."[60]

Dr. John Gregory, more realistic, told his daughters that "The love of dress is natural to you, and therefore it is proper and reasonable."  He warned, however, that extravagant apparel signified to the masculine eye "Vanity, levity, . . . [and] folly" in the wearer, and advised instead "An elegant simplicity."  Concerned over the future of his girls, already deprived of their mother and soon, he feared, to lose his guidance as well, the ailing physician spelled out his advice plainly.  Good taste, he said, "will direct you to dress in such a way as to conceal any blemishes, and set off your beauties, if you have any, to the greatest advantage."  In applying the latter rule, however, circumspection was required, especially as to décolletage.  "A fine woman shews her charms to most advantage, when she seems most to conceal them.  The finest bosom in nature is not so fine as what imagination forms."[61]

In the adornment of the mind as well as of the body moral

60 Molly Tilghman of Maryland, quoted in ibid., 135.

61 Gregory, Father's Legacy, 22-23.

and masculine standards were inextricably mixed. Every
author urged woman to devote part of her leisure to improving
reading, realizing that her formal training in school had
likely been scanty or frivolous or both. "Be all ardour,"
the Rev. Dr. Fordyce exhorted his female hearers, "to emu-
late those excellent ones of your sex" who possessed "a mind
devoted to wisdom, and ennobled by knowledge." Nevertheless
Fordyce and others made it clear that it was not intellectual
but emotional qualities that the world valued in women.
"Nature," he declared, appears to have formed the faculties
of your sex, for the most part, with less vigour than those
of ours. . . ." Yet "I would by no means insinuate," he continued,

> that you are not capable of the judicious
> and the solid, in such proportion as is
> suited to your destination in life. This,
> I apprehend, does not require reasoning
> or accuracy, so much as observation and
> discernment. Your business chiefly is to
> read Men, in order to make yourselves
> agreeable and useful. It is not the ar-
> gumentative, but the sentimental talents,
> which give you that insight, and those
> openings into the human heart, that lead
> to your practical ends, as women.

In this her proper study, however, womankind could "derive
great assistance from books."[62]

Education also served other practical purposes. Besides

---

62 Fordyce, Sermons to Young Women (Philadelphia, 1787), 170,
161-162.

enabling women to fathom the masculine mind, suitable reading would furnish them with material for conversation --
"Reflections and Sentiments," as Richard Steele put it,
"proper for the Companions of reasonable Men." It would also stiffen the moral character, making them less dependent
on empty amusements and "more superior to every thing corrupting and dangerous."[63]

As to exactly what women should read to reap these benefits, most of the male writers were vague. Mrs. Chapone,
however, devoted a third of her book to detailed instructions
on this point. This cultivated lady regarded reading as "the
sincerest of pleasures" and wished nothing so much for her
sex as that they acquire "a taste for intellectual improvement." Sensibly realizing, however, that most young women
would quail at the thought, Hester Chapone urged her readers
not to be discouraged by a modest opinion of their capacities.
She also quieted their fears that study would turn them into
female pedants, making them a laughing stock and frightening
men away. Mrs. Chapone's program, as it turned out, was very
limited, consisting chiefly of history ("more materials for
conversation are supplied by this kind of knowledge, than by
almost any other") and poetry (to cultivate "The faculty, in
which women usually most excel, . . . that of imagination").

---

63 Steele, The Tatler, No. 248, quoted in Rae Blanchard,
   "Richard Steele and the Status of Women," Studies in
   Philology, XXVI (July, 1929), 341; Fordyce, Sermons, 160.

She did not advise the study of the learned languages; modern literature would be "more than sufficient to store your mind with as many ideas as you will know how to manage."[64]

In exceptional cases these rules might be suspended. No one would bar from abstruser studies "those ladies, whom Nature, not confining herself to her customary operations, has endowed with any signal strength of genius." "But if you happen to have any learning," Dr. Gregory advised, "keep it a profound secret, especially from the men, who generally look with a jealous and malignant eye on a woman of great parts, and a cultivated understanding."[65]

No girl's training was complete without a careful grounding in religion. On this the best authories were firm. They had an uphill fight, however, for the eighteenth century was an age of little faith. Many mothers, The Ladies Calling complained, "though nicely curious in other parts of their Daughters breeding," completely neglected to teach them piety, considering this not only unnecessary but "ungentile, below the regard of Persons of Quality." To impress on the female mind the importance of religion their advisers characteristically resorted to practical arguments. Dr. Gregory observed that women particularly required this kind of solace. Sorrow

64 Chapone, Letters on the Improvement of the Mind (Boston [1782]), 250, 193, 195. "That men are frighted at Female pedantry, is very certain," declared Fordyce. (Sermons, 176.)

65 Fordyce, Sermons, 168; Gregory, Father's Legacy, 15.

and suffering often fell to their lot, yet they were denied
the masculine relief of plunging into business or riotous
living to forget personal troubles. Dr. Fordyce offered the
further inducement that "the considerations of Religion will
conduce mightily to support and cheer you under the restraints
of sobriety and decorum" which good society imposed on the
sex.[66]

Men, whose conduct lay under no restraint whatever, did
not need this consolation and were not expected to seek it.
Nevertheless, Gregory warned, "Women are greatly deceived when
they think they recommend themselves to our sex by their indifference about religion. Even these [sic] men who are themselves unbelievers, dislike infidelity in you." Irreligion
in a woman seemed hard and unfeminine. Furthermore, it was
likely to raise doubts in a man's mind regarding her virtue.[67]

With a good understanding and sound principles a young
lady could be counted on to display "a determined resolution
and steadiness" on all important points of conduct. In other
respects, however, she was expected to exhibit, in Steele's

---

66 The Ladies Calling, 218-219; Gregory, Father's Legacy, 9;
Fordyce, Sermons, 216.

67 Gregory, Father's Legacy, 13. Benjamin Franklin also seems
to have reserved religious skepticism for his own sex; regarding his daughter Sally he wrote home from England in
1758, "I hope she continues to love going to church, and
would have her read over and over again . . . the Lady's
[sic] Library." Franklin to Deborah Franklin, The Works
of Benjamin Franklin, Jared Sparks, ed. (Boston, 1838),
VII, 166-167.

words, a "gentle softness" and "tender fear."[68] An appearance of fragility would add to these feminine charms. Dr.
Gregory wished his daughters to enjoy good health, but since
men "so naturally associate the idea of female softness and
delicacy with a correspondent delicacy of constitution," he
advised them not to call attention to physical vigor.[69]

In her deportment towards men, the young lady's mentors
counseled a modest reserve.[70] This was particularly essential
in courtship. It was most indelicate for a girl to allow any
hint of her feelings to escape until a suitor had formally

---

68 Gregory, Father's Legacy, 24. Steele is quoted in A. R.
   Humphreys, "The 'Rights of Woman' in the Age of Reason,"
   Modern Language Review, XLI (July, 1946), 260.

69 Gregory, Father's Legacy, 21. Dr. Gregory was often
   criticized for this passage by later writers who forgot
   that he had also (pp. 20-21) urged his girls to take out-
   door exercise, to "give vigour to your constitutions,
   and a bloom to your complexions." He merely wished them
   not to give an impression of being Amazons ("when a
   woman speaks of her great strength, her extraordinary
   appetite, her ability to bear excessive fatigue, we re-
   coil . . . in a way she is little aware of."). Unfortunately eighteenth century ladies tended to heed the
   advice to appear fragile rather than the injunctions to
   take exercise. The well-to-do in America as well as in
   England increasingly went for their outings in carriages
   rather than on foot or horseback (Spruill, Women's Life,
   108-109) with the result that delicate health was tend-
   ing to become a fact as well as an attitude.

70 A man preferred to worship his angel from afar, Dr. Gregory informed his daughters. If a young lady insisted on
   forcing her charms on men by making herself conspicuous
   in public places and conversing with bold masculine freedom, he warned, "she may soon reduce the angel to a very
   ordinary girl." Father's Legacy, 18-19.

declared himself.[71] She should if possible even restrain
herself from falling in love until she had "received the
most convincing proofs of the attachment of a man of such
merit, as will justify a reciprocal regard." This policy
would protect her against the designs of unscrupulous males
whose aim was seduction rather than wedlock. Once a man of
worth had declared himself, however, it was neither honorable
nor humane to "let him linger in a miserable suspense" as to
whether she intended to accept him.[72]

This latter rule seems to have been honored mostly in
the breach, if one can judge from the strictures on coquettes,
whom the eighteenth century seemed to consider almost as dangerous to the male sex as seducers to the female. A belle

---

71 George Washington explained to his stepdaughter that "The
declaration, without the most indirect invitation of yours,
must proceed from the man to render it permanent and valuable." Quoted in Spruill, Women's Life, 149. Dr. Gregory
was even dubious about revealing one's feelings after marriage, especially if the man were violently in love. "If
you love him, let me advise you never to discover to him
the full extent of your love, no, not although you marry
him. . . . Violent love cannot subsist, at least cannot be expressed, for any time together, on both sides;
otherwise the certain consequence, however concealed, is
satiety and disgust." Father's Legacy, 32. This piece
of advice, like the doctor's remarks on health, was also
much criticized by later writers, who forgot that he
counseled this concealment only in special cases. Mrs.
Chapone, for instance, declared that this was "a precept
which does no honour to his own sex, and which would take
from ours its sweetest charms, simplicity and artless
tenderness." "A Letter to a New-Married Lady," The Works
of Mrs. Chapone (Boston, 1809), IV, 83-84.

72 Gregory, Father's Legacy, 37, 32.

with a flock of suitors could afford to spin out the game,
strewing broken hearts along her path for several years before bestowing her hand upon the likeliest candidate.[73]

"Let us not dissemble the truth," pronounced the Rev.
Dr. Fordyce, reflecting philosophically upon eternal veri-
ties. "The greater part of either sex study to prey upon one
another. The world, in too many instances, is a theatre of
war between men and women. Every stratagem is tried, and
every advantage taken, on the side of both. On the side of
the former, strength and daring are joined to art and ambition, in which the latter abound." The situation, he said,
reminded him of relations between England and France, where
"a general truce is always short, and a national peace never
secure."[74]

After marriage the war between the sexes took on a different form. Against the husband's authority was now pitted
the wife's feminine wiles. Men, Lord Halifax explained, were

---

73 Some observations by a Maryland girl on a case of this
kind are instructive. The hard-hearted young lady in
question had just accepted a suitor who had been wooing
her for three years against stiff competition. "Her
reign has been brilliant," Molly Tilghman remarked, "and
she has clos'd it in very good time, while her train was
undiminish'd. It is a nice point for a Belle to know
when to marry, and one in which they are very apt. She
understood the matter." Quoted in Spruill, Women's Life,
149.

74 Fordyce, Sermons, 232-233.

appointed to be the lawgivers and therefore "had the better share of Reason bestow'd upon them. . . ." Nevertheless, after impressing on his daughter the duty of wifely submission he assured her that she was far from helpless in the combat. "You have more strength in your Looks," he declared, "than we have in our Laws, and more power by your Tears, than we have by our Arguments."[75]

Halifax's book was largely a treatise on how to handle a difficult husband. Smiles and flattery would work with a bad-tempered man, he advised; appeals to vanity or ambition with a tight-fisted one. A weak man could easily be governed with a tactful hand. If one's husband proved unfaithful, however, one could only pretend not to notice.[76] "You are to consider," Halifax instructed, that "you live in a time which has rendered some kind [sic] of Frailties so habitual, that they lay claim to large Grains of Allowance." Such misconduct was "in the utmost Criminal" in a woman. "Next to the danger of committing the Fault yourself," however, he warned, "the greatest is that of seeing it in your Husband. Do not seem to look or hear that way."[77]

---

75 Quoted in Spruill, Women's Life, 216.

76 Ibid., 216-217.

77 Halifax, Advice to a Daughter, quoted in Blanchard, "Richard Steele and the Status of Women," Studies in Philology, XXVI, 344. The Ladies Calling (p. 183) gave similar counsel, urging the wife to abstain from all "virulencies and reproches [sic]."

When the best authorities had to give this advice, marriage had indeed fallen upon evil days. Far from being glorified as in Puritan times, it had become, in Restoration London at least, a target for ribald wit, being usually presented on the stage as a boresome state from which both wife and husband were eager to escape into illicit adventure. The hero of a Restoration comedy was most often a gay rake who had "but one Reason for setting any Value on the Fair Sex."[78] Evidently no one thought it amiss when after intrigues with various mistresses and erring wives this glamorous gentleman climaxed his career by marriage with a virtuous maiden. And the drama's picture of society, though highly artificial, was not so unrealistic as it might seem. Gentlemen not only in London but in the colonies kept mistresses, acknowledged illegitimate children, and carried on amorous intrigues freely. Nor did good society close its doors to them -- or prevent its carefully reared daughters from becoming their wives.[79]

---

78 The Tatler, No. 53, quoted in Blanchard, "Richard Steele and the Status of Women," 333. Sherburn's account of Restoration comedy in A Literary History of England, 762-779, is useful.

79 Spruill, Women's Life, 174ff. This kind of immorality seems to have been most prevalent in the South (though Benjamin Franklin had a natural son whom he raised in his own family in Philadelphia). One writer in a South Carolina newspaper in 1738 complained that even "professed Friends to Religion and Virtue" would welcome in their homes "an abandon'd Fellow, who has been often over-run with a polite Disorder, debauched two or three innocent Virgins or kept half a dozen Negro Wenches in the Face of the Sun." (Quoted in Spruill, Women's Life, 174.) The

No writers condoned these masculine peccadilloes, however much they might preach resignation to the injured wife. Richard Steele stoutly maintained "that Chastity is . . . as much to be valued in Men as in Women."[80] Samuel Richardson in all his novels crusaded against the double standard of morality, making his heroes into faithful paragons of the domestic virtues, not unlike his heroines. He did succeed in casting a permanent slur upon the gay rake;[81] after Richardson's harrowing picture of Clarissa Harlowe's sufferings at the hands of Lovelace this character appeared henceforth in fiction as a villain of the deepest dye. Whether he met with similar disapproval in real life, however, is another question. If the vast popularity of novels about seduction in post-Revolutionary America is any proof, the double standard continued to flourish.

Marriage, however, regained some of its former dignity.

---

handbooks instructed young ladies to make careful inquiries among their friends about a suitor's character and reputation before accepting him (Mrs. Spruill cites a list of questions George Washington gave his stepdaughter to ask, pp. 153-154). Yet such was the glamor of the "libertine" that a popular adage maintained "A reformed rake makes the best husband" -- an idea advisers to young women spent much time refuting. See, for instance, Fordyce, Sermons, 82-84; Gregory, Father's Legacy, 43 ("A rake is always a suspicious husband, because he has only known the most worthless of your sex. He likewise entails the worst of diseases on his wife and children, if he has the misfortune to have any.")

80 Quoted in Blanchard, "Richard Steele and the Status of Women," 349.

81 Brian W. Downs, Richardson (London, 1928), 169.

Richard Steele turned the tables on the Restoration wits by
devoting his own considerable talents in that line to praise
of the married state.[82]  And Benjamin Franklin, following
the Tatler and Spectator's lead or perhaps merely his own
common sense, put up an able defense of the matrimonial life.
The husband, to be sure, would have to rectify the defects in
his wife's education before he could take pleasure in her
company.[83]  Once this was accomplished, however, he thought
marriage could afford "as much real felicity, and as refined
an enjoyment of life, to its latest period, as any other
scheme can justly lay claim to."[84]

Franklin envisaged a partnership based on "an union of
minds, a sympathy of affections, a mutual esteem and friendship for each other."  He saw no justification for the arbitrary power which the common law gave a man over his wife,
declaring that "there is no such kind of dominion derived
from either reason or nature" and that its exercise would only
make married life "uncomfortable and miserable."  Nevertheless

---

82 Sherburn quotes a contemporary's remarks on this feat in
A Literary History of England, 874.

83 It was best to begin this program during courtship.  In
paying his addresses to a young lady Franklin advised
the suitor to avoid the fulsome flattery dictated by
custom.  He would favor her instead with "solid and practical reflections" and would suggest also "recommending
the perusal of elegant and improving books."  This would
"drive out . . . that little narrow spirited way of thinking, . . . which is too much the characteristic of many
women."  Reflections, 30.

84 Ibid., 9.

a successful marriage in his view depended upon the husband's having "a superior degree of knowledge and understanding," which would automatically influence his wife to submit to his guidance. "Nature, and the circumstances of human life," he observed, "seem indeed to design for man that superiority. . . ."[85]

Franklin devoted considerable attention to the wife's management of the household, advising her to steer a middle course between the extremes of extravagance and parsimoniousness. The house, he directed, should be run with quiet order, with a minimum of bustle and scolding of servants[86] -- advice obviously pertinent to middle-class townswomen whose standard of living was rising.

In this domestic area Franklin spoke from American experience, though in its treatment of other subjects his pamphlet could easily have passed for an English work. The British manuals were directed to an upper class family settled in its habits of living and possessed of sufficient wealth so that the wife in many cases had only a remote connection with household affairs. Mrs. Chapone, to be sure, devoted

---

85 Ibid., 43-45.

86 Ibid., 66-69. Franklin particularly disliked an excess of virtue in housecleaning: "Some women have such amphibious dispositions, that one would think they chose to be half their lives in water: There is such a clatter of pails and brushes, such inundations in every room, that a man cannot find a dry place for the sole of his foot. . . ."

a sensible chapter to "Economy," declaring that this skill "ought to have the precedence of all other accomplishments." She admitted, however, that it was "too often wholly ne- glected in a young woman's education," so that she went from her father's house to her husband's without the slight- est practical experience.[87] The women in Dr. Fordyce's fashionable congregation evidently regarded the domestic arts as "below their notice," a mortifying sign, he said, of "the declension of the age." Even the exceptional mistress who supervised her establishment properly spent relatively little time on these duties. "The necessary orders, and examina- tions into household affairs," Mrs. Chapone directed, "should be despatched, as soon in the day, and as privately as pos- sible, that they may not interrupt your husband or guests, or break in upon conversation, or reading, in the remainder of the day."[88]

In America most women of "rank and affluence"[89] had no heavier responsibilities than their English counterparts. They too had housekeepers and, especially in the South, large numbers of servants. George Washington felt a house- keeper or steward was absolutely essential at Mount Vernon, writing on one occasion when looking for a replacement that

87 Chapone, Letters on the Improvement of the Mind, 153.

88 Fordyce, Sermons, 125, 135; Chapone, Letters, 162.

89 Fordyce, Sermons, 125.

Mrs. Washington's "fatigue and distress for the want of one
were so great that the matter of salary would be of no consideration." Many husbands, too, like Washington, took an
active part in running the household, keeping the accounts,
ordering clothing and furniture, and even handling the family's
social correspondence.[90]

Eighteenth-century gentlemen took pride in relieving their
wives of domestic burdens, believing themselves truly liberal
in their attitudes toward the sex. The writers of the manuals of the 1760's and 1770's felt their conceptions of
woman's place to be a notable advance over that of previous
generations. Dr. Gregory called his daughters' attention to
the "honourable point of view [in which] I have considered
your sex; not as domestic drudges, or the slaves of our
pleasures, but as companions and equals. . . ."[91] This did
not mean, Dr. Fordyce explained, that women should share
men's activities: "you yourselves, I think, will allow that
war, commerce, politics, exercises of strength and dexterity,
abstract philosophy, and all the abstruser sciences, are most
properly the province of man." Women were clearly intended
"to be a kind of softer companions, who, by nameless

---

90 Spruill, Women's Life, 77-79.

91 Father's Legacy, 7-8. Dr. Fordyce had the same consciousness of superior virtue. "To divert fancy, to gratify desire, and in general, to be a sort of better servants, are
all the purposes for which some suppose your sex designed.
A most illiberal supposition!" Sermons, 123.

delightful sympathies and endearments, might improve our
pleasures and soothe our pains; to lighten the load of domestic cares, and thereby leave us more at leisure for rougher
labours, or severer studies; and finally, to spread a certain
grace and embellishment over human life." Only an ignorant
barbarian could hold any other opinion.[92]

The effect of this eighteenth-century climate of opinion
upon women who had the leisure to read books was naturally to
discourage any constructive activity outside the home. The
economic incentive, largely responsible for the public appearances of upper-class women in the pioneer generation, had
disappeared, and without this practical competition the the-
orists had a free hand to dictate the terms of a lady's existence.

Middle-class townswomen in the colonies still carried
on their tidy business ventures as they had in the pioneer
era. In fact it has been said that just before the Revolution
nearly ten per cent of the Boston merchants were women.[93]
Continuing the old crafts and trades, they added new ones
to cater to the rising demand for luxuries, doing commercial
dressmaking, fine laundering and dry cleaning, fancy baking,

---

92 _Sermons_, 161, 123-124.

93 Dexter, _Colonial Women of Affairs_, 38.

pickling and preserving.  Others answered the call for education in the niceties of gracious living by setting up boarding and day schools for girls, hiring masters to give the actual instruction.[94]

A few women of good birth were still making names for themselves in business management just before the Revolution. Mrs. Mary Alexander ran a large provision house in New York and at one time during the French and Indian wars received a contract to supply the British troops.  Her mother and grandmother had also been merchants, and this tradition and the family wealth undoubtedly smoothed the way for Mrs. Alexander's career.  She was a social leader in the city as well and for a long time the only personage beside the governor to drive a two-horse coach.[95]

Gentlewomen in reduced circumstances might also go into business without affecting their social standing.  Mrs. Susannah Sheaffe, widow of a public official in Boston, was set up in the grocery business by friends in 1771, made a success of the enterprise, and married off all her five daughters to distinguished men.  In the South widows of good family who were left without resources sometimes turned their large homes into public houses.  These became widely known for the quality of their hospitality and often were centers of

---

94 Ibid., chs. 3, 5; Spruill, Women's Life, 257.

95 Dexter, Colonial Women of Affairs, 105-106, 184.

community social life.[96]

The South, too, continued to produce capable women plantation managers. Notable among them was Eliza Lucas Pinckney,
in some respects the most interesting woman of the colonial
period. In 1739, when she was only seventeen, her father, a
British army officer stationed in the West Indies, left her
in charge of his extensive South Carolina property. Eliza
had been brought up in England in the home of a family friend,
and since her father disapproved of girls' wasting time on
elaborate needlework,[97] she had probably received a somewhat
more sensible education than most young ladies of her day.
In any case she had a practical and inquiring turn of mind
and real executive talent, with a thorough grasp of the needs
of the Carolina economy.

> I have the business of 3 plantations
> to transact [she wrote the friend who had
> raised her in England] w$^{ch}$ requires much
> writing and more business and fatigue of
> other sorts than you can imagine, but least
> you should imagine it too burthensom to a
> girl at my early time of life, give mee
> leave to assure you I think myself happy
> that I can be useful to so good a father.
> By rising very early I find I can go
> through with much business, but least you
> should think I shall be quite moaped with
> this way of life, I am to inform you there
> is two worthy Ladies in C$^{rs}$ Town, Mrs.
> Pinckney and Mrs. Cleland who are partial
> enough to mee to wish to have mee with them,
> and insist upon my making their houses my
> home when in Town. . . .[98]

---

96 Ibid., 183-184; Spruill, Women's Life, 301-302.

97 Harriott Horry Ravenel, Eliza Pinckney (New York, 1909), 11.

98 Ibid., 6.

Eliza had inherited her father's interest in experimental agriculture, and what time she could spare from routine plantation concerns, tutoring her younger sister and the Negro children, and caring for her invalid mother, she devoted to planting seeds and cuttings which Colonel Lucas sent her.

> I have planted a large figg orchard, with design to dry them, and export them [she wrote to a girlish friend in Charlestown]. I have reckond my expence and the prophets to arise from those figgs, but was I to tell you how great an Estate I am to make this way, and how 'tis to be laid out, you would think me far gone in romance. Y^t good Uncle I know has long thought I have a fertile brain at schemeing, I only confirm him in his oppinion; but I own I love the vegitable world extreamly.[99]

She also tried ginger, cotton, alfalfa, and cassava root (the source of tapioca) but informed her father that she had best hopes for indigo, a leafy plant which in those days before the invention of aniline dyes was the valued source of the color blue. Indigo cultivation required constant care, and the processing of the leaves into small cakes of marketable dye was an unpleasant and tricky job. Eliza had considerable trouble obtaining seed from her father in time to raise a crop before frost. She had even worse luck with an expert from the islands, sent by the colonel to teach her the method of dye-extraction, who deliberately spoiled the cakes in an attempt to prevent the prospective competition

---

99 Ibid., 31-32.

of Carolina indigo with the product of his native place.
Nevertheless by 1744 she managed to raise a good crop, which
she devoted to seed, distributing it among her neighbors.
Three years later the colony had a crop large enough to ex-
port, and indigo soon became the staple upon which, together
with rice, the colony's prosperity rested until the end of
the century.[100]

In the year of Eliza's final success with indigo culture,
she married Colonel Charles Pinckney, later chief justice of
South Carolina and colony commissioner in London, and widower
of the Mrs. Pinckney who had extended Eliza such cordial in-
vitations to Charleston.  The bride's father who, according
to her biographer, seems to have had "misgivings lest his
managing daughter should attempt to be also a managing wife,"
wrote Eliza a letter of advice on the proper attitude for her
new situation, to which she replied,

> I assure you t'is not more my duty than
> my inclination to follow it; for making
> it the business of my life to please a man
> of Mr. Pinckney's merrit even in triffles,
> I esteem a pleasing task: and I am well as-
> sured the acting out of my proper province
> and invading his, would be an inexcusable
> breach of prudence; as his superiour under-
> standing, (without any other consideration,)
> would point him to dictate, and leave me
> nothing but the easy task of obeying.[101]

The two were very congenial; Colonel Pinckney valued her

---

100 Just before the Revolution, South Carolina was exporting
over a million pounds of indigo a year. Ibid., 106-107.

101 Ibid., 100.

abilities enough to enlist her aid both in the management of
his plantations and the education of their children.  She
continued to administer her father's property as well, attempted the culture of flax and hemp at his behest, with
indifferent success, and became interested in tree planting
and the cultivation of silkworms.  From this latter experiment she produced enough silk to make three dresses of lus-
trous brocade, one of which she presented to the Princess of
Wales, mother of George III, during the Pinckneys' residence
in London in the 1750's.[102]  She also raised a daughter and
two sons, Charles Cotesworth and Thomas, and lived to see one
a framer of the United States Constitution and the other
United States ambassador to England before her death in 1793.
President George Washington at his own request acted as one
of her pallbearers.[103]

Eliza Pinckney, like Anne Hutchinson, rose easily above
the conventional restrictions on women's activities; she would
have left an impression on any period.  In general, however,
"the eighteenth century saw a decline in the vigor and self-
reliance of women in wealthier families and a lessening of
their influence in public matters."[104]  The historian of

102 Ibid., 130-131.

103 Ibid., 317.  See Spruill, Women's Life, 308ff., for a good
    shorter account of Mrs. Pinckney.

104 Spruill, Women's Life, 241.

women in the Southern colonies notices in the petitions and requests made by women to public officials in the eighteenth century a consciousness of sex, anxious disclaiming of ability to understand politics, and an apologetic manner for presuming to meddle in such affairs, quite different from the sturdy directness of Margaret Brent's petitions and those of the women rebels in Bacon's uprising. These later ladies had taken well to heart the Spectator's admonition that political activity was "repugnant to the softness, the modesty, and those other endearing qualities . . . natural to the fair sex."[105]

---

[105] Quoted in ibid., 243-244.

Chapter Two

THE REVOLUTIONARY ERA AND WOMAN'S RIGHTS, 1776-1800

Chapter Two

THE REVOLUTIONARY ERA AND WOMAN'S RIGHTS, 1776-1800

The onset of the revolution brought to an end the halcyon days of aristocratic society in America. This of course was by no means the intention of the patriot leaders who launched the rebellion. They planned merely a political revolution, and only so much of that as was necessary to overthrow British rule. They contemplated no upheaval in the social order, no abandonment of settled custom -- the elaborate dress, the careful distinctions of rank, the moralistic insistence on propriety and manners. But the philosophy with which they justified their cause, the constant talk of natural law and the rights of man, was bound to inspire other challenges to the established order. Democratic ideas, once set in circulation, would inevitably gather strength, and later converts might apply them in realms far removed from the province house and the customs house -- perhaps even in the home.

These changes came slowly. Aristocratic habits and the prestige attached to them died hard, and particularly where women were concerned. The eighteenth-century ideal of womanhood would remain the standard in America for years to come. The manuals of Drs. Gregory and Fordyce, classic champions of that creature of delicacy and ornamental grace, were as popular after the Revolution as before. Yet this standard

65

now for the first time began to be questioned, both by liber-
als and conservatives. The closely related idea of submission also came under attack. It was no accident that the
term woman's rights was born in the revolutionary era.


To women's actual lives the War of Independence brought
the disruption characteristic of all wars -- the separations,
the inflation, the shortages -- but it did not alter popular
ideas about women's place. Standards of behavior were
slightly relaxed; journalists previously much given to inculcating the importance of retiring modesty now applauded the
young ladies who formed associations to refuse the addresses
of any but patriot suitors, even printing their names in the
papers along with spirited letters from wives so stirred by
America's wrongs that they longed to take up sword and join
their husbands in the field.[1] Lower-class women actually did
follow husbands or lovers to the army, where they formed the
disorderly band of camp-followers which was one of Washington's
headaches. Some of these managed to be of service as nurses
in the field hospitals, however, and a few Molly Pitchers and
Deborah Sampsons actually bore arms. But ladies confined their
efforts to collecting money, food, and clothing for the

---

1 Julia Cherry Spruill, Women's Life and Work in the Southern
  Colonies (Chapel Hill, 1938), 345.

soldiers, with great bustle and publicity which elicited jeers from the London papers and jokes from their indulgent menfolk. A group of Philadelphia dames who had raised a sum for the Pennsylvania forces, however, showed a sense of propriety by sending with the money a note to General Washington asking him to use it as he thought best, since they "knew nothing of affairs of State." The average woman, of course, served her country in the traditional domestic sphere, by putting social pressure on neighbors of wavering loyalty, boycotting British manufactures and buying American, and keeping her home going for some ten years in a badly dislocated economy.[2]

Though most women thus left politics to the men, there were some exceptions, notably among the women of the prominent patriot families. Living in a tense and exciting atmosphere dominated by political talk, several of them fully shared their husbands' concerns and became shrewd observers of public events whose counsel was highly valued. Many plans, for instance, were "Laid, Discussed, and Digested"[3] at the Adams fireside in Braintree, Massachusetts, especially when John and Abigail Adams entertained their close friends and fellow-republicans James and Mercy Warren of Plymouth. Mrs. Adams, a contemporary later recalled, "had a distinct view

---

2 Elizabeth Cometti, "Women in the American Revolution," New England Quarterly, XX (September, 1947), passim.

3 Mercy Warren to John Adams, December 15, 1778, Warren-Adams Letters (Boston, 1917-1925), II, 80.

of our public men & measures & had her own opinions which
she was free to disclose but not eager to defend in public
circles."[4] Mrs. Warren, sister of the renowned orator James
Otis and wife of another radical leader, was less retiring.
Proud of her literary gifts, she vented her enthusiasm for
the cause in poems celebrating Revolutionary triumphs, satirical plays attacking the hapless Tory officialdom, and finally,
in her later years, a strongly partisan History of the American Revolution.

The talk of freedom, equality, and human rights, so much
in the air through these days of revolution, could not fail
to set vigorous and clear-headed women like Abigail Adams and
Mercy Warren to thinking about the implications of these doctrines for their sex. "I long to year that you have declared
an independency," wrote Abigail to John Adams in March of
1776.

> And, by the way, in the new code of laws
> which I suppose it will be necessary for
> you to make, I desire you would remember
> the ladies and be more generous and favor-
> able to them than your ancestors. Do not
> put such unlimited power into the hands
> of the husbands. Remember, all men would
> be tyrants if they could. If particular
> care and attention is not paid to the ladies,
> we are determined to foment a rebellion, and
> will not hold ourselves bound by any laws in
> which we have no voice or representation.

Adams had to laugh at his wife's parody of the revolutionary

---

[4] William Bentley, The Diary of William Bentley, D. D. (Salem,
1905-1914), IV, 557.

talk of the day.

> We have been told that our struggle has
> loosened the bonds of government every-
> where; that children and apprentices were
> disobedient; that schools and colleges
> were grown turbulent; that Indians slight-
> ed their guardians, and negroes grew inso-
> lent to their masters. But your letter was
> the first intimation that another tribe,
> more numerous and powerful than all the
> rest, were grown discontented. This is
> rather too coarse a compliment, but you are
> so saucy, I won't blot it out.

Abigail reported the interchange to Mercy Warren. "He is very

sausy to me, in return for a List of Female Grievances which

I transmitted to him. I think I will get you to join me in

a petition to Congress.[5]

Later generations of readers, thinking of the woman's

suffrage movement of their own times, assumed that the

sprightly Mrs. Adams was demanding political rights for her

sex. Actually such an idea was so out of keeping with the

eighteenth-century conception of woman's sphere and character

that people never even joked about it. Abigail Adams, under

her raillery, was concerned rather with married women's help-

less position under the "Laws of England which gives such

---

5 Abigail to John Adams, March 31, 1776, Familiar Letters of
John Adams and his Wife, Abigail Adams, during the Revolution, Charles Francis Adams, ed. (New York, 1876), 149-150;
Mary Sumner Benson, Women in Eighteenth-Century America
(New York, 1935), 247; John to Abigail Adams, Familiar
Letters, 155; Alice Brown, Mercy Warren (New York, 1896),
238. The Adams letters edited by Charles Francis Adams
were freely altered in the light of the genteeler standards of a later day, and the printed versions probably
often do not follow either the spelling or the phraseology
of the originals.

unlimited power to the Husband to use his wife Ill."[6]  Under
the common law which the English colonists had transplanted
to America, and which continued to govern the married
woman's status well into the nineteenth century, a husband
had complete control over his wife's person (including the
right of chastisement), over their children, and over any
property she brought to the marriage or might acquire after-
wards.  In a legal sense, the wife did not exist.  American
custom had slightly ameliorated these laws, occasionally by
recognizing pre-nuptial contracts allowing the wife to retain her property; rigidly safeguarding the widow's dower
rights (to a third of her husband's real estate during her
lifetime and a third of his personal property); and requiring
the wife's consent to any sale of land by her husband.  American lawmakers also sometimes relieved the legal straits of
married women in business by special enactments permitting
them to bring legal action with the same complete freedom enjoyed by spinsters and widows.  Furthermore, for the victims
of intolerable marriages, divorce was very slightly easier to
obtain in America than in Europe.[7]

Happy wives like Mesdames Adams and Warren, of course,
had little need of these measures of protection.  As Abigail
correctly observed, "Men of sense in all ages abhor those

---

6 Brown, Mercy Warren, 238-239.

7 Benson, Women in Eighteenth-Century America, 232-241.

customs which treat us only as the vassals of your sex." And
there was considerable wisdom in John's jesting remark that
"our masculine systems . . . are little more than theory. . . .
In practice you know we are the subjects." Yet less loving
and magnanimous husbands might exercise oppressive sway, unrestrained by law, and abused wives, especially in the lower
classes of society, could suffer mental and physical cruelty,
and watch their family's goods being gambled or drunk away,
with no recourse. Perhaps Mrs. Adams knew such cases in her
neighborhood; perhaps she had had some experience herself of
the difficulty of a wife's legal position in transacting
business for her husband. In any case, "as there is a
Natural propensity in Human Nature to domination," she wrote
Mercy Warren, "I thought the Most Generous plan was to put it
out of the power of the **Arbitrary** & tyranick to injure us
with impunity by establishing some Laws in our Favour upon
just & Liberal principals."[8]

Neither lady questioned the theory of submission. Mrs.
Warren would readily have concurred with her friend's belief
that "the all-wise Creator made woman an help-meet for man,
and she who fails in these duties does not answer the end
of her creation." Yet their private solicitude for the
condition of their sex, their conscious dignity, and their

---

8 Abigail to John Adams, March 31, 1776, Familiar Letters, 150;
  John to Abigail Adams, April 14, 1776, Ibid., 155; Brown,
  Mercy Warren, 239.

faith in education put Abigail Adams and Mercy Warren in the forefront of a slowly advancing enlightenment of opinion. "I can hear of the brilliant accomplishments of any of my sex with pleasure," said Mrs. Adams, "and rejoice in that liberality of sentiment which acknowledges them. At the same time, I regret the trifling, narrow, contracted education of the females of my own country."[9] And Mercy Warren suggested to a sensitive young lady, somewhat discouraged by her lot, that

> While we own the Appointed Subordination
> (perhaps for the sake of Order in Families)
> let us by no Means Acknowledge such an In-
> feriority as would Check the Ardour of our
> Endeavours to equal in all Accomplishments
> the most masculine Heights, that when these
> temporary Distinctions subside we may be
> equally qualified to taste the full Draughts
> of Knowledge and Happiness prepared for the
> Upright of every Nation & Sex. . . .[10]

During the decade after the Revolution Americans who had become interested in political and social questions began to explore the writings of the eighteenth-century French philos- ophers. These writers -- Voltaire, Rousseau, Turgot, Con- dorcet and the rest -- had been little known in the colonies.

---

9 Abigail Adams to Mrs. _____ Shaw, June 5, 1809, Letters of Mrs. Adams, Charles Francis Adams, ed. (Boston, 1840), II, 265; Abigail to John Adams, June 30, 1778, ibid., I, 127.

10 Brown, Mercy Warren, 241-242.

The wartime alliance, however, had opened the way for ideas
as well as military aid from France, and Americans now found
much that was congenial in the works of the philosophes.

Indeed, the faith in progress and the perfectibility of
man and human institutions which these spokesmen of the Enlightenment proclaimed was working in the mind of all the
western world in this latter part of the eighteenth century.
Americans like Jefferson had imbibed it earlier from the
English philosopher John Locke, drawing strength for their
resolve to overthrow British tyranny and establish a government better calculated to promote their welfare.  The French
philosophes, seeking to cure their own ills, were also pressing
the reform of political institutions.  But Americans, with
their revolution safely behind them, could learn more from
other aspects of the philosophes' thinking, particularly from
their program for the gradual regeneration of society through
education.

The leading figure in this phase of the movement was
Jean Jacques Rousseau.  It was his treatise in fictional form,
the Émile, which, contemporaries agreed, started the "passion
of authors and readers for the composition and perusal of
Systems of Education" so characteristic of the age.[11]  Rousseau

---

11 Alexander Fraser Tytler, Lord Woodhouselee, Memoirs of the
   Life and Writings of the Honourable Henry Home of Kames
   (Edinburgh, 1814), II, 280.

proposed to replace the traditionally repressive discipline of childhood with a highly individualistic system in which instruction and restraint would be largely left up to nature, the child learning from experience rather than books. To be sure, he confined these liberal views to his own sex, believing convention the safest guide for females. Women were bound to benefit indirectly, however, from the widespread interest aroused by the French philosopher's novel, progressive scheme. Moreover, in the Social Contract, his radically democratic treatise on government, Rousseau insisted upon the necessity of public education for all citizens to insure the wise working of the popular will, an ideal which held the seeds of free and equal education for both sexes.

Spurred by this intellectual enthusiasm, popular sentiment both in Britain and the United States was beginning in the 1780's to arouse from its long indifference to women's education. Boarding and day schools, to be sure, had flourished in the mother country for some hundred and fifty years, and in the colonies for two generations before independence, but the instruction was largely confined to the accomplishments and graces of polite society. In the 1780's, however, certain English schools began to offer a solider curriculum,[12] while Americans, under the stimulus of burgeoning national pride, made decided improvements in the schooling of girls, both at the elementary and secondary level.

---

12 Gardiner, English Girlhood at School, 347.

In former years, the only classroom the average girl ever saw was in the home of some neighbor who ran a "dame-school" to teach tiny children to read. The well-to-do in the large towns might continue their studies at an "adventure school," the private undertaking of some individual, often a European refugee, who capitalized on special skill in languages or fancy work to earn a precarious living. Uneven as this instruction was, it had gradually created a demand for public provision for elementary education. The old town schools (roughly comparable to the public primary schools of today) now began to admit girls as well as boys.[13] As an elderly educator described it many years later, "After the close of the revolution, in 1783, females over ten years of age, in populous towns, were sometimes . . . placed in the common schools, and taught to write a good hand, compose a little, cipher, and know something of history. The cause of female education was thus considerably advanced."[14]

In addition to these public schools, American culture was now broad enough to support some permanently organized instruction at a higher level for young ladies who could afford it. The result was the establishment of academies for girls, privately run but often incorporated by the states.

---

13 Benson, Woman in Eighteenth-Century America, 136; Thomas Woody, A History of Women's Education in the United States (New York, 1929), I, chs. 4, 5, 6, passim.

14 Senex, pseud., "Female Education in the Last Century," American Annals of Education, I (November, 1831), 524-525.

"When, at length, academies were opened for female improvement in the higher branches," wrote the same commentator,
"a general excitement appeared in parents, and an emulation
in daughters to attend them. Many attended such a school one
or two quarters, others a year, some few longer. . . . The
love of reading and habits of application became fashionable. . . ."[15]

The two most famous of these early academies were founded in the mid-'eighties, in Philadelphia by John Poor, and
in Boston by Caleb Bingham, who wrote a special text for his
pupils entitled The Young Lady's Accidence; or, a Short and
Easy Introduction to English Grammar. Several young men who
subsequently made notable contributions to American intellectual life also ran schools for girls during these years:
Timothy Dwight, later president of Yale, Jedidiah Morse,
pioneer geographer, and Noah Webster of dictionary fame.[16]

A very popular academy conducted near Boston by Mrs.
Susanna Haswell Rowson, former actress and a writer of novels,
offered musical instruction of high caliber, featuring German
teachers and a piano, one of the first of these instruments
seen in America. In between novels, Mrs. Rowson composed
geography and history textbooks for her pupils. Girls came

---

15 Ibid., 525-526; Woody, History of Women's Education, I,
chs. 7, 8.

16 Benson, Woman in Eighteenth-Century America, 137-155; Woody,
History of Women's Education, I, 154, 236, 333-340.

to her "from every part of the United States, and from the
British Provinces in North America and the West Indies," one
of them writing home that Mrs. Rowson was "so mild, so good,
no one can help loving her; she treats all her scholars with
such a tenderness as would win the affection of the most
savage brute."[17]

Both Mrs. Rowson's school and John Poor's academy regularly enrolled a hundred pupils. The young ladies exhibited
their scholastic prowess at intervals in public examinations,
attended by the parents and trustees. Of one of these occasions at Poor's academy an eminent Philadelphian wrote
enthusiastically,

> it is not easy to conceive how any thing
> of the kind could have been more perfect.
> In reading, in writing, in arithmetic, in
> geography, in English grammar, and in com-
> position, such specimens were given of pro-
> ficiency not confined to a few individuals,
> but spreading . . . through the classes in
> general, as even in this city would not a
> few years ago have been conceived practica-
> ble.

"Let it suffice to say," added another visitor, "that such
academical improvements, tend to mollify the temper, refine

---

17 Elias Nason, A Memoir of Mrs. Susanna Rowson (Albany,
   1870), 98, 102; Samuel L. Knapp's memoir of Mrs. Rowson,
   in her Charlotte's Daughter (Boston, 1828), 10; Eliza
   Southgate to Dr. Robert Southgate, February 13, 1798,
   A Girl's Life Eighty Years Ago (New York, 1887), 17.
   Equally popular was Miss Sarah Pierce's school conducted
   from 1792-1833 in Litchfield, Conn. See Woody, History
   of Women's Education, I, 340; Emily Noyes Vanderpoel,
   comp., Chronicles of a Pioneer School (Cambridge, 1903)
   and More Chronicles of a Pioneer School (New York, 1927).

the manners, amuse the fancy, improve the understanding, and
strengthen virtue . . . to lay a foundation for a life of usefulness and happiness here, and if rightly improved, for a
blessed immortality hereafter."[18]


The general interest in girls' education and the patriotic fervor rampant during these years prompted several Americans
to commit their ideas to print, the first important native
writers about women's training and sphere since Cotton Mather
and Benjamin Franklin. Dr. Benjamin Rush, America's foremost
physician and an enthusiastic advocate of social reform, delivered his Thoughts upon Female Education to the graduating class
of a Philadelphia academy in 1787. The address established
him as a leader in the new movement and was regarded as authoritative well into the next century. About the same time Noah
Webster, erstwhile schoolmaster with whom education was a lifelong concern, was getting out an American Magazine in New York.
During the one short year of its existence Webster devoted more
space to women than any previous American periodical,[19] repeatedly declaring that the female mind had been too much

---

18 The Rise and Progress of the Young Lady's Academy of Philadelphia (Philadelphia, 1794), 16-17, 24-26, quoted in Woody,
History of Women's Education, I, 334, 335.

19 Frank Luther Mott, A History of American Magazines (Cambridge, 1930-1938), I, 105.

neglected. In 1790 Webster and Rush gained a new recruit in the Reverend Enos Hitchcock, a public-spirited Providence clergyman of liberal views who published in that year two volumes of imaginary Memoirs of the Bloomsgrove Family (dedicated to Martha Washington) which expounded his ideas on the education of girls.

On all important points doctor, editor, and minister were in essential agreement. All three had studied Rousseau, Hitchcock having borrowed from Émile its fictional framework as well as some of its philosophy. Being practical Americans, however, and intensely patriotic, they took over chiefly the broad theories most meaningful for their own country. Rousseau provided intellectual support for the democratic faith the American Revolution had taught them, and his argument for popular education served likewise to confirm their conviction that the success of the republican experiment depended upon the enlightenment of the people. Most of his specific suggestions for educational practice, however, they regarded as eccentric, though his emphasis on a utilitarian training appealed strongly to their sense of the young nation's needs. Pondering various ideas for a distinctively American educational system, all of them were struck with the importance of properly training their countrywomen. By their influence on manners, Webster pointed out, women set the moral tone of society. As mothers, moreover, they molded the character of youth during the formative years; "their own education should therefore

enable them to implant in the tender mind, such sentiments
of virtue, propriety, and dignity, as are suited to the freedom of our governments."[20]

Rush and Hitchcock joined with Webster in disapproving
what they considered the disproportionate amount of time which
girls, especially in the larger towns, devoted to the polite
accomplishments of French, music, drawing, and dancing. "The
education of females, like that of males," Webster said,
"should be adapted to the principles of the government, and
correspond with the stage of society" in which they live. "In
America, female education should have for its object what is
useful." Rush listed certain distinctive features of women's
life which, he felt, made it "incumbent upon us to make ornamental accomplishments yield to principles and knowledge."
Thus, early marriage made the time available for girls' training too short to be wasted on fripperies. Moreover, a wife
often had to help manage her husband's property, for which she
needed some practical business training. Since his affairs
often called him from home, she must also be able to educate
their children alone. Lastly, she could never count on having trained servants and so must learn to be adept in domestic
matters. To meet these needs Rush prescribed a practical education in English, "figures and bookkeeping," geography and

---

20 Noah Webster, A Collection of Essays and Fugitiv [sic]
Writings (Boston, 1790), 27-28.

history, Christian principles, and a smattering of science
(which might be applied in cooking), along with singing and
dancing for exercise.[21]

Rush and Hitchcock particularly commended the day-academy
plan. "By the separation of the sexes in the unformed state
of their manners," the doctor declared, "female delicacy is
cherished and preserved. Here the young ladies may enjoy all
the literary advantages of a boarding-school, and at the same
time live under the protection of their parents."[22] Hitchcock
thought the existing boarding schools were unsuitable, having
taught girls "to dissemble gracefully, rather than to think or
act virtuously," and he prophetically wished "that academies
for the education of females, . . . may be the future boarding
schools of America." In these institutions girls could be
"directed to such studies, as have a tendency to enlarge the
understanding, without the labor of close investigation; to
entertain the mind, while they direct the affections of the
heart."[23]

Obviously these writers still retained some of the older

---

21 Ibid., 28; Benjamin Rush, Thoughts Upon Female Education
(Boston, 1787), 5-7, 7-12. Rush was the first American to
advocate the teaching of science to women, in his Syllabus
of Lectures Containing the Application of the Principles of
Natural Philosophy and Chemistry to Domestic and Culinary
Purposes (Philadelphia, 1787).

22 Rush, Thoughts Upon Female Education, 22.

23 Enos Hitchcock, Memoirs of the Bloomsgrove Family (Boston,
1790), II, 24, 9ln, 25.

eighteenth-century outlook. Though Hitchcock, for instance, declared unequivocally his faith in women's mental ability -- "The idea of inferiority on the part of your sex, I renounce with indignation" -- he nevertheless thought their subordination to men ordained by nature in order that "the modesty and delicacy which is the glory of the sex, and the palladium of virtue, may be preserved."[24] Webster felt that learning might be a very agreeable accomplishment, but he did observe that "a strong attachment to books in a lady, often deters a man from approaching her with the offer of hiz [sic] heart."[25] And Rush, who had received part of his medical training under Dr. John Gregory at Edinburgh, so much admired his teacher's ideas about women that he presented a copy of the Father's Legacy to Abigail Adams for her daughter's use.[26]

Thus these men looked both to the past and to the future. The philosophy of the Enlightenment had brought them to realize the importance of women's influence in a democratic society, yet they did not question the aristocratic eighteenth-century canon of female behavior, for all its inhibiting effect on

---

24 Ibid., II, 15, 16-17, 44.

25 Webster, Collection of Essays, 410.

26 Benson, Woman in Eighteenth-Century America, 142.

women's minds. In no sense radical thinkers, they were rather practical Americans with a progressive bent, combining experience with idealism into a workable program which improved on existing conditions without requiring any thoroughgoing change.

It remained for the second and more violent revolution of the era, France's in 1789, to call forth a champion of the sex who could carry the democratic theories of the Enlightenment to their logical extreme. The Englishwoman Mary Wollstonecraft performed this feat in 1791, with a force and brilliance that provoked discussion on both sides of the Atlantic. Her sensational book gave the woman's rights movement of the next century its name and inspired many of its leaders.


Mary Wollstonecraft was one of a long line of women who, by sheer force of intellect and character, had maintained their individuality and lived their own lives in a society hostile to such unconventional behavior. She made her way, however, at the cost of a struggle such as none of her predecessors had known. It was this struggle, together with her particular combination of intellect and strong emotion, that made her a militant feminist, the first of the genus as well as probably its most original mind. The story of her influence on women's social progress, however, is one of the ironies of history, for her liberalism, too thoroughgoing for the times, was misunderstood and backfired against her cause. For years

after her death, her name evoked in popular thought a picture
of social license appalling to the respectable, a potent
weapon for opponents of women's rights, both in England and
America.

Since Mary's work was uniquely influenced by the events
of her life, it is necessary to treat her history in some detail. In her short lifetime she witnessed or experienced nearly all the disabilities to which women were subject. She was
born into a respectable middle-class family with reasonable expectations of prosperity, her father having inherited a modest
fortune. But Mr. Wollstonecraft, a restless, unstable character, constantly shifting from one part of the country to another to undertake new schemes, soon dissipated his means.
While his improvidence was impoverishing his family, his violent temper and fits of brutality were devastating it. Mary
was devoted to her mother -- the first of a series of strong
attachments characteristic of her nature -- and would often
"throw herself between the despot and his victim, with purpose
to receive upon her own person the blows . . . directed against
her mother," or lie all night on the floor outside her parents'
door when "she apprehended that her father might break out into
paroxysms of violence."[27] Her weary mother, however, was quite
indifferent to her devotion, and between lack of maternal

27 William Godwin, Memoirs of the Author of a Vindication of
   the Rights of Woman (London, 1798), 9-10.

affection and her father's tyranny, Mary's girlhood passed
in a state of constant frustration, equally galling to her
sensitive feelings and to her intellectual sense of justice.[28]

At nineteen the family poverty helped her overcome her
parents' genteel objections to her going to work. There were
only two obvious employments for young women of her class:
teaching and being a companion. Trying the latter first, she
survived two years with an autocratic old lady in Bath, who
later confessed that Mary was "the only person that had lived
with her in that situation, in her treatment of whom she had
felt herself under any restraint."[29] Mary left this job to
nurse her mother through a lingering illness which ended in
death. The next to appeal to Mary's humanity was her sister
Eliza, who, married to a younger edition of their father, had
been driven to the edge of insanity. Braving the rigors of the
law, Mary kidnapped Eliza from her husband and hid her in London, out of his reach, until a separation was arranged. By
this time life under Mr. Wollstonecraft's roof had become intolerable, and besides the hapless Eliza, Mary had another
fainthearted sister, Everina, to provide for. This time she
started a school. The three girls had received only a meager

---

28 The reflections on parent-child relationships which grew
   out of this experience she incorporated into her A Vindication of the Rights of Woman (London, 1792), chs. 10, 11.

29 Godwin, Memoirs, 26.

education, but Mary had enlarged her mind with considerable
miscellaneous reading.  She seems to have had a flair for
teaching, winning her pupils' affection with some of the maternal kindness and sympathy which her own childhood had missed,
and endeavoring to stimulate their minds to thought rather than
drilling them by rote.[30]  Her scanty resources, however, were
hardly sufficient for such an undertaking.  Despite the hard-
est sort of work,  Mary was soon harassed with debts and un-
paid bills, and during her absence on another errand of mercy,
the school fell apart in the hands of Eliza and Everina.

Mary next found a job as governess in a wealthy family
in Ireland.  For a year she endured the meanness and snubs of
this position -- in the Britain of 1787 little better than
that of a servant -- until discharged by her employer, a fashionable woman who lavished all her affection on dogs and then
resented her daughters' fond attachment to their governess.[31]
Mary, now determining on a new departure, repaired to London
to try her hand at writing.  In the next few years of literary
hack-work she managed by rigid economy to maintain herself,
finance special training for her two sisters and two brothers
to fit them for a livelihood (Eliza and Everina as governesses),
and all this while helping to support her indigent father as
well.

---

30 See her Vindication, ch. 12.

31 Ibid.

Experiences like this had crushed the spirit of many other women. But Mary, in the words of William Godwin, her first biographer, possessed "a firmness of mind, an unconquerable greatness of soul, by which, after a short internal struggle, she was . . . accustomed to rise above difficulties and suffering."[32] Her capacity for strong feeling had sharpened the pain of her experiences and made her a prey to melancholy, but at the same time it disposed her to rebel, rather than submit to oppression. Her acquaintance in London with a circle of liberal reformers and natural-rights philosophers, including the Unitarian scientist Dr. Joseph Priestley and Thomas Paine, handyman of revolutions, directed her sympathies into broad social channels.

In 1790, believing ardently in the libertarian principles of the French Revolution, then two years underway across the channel, she read Edmund Burke's reactionary Reflections on the Revolution in France with shock and indignation, and undertook a public rebuttal of the eminent orator-statesman's appeal to traditionalism. Her vehement Vindication of the Rights of Man attracted wide attention and applause. With new confidence in her powers she threw herself into a work for which all her life and thought had been in a sense the preparation, and in 1791 published A Vindication of the Rights of Woman.

---

32 Godwin, Memoirs, 38.

In this book Mary Wollstonecraft concentrated on the
plight of that portion of mankind whose interests she had most
at heart and whose freedom she most earnestly desired.  In
the course of her argument she made certain suggestions which
in a general way anticipated the aims of the woman's rights
movement of the next century: equal education, wider opportunities of employment and more adequate pay, the removal of
legal and political disabilities.  Later biographers seized
upon these "modern" aspects of her thought as most meaningful
for their own times and problems, and some hailed her as the
prophet of the woman's rights' crusade.  This she certainly
was in her fearlessness and humanitarian zeal, and even in her
clever use of propaganda devices.  But it never occurred to
her to push specific reforms, because the women of her generation were not ready for them.  They needed first to gain self-
respect and self-confidence.  To this end Mary held up before
their fearful or foolish minds the revolutionary ideals of
liberty and equality, urging upon them the revolutionary faith
that these could be attained by the mere unfettered exercise
of the human reason.  She appealed to "reasonable men" as well,
entreating them "to emancipate their companion, to make her a
help meet for them!"

> If she be not prepared by education to be-
> come the companion of man, she will stop the
> progress of knowledge and virtue; for truth
> must be common to all, or it will be ineffi-
> cacious . . . . And how can woman be expect-
> ed to co-operate unless she know why she ought

> to be virtuous? unless freedom strengthen
> her reason till she comprehend her duty,
> and see in what manner it is connected
> with her real good.[33]

Mary addressed her message to the women of the middle classes in England as the chief hope for the redemption of their kind. The fine ladies of rank she considered to be enervated by the wealth which insured them respect and obeisance without the necessity of toil. Of true dignity and virtue she thought she had seen more in low life: "Many poor women maintain their children by the sweat of their brow, and keep together families that the vices of the fathers would have scattered abroad; but gentlewomen are too indolent to be actively virtuous, and are softened rather than refined by civilisation." The middle orders seemed to be in the most promising state, but they yearned after the vain pleasures of the rich, and would "sacrifice everything to tread on their heels. . . . Women, in particular, all want to be ladies. Which is simply to have nothing to do, but listlessly to go they scarcely care where, for they cannot tell what."[34]

A few strong-minded women before her had deplored the spineless character of the sex as the cause of the vanity and folly so often satirized by men. The Englishwoman Mary Astell in 1697 had called for "a sort of Bravery and Greatness of

---

33 Vindication, 342, vi-vii.

34 Ibid., 167, 337.

Soul, which does more truly ennoble us than the highest Title, and it consists in living up to the dignity of our Natures. . . This is the richest ornament and renders a Woman glorious in the lowest Fortune."[35] Mary Astell and others had labored to improve the education of woman, seizing upon her intellectual deficiencies as the most obvious bar to her rise both in her own estimation and that of society. While Mary Wollstonecraft fully recognized the importance of intellectual training, her primary concern was with education in a larger sense: the formation of the individual character, for better or worse, by pressure from the whole complex of social forces. Speaking in the idiom of her group, she declared that these forces had put woman everywhere in chains, making her a slave not only as her mother had been to Mr. Wollstonecraft, but as the rich Irishwoman who had employed her as governess had been in a society and class which gave her no incentive to be otherwise than vain and silly.

Mary's radical mind, from which her harsh life had ripped the sentimental fallacies that made other women accept this subjection, then probed to the fundamental cause of the tyranny, exposing in angry analysis the whole structure of false distinctions of sex. She singled out for special castigation the books by men like Fordyce and Gregory, whose sole purport was to "render women pleasing at the expence of every solid

35 Gardiner, English Girlhood at School, 379.

virtue."[36]

> Considering females rather as women than
> human creatures, . . . [they] have been
> more anxious to make them alluring mistres-
> ses than affectionate wives and rational
> mothers; and the understanding of the sex
> has been so bubbled by this specious homage,
> that the civilised women of the present cen-
> tury, with a few exceptions, are only anxious
> to inspire love, when they ought to cherish
> a nobler ambition, and by their abilities and
> virtues exact respect.[37]

Mary thought this eagerness to please men accounted for
the emphasis in girls' education on polite accomplishments
rather than on studies for disciplining the mind and culti-
vating the judgment. She protested the idea that the sexes
had unlike minds, as evinced, for example, by the "natural
fondness" of little girls for dress, dolls, talk, and other
"feminine" pursuits. This false belief, together with opinions like Dr. Gregory's that the appearance of delicacy made
women more attractive, was responsible for condemning women
to a sedentary life that ruined health and unfitted her for
her real duties in life. And physical helplessness naturally
produced mental helplessness, a condition further encouraged
by these writers' insistence that her mind was primarily an
organ of feeling rather than of reason. Thus it was not surprising that women "become the prey of their senses, delicately
termed sensibility, and are blown about by every momentary gust

36 Vindication, 38-39.

37 Ibid., 2.

of feeling. . . ."[38]

> Fragile in every sense of the word,
> they are obliged to look up to man for
> every comfort. In the most trifling dangers
> they cling to their support, with parasitical
> tenacity, piteously demanding succour; and
> their natural protector extends his arm, or
> lifts up his voice, to guard the lovely tremb-
> ler -- from what? Perhaps the frown of an
> old cow, or the jump of a mouse; a rat would
> be a serious danger. In the name of reason,
> and even common-sense, what can save such be-
> ings from contempt; even though they be soft
> and fair.[39]

As debilitating to character as this mental incompeten-

cy, Mary thought, was the special code of moral virtues and

rules of behavior prescribed for her sex in the standard

handbooks. (For how could their virtues differ, "if virtue

has only one eternal standard?")[40] She quoted passages

from these writings, urging women to cultivate cunning and co-

quettish arts and wiles; recommending docility, gentleness,

and modesty; emphasizing strict propriety of conduct and the

importance of maintaining an unblemished reputation. These

she regarded solely as devices to enhance women's sex appeal.

Gentleness thus became "the submissive demeanour of dependence,

the support of weakness that loves, because it wants protection;

and is forbearing, because it must silently endure injuries."

And their modesty she condemned as only the affectation of

---

38 Ibid., 129.

39 Ibid., 133.

40 Ibid., 49.

modesty, a "fig leaf borrowed by wantonness" to "give a zest
to voluptuous enjoyments."[41]

For the same reason chastity had come to be so overprized
in women that it had become the sole element essential for preserving their reputation. As long as they observed the rules
of decorum and retained their sexual virtue, society absolved
them of all other moral obligations. "If the honour of a
woman, as it is absurdly called, be safe, she may neglect every social duty; nay, ruin her family by gaming and extravagance; yet still present a shameless front. . . ."[42] On the
other side of the shield was men's exemption from this chastity
code, so complete that they might even boast of their triumphs
over women, while weak, dependent woman, educated only to
please, must assume both the burden of responsibility in re-
sisting passion and the blame for any transgression.[43] This
illogical view of the relations between men and women Mary
could not too strongly deplore. Marriage never would be held
sacred, she asserted, nor serve as "the cement of society,"
until women were prepared to be the companions of men rather
than their mistresses. Nor was "a being who, from its infancy,
has been the weathercock of its own sensations" fit to discharge

41 _Ibid._, 106, 65, 286.

42 _Ibid._, 311-312.

43 _Ibid._, 283-284.

the duties of motherhood.[44]

Mary Wollstonecraft had no wish to take women out of the home. She was not primarily concerned with the fate of individuals like herself ("let it be remembered, that for a small number of distinguished women I do not ask a place") but with persons in the ordinary walks of life.[45] If the men who had labored so earnestly in their writings to keep women domesticated had really persuaded them, even by the working sinisterly on their feelings, "to stay at home, and fulfil the duties of a mother and mistress of a family," Mary said, she would have hesitated to oppose their opinions. But experience showed that the common neglect of woman's understanding had made her either irresponsible, so that she abandoned home tasks for the pursuit of pleasure, or a mere "square-elbowed family drudge," little more than a trusty servant to her husband.[46]

Constructive employment, Mary thought, might do much to raise her sex's self-respect and standard of values. "Gardening, experimental philosophy, and literature, would afford them subjects to think of and matter for conversation, that in some degree would exercise their understandings." They might study politics and keep themselves informed on the events of the day, or learn the art of healing and practice as physicians, nurses

---

44 Ibid., 381, 147.

45 Ibid., 69, 168-169 and n., 136.

46 Ibid., 137-138, 142-145.

and midwives.

> Business of various kinds, they might
> likewise pursue, if they were educated in a
> more orderly manner, which might save many
> from common and legal prostitution. Women
> would not then marry for a support, as men
> accept of places under Government, and ne-
> glect the implied duties; nor would an at-
> tempt to earn their own subsistence, a most
> laudable one! sink them almost to the level
> of those poor abandoned creatures who live
> by prostitution. For are not milliners and
> mantuamakers reckoned the next class?

"The few employments open to women, so far from being liberal,

are menial; . . . when a superior education enables them to

take charge of the education of children as governesses,"

they found their position painfully humiliating. It was a

very defective government, Mary thought, "that does not pro-

vide for honest, independent women, by encouraging them to fill

respectable stations."[47]

Some time or other, she hoped, society would be different-

ly constituted. If women were to become truly virtuous and

useful, they must be educated after the same model as men and

in comradeship with them; they must have "a civil existence

in the State, married or single," and be equipped to earn their

own living. "For how can a being be generous who has nothing

of its own? or virtuous who is not free?" This new woman

would be a devoted, intelligent wife intent on managing her

household, educating her children, and assisting her neighbors,

---

47 Ibid., 165-166, 337-339.

as well as a responsible citizen.[48]


The public received the <u>Vindication of the Rights of
Woman</u> with amazement. It was immediately reprinted in America and translated into French and German, giving Mary Wollstonecraft an international reputation. No one could be indifferent to a work so impassioned and so revolutionary. Her
own circle hailed it with enthusiasm. Mary had already won
their respect and affection; they now honored her for the
courage, sincerity, and acumen with which she had analyzed one
glaring defect of the social order they so earnestly wished to
reform. Most people, however, were shocked, especially at
her branding the homage traditionally rendered the sex a kind
of leering insult. Some were curious to get a look at this
woman who wrote as straightforwardly as a man, with none of
the apologetic consciousness of sex which imbued the work of
other women writers. Expecting to find "a sturdy, muscular,
raw-boned virago," said William Godwin, ". . . they were not
a little surprised, when, instead of all this, they found a
woman, lovely in her person, and in the best and most engaging
sense, feminine in her manners."[49]

But conservatives shunned her book as a moral plague. To

---

[48] <u>Ibid</u>., 333, 339. Mary Wollstonecraft described her educational ideas at length in ch. 12.

[49] Godwin, <u>Memoirs</u>, 83.

them the existing distinctions of sex were as essential to the
stability and well-being of society as the distinctions of
class. As they watched the growing violence of the French
Revolution, fear seized them that the writings of Mary
Wollstonecraft and her friends would spread the contagion to
England. Horace Walpole thanked "Providence for the tranquil-
lity and happiness we enjoy in this country, in spite of the
philosophizing serpents we have in our bosom, the Paines, the
Tookes, and the Wollstonecrafts. . . . We have had enough of
new systems, and the world a great deal too much already."[50]
Many refused even to read the book, particularly happy, sheltered women who could not see what the fuss was all about.
The moralist Hannah More, a stalwart defender of the established
order during this turbulent decade, expressed the view of this
group in a letter to Walpole.

> I have been much pestered to read the
> 'Rights of Women,' but am invincibly resolved
> not to do it. Of all jargon, I hate metaphys-
> ical jargon; beside, there is something fan-
> tastic and absurd in the very title. How many
> ways there are of being ridiculous! I am sure
> I have as much liberty as I can make a good use
> of, now I am an old maid; and when I was a
> young one I had, I dare say, more than was good
> for me. If I were still young, perhaps I should
> not make this confession; but so many women are
> fond of government, I suppose, because they are
> not fit for it. To be unstable and capricious,
> I really think, is but too characteristic of our

---

50 In a letter to Hannah More, August 21, 1792. William Roberts, Memoirs of the Life and Correspondence of Mrs. Hannah
More (New York, 1835), I, 417-418.

> sex; and there is, perhaps, no animal so much
> indebted to subordination for its good behav-
> ior as woman.[51]

To people like this -- and in 1791 they were the vast
majority of all articulate persons -- it seemed that a woman
who asked for greater freedom wanted it for questionable ends.
Their suspicion appeared to be fully justified by the events
of Mary Wollstonecraft's remaining years. In Paris, where she
had gone for a closer view of the revolution, she formed a
connection in 1793 with an American adventurer named Gilbert
Imlay. They lived together for nearly two years; Mary had a
child and was happy for the first time in her life. She herself considered their relationship "as of the most sacred nature,"[52] but Imlay tired of the affair and he gradually deserted her. In her despair she tried to commit suicide by drowning
in the Thames. But six months after the final break with Imlay, fortune turned briefly in her favor. In the radical
philosopher William Godwin she found a worthy lover and an
intellectual equal. They were not married at first, sharing
a distaste for "those consequences which the law of England
annex to the relations of husband and wife,"[53] but when Mary
became pregnant they bowed to convention. In September of
1797, after a year of unbroken happiness with Godwin, Mary

---

51 1793. _Ibid._, 427.

52 Godwin, _Memoirs_, 107.

53 _Ibid._, 158.

died following the birth of their child.

Throughout her life, wrote her husband, she had "trampled on those rules which are built on the assumption of the imbecility of her sex; and had trusted to the clearness of her spirit for the direction of her conduct, and to the integrity of her views for the vindication of her character."[54] But the times would not grant a woman such immunity, nor judge a woman's literary work solely on its own merits. Mary's violations of the moral code ruined both her personal reputation and that of her Vindication. Conservatives who had refused to read the book because of Mary's known radicalism now advertised her career as paramour and unwed mother as the natural consequence of her philosophy. The fate of her book was a fitting conclusion to the frustration of her life, for instead of persuading her contemporaries or their posterity to improve the status of women, she stiffened resistance to change. Long after the hysteria of the French Revolution had subsided, upholders of the status quo both in England and America continued to smear every effort to secure "woman's rights" with the moral stigma attached to the name of Wollstonecraft.

54 Godwin, Memoirs of the Author of a Vindication of the Rights of Woman, 2nd edition (London, 1798), 155. Godwin's is still the most satisfactory brief account of her life. H. N. Brailsford, Shelley, Godwin and Their Circle (London, 1913), discusses the intellectual background of her thought. Rosalie G. Grylls, William Godwin and his World (London, 1953) is a sympathetic but detached modern evaluation of Godwin and his associates.

The powerful logic of Mary's argument might have sur-
mounted even this obstacle, however, if it had been cast in
effective literary form.  But in her excitement she had been
too impatient to prune and polish her sentences, or arrange
her thoughts in orderly sequence.  She gave to the public a
450-page jungle of repetitious and rank verbiage, and few
people since her day have plowed their way through it who were
not already converts to her doctrines.  These individuals considered themselves rewarded by the apt phrases scattered
through the book and the inspiration of her comprehensive
statement of human rights, but her work was of little use as
propaganda for the unenlightened.

Mary Wollstonecraft's object was eventually accomplished,
but hardly in the way she had envisioned.  Her insistence that
women should be equipped for self-support showed that she par-
tially understood the economic basis of social freedom.  She
did not, however, realize that a change in economic conditions,
rather than a vague general good will, would be necessary to
provide those jobs with which women could earn their own living,and with it the world's respect.  Such prescience, of
course, could not fairly be expected of her, since the liberal
thought of her day rested its hopes for social improvement on
political freedom and a confidence in the essential goodness
of human nature which seems unrealistic to the twentieth-
century mind.  In the slow course of time, women grew out of
the vices and weaknesses Mary Wollstonecraft attacked in the

England of her day, and out of the same follies so far as they existed in America. But they achieved dignity and independence of mind through a series of piecemeal reforms and by a cautious advance into new activities, carried out as shifting economic conditions permitted, rather than under the sovereignty of reason in a brave new world, according to the faith of the eighteenth-century philosophers.

America caught the French Revolutionary fever in the 1790's but, having recently been inoculated by its own rebellion, got off with a light case. Fresh from their own political and social reforms, the citizens of the United States took a personal interest in the first lively stirrings of democracy abroad. The exciting events in France were celebrated in poems and patriotic addresses, public feasts and parades. Clubs were formed to foster republican principles, and the man in the street adopted the revolutionary slang and its popular songs. Yet before the middle of the decade enthusiasm had begun to wane. The Reign of Terror revealed a more savage France than Americans could stomach, and its leveling principles and rude trampling on religion shocked all but the most radical.

For a few years, however, Americans breathing this heady atmosphere gave the liberal theories blowing in from Europe a hospitable reception. While the spell lasted many thoughtful citizens read Mary Wollstonecraft's <u>Vindication</u> and appraised

it on its own merits, respecting her idealism and sincerity
even when they could not swallow all her doctrines. The editors of a ladies' magazine begun in Philadelphia in 1792
embellished their first volume with a frontispiece which depicted the Genius of the Magazine kneeling before Liberty and
presenting her with a copy of the Rights of Woman, and one of
the early numbers of the periodical offered a lengthy review of
Mary's book. The reviewer had "perused this volume with great
pleasure," finding "a vast variety of reflections, solid and
entertaining," which he did not hesitate to recommend, even
though "we cannot wholly agree with our fair authoress in all
the points she contends for."[55]

The Lady's and Gentleman's Pocket Magazine of Literature
and Polite Amusement, in its first issue published in New York
in 1796, urged female readers to ponder the rights and duties
discussed by "that eminent champion of her sex, Mary Wollstonecraft Godwin." The co-editor of this periodical, an active
member of the local republican club, could conceive of "nothing
of higher importance to a nation than the education, the habits,
the amusements of the Fair Sex"; he proceeded in his next number to advocate government founding and support of female

---

55 Lady's Magazine and Repository of Entertaining Knowledge,
I, 190; Bertha M. Stearns, "Early Philadelphia Magazines
for Ladies," Pennsylvania Magazine of History and Biography,
LXIV (October, 1940), 481-482.

academies and universities, to be staffed entirely by women.[56]

Whether attracted by publicity of this sort or by simple curiosity, a number of American women got hold of Mary's book, at least a few finding that her bold arguments crystallized views they themselves had vaguely entertained. A twenty-three-year-old Massachusetts widow flouted the proprieties to enter upon a correspondence with a masculine friend because she could see no reasonable objection to such a course, and promptly engaged him in a discussion of the arresting topic.

> I am gratified extremely to find you disposed to consider woman as 'rational and human.' That we do not more frequently conduct like reasonable beings is the fault of man; who, by the attention he pays to the exterior, seldom fails to convince us the more difficult attainments of moral and intellectual excellence may be easily dispensed with, provided the person be pretty, and the air and dress fashionable.[57]

Eliza Southgate, a gay young miss of a prominent Maine family, found time amid her whirl of visits and balls for an attempt to convince a male cousin of the advantages of more thorough

---

56 Bertha M. Stearns, "Early New York Magazines for Ladies," New York History, XIV (January, 1933), 36-37; Stearns, "Before Godey's," American Literature, II (November, 1930), 250; Eugene P. Link, Democratic-Republican Societies, 1790-1800 (New York, 1942), 58n. Miss Stearns has raised the possibility that these articles in Philadelphia and New York magazines recommending Mary Wollstonecraft's work may have been written by Charles Brockden Brown. "A Speculation Concerning Charles Brockden Brown," Pennsylvania Magazine of History and Biography, LIX (April, 1935), 99-105.

57 Mary Wilder van Schalkwyck to Ebenezer Rockwood, February 18, 1803, Elizabeth A. Dwight, Memorials of Mary Wilder White, Mary Wilder Tileston, ed. (Boston, 1903), 110.

and systematic education for girls.  "The cultivation of the powers we possess, I have ever thought a privilege (or I may say duty) that belonged to the human species, and not man's exclusive prerogative.  Far from destroying the harmony that ought to subsist, it would fix it on a foundation that would not totter at every jar."[58]

Most articulate of these thoughtful women was a Gloucester matron with literary ambitions whose pen name "Constantia" was a familiar sight to readers of Boston magazines in the 1780's and '90's.  Judith Sargent Murray belonged to the generation of Mercy Warren and Abigail Adams, with whom she was in fact acquainted.  Born of a prominent seafaring family, she showed an early interest in study and, like Mercy Otis, was allowed to share her brother's lessons as he prepared for Harvard.[59] In her twenties she was "seized with a violent desire to become a writer."  Unable to overcome "this unaccountable itch for scribbling,"[60] which even kept her awake at night, she turned

---

58 Eliza Southgate to Moses Porter, June 1, 1801, A Girl's Life Eighty Years Ago, 60-61.

59 Vena B. Field, Constantia, A Study of the Life and Works of Judith Sargent Murray (University of Maine Studies, ser. 2, no. 17, Orono, 1931), 15-16.

60 Judith Sargent Murray, The Gleaner (Boston, 1798), I, 14.

out "poetry by the acre"[61] and tried her hand at the drama,
finally hitting her stride in the urbane periodical essay
which Addison and Steele had made popular at the beginning of
the century.

Like many another would-be authoress both before and
after her time, Judith Murray quickly discovered that only a
few steps out of the domestic sphere confronted her with the
woman question. During the American Revolution, following the
same train of thought that prompted Mesdames Warren and Adams
to wish for reforms in the laws affecting married women and
to deplore the narrow education females received, she wrote
an essay arguing that the sexes had equal minds, and calling
for more thorough training for girls. Friends to whom she
showed the piece probably thought it too vehement;[62] at any
rate, it did not appear in print for another decade. In the
meantime she published in the Gentleman and Lady's Town and
Country Magazine, the first woman's journal in the United
States, a few "Desultory Thoughts" suggesting that if parents
encouraged a healthy self-respect in their daughters, they
might think twice before rushing into marriage simply to gain
social prestige and avoid spinsterhood.[63]

---

61 According to a lively young cousin, quoted in Field, Constantia, 45.

62 Judith Sargent Murray, "On the Equality of the Sexes,"
Massachusetts Magazine, II (March, April, 1790), 132.

63 "Desultory Thoughts upon the Utility of Encouraging a De-
gree of Self-Complacency, Especially in Female Bosoms,"
The Gentleman and Lady's Town and Country Magazine, I
(October, 1784), 251-253.

Like most New Englanders of her class, Mrs. Murray became a staunch Federalist during the 1790's, believing that
the Revolution had carried the country far enough toward democracy. Moreover, by the time Mary Wollstonecraft's book
came to her hands, the excesses of the French Revolution were
demonstrating the truth of her conviction that "There is no
calculating the disorders which may result from relaxing the
series of subordination."[64] Judith Murray nonetheless had the
gift of tolerance, which she probably owed to her experience
as a member of an unpopular religious sect, the Universalist
church, whose American founder John Murray was her second husband. Hence, though the Vindication of the Rights of Woman
had obviously been inspired by political principles which she
reprobated, Mrs. Murray was able to appreciate the merits of
Mary's message, finding, indeed, that it strengthened convictions which she had long held.[65]

---

[64] The Gleaner, I, 264.

[65] In her essays on political subjects she always deplored the
acrimonious party feeling of the '90's, urging that followers of Mr. Jefferson be considered "misguided sons of liberty" rather than "disorganizers of government" or "friends
to anarchy," and insisting that there were many worthy
characters in the opposite camp. For instance, she considered Mrs. Catharine Macaulay, the radical Whig historian,
a person "of no inconsiderable merit, nothwithstanding her
equalitarian views," and Mercy and James Warren's allegiance
to Jeffersonian principles (to them the logical outgrowth
of the Revolutionary philosophy) did not diminish her respect for "the elegantly moral poetess, and faithful historian, who [stands] at the head of female literature in
this new world. . . ." The Gleaner, I, 263, III, 182, 184.
The opinions of Republican Mercy Warren and Federalist Abigail Adams on Mary Wollstonecraft do not seem to have survived.

Further encouraged by the signs of growing public interest in female education, she devoted four essays in a series
she was writing for the Massachusetts Magazine, or Monthly
Museum of Knowledge and Rational Entertainment to a manifesto
of woman's equality with man. One of the most popular features
of this leading Boston periodical, "Constantia's" essays were
collected in 1798 into three volumes entitled The Gleaner, and
published with a fulsome dedication to President John Adams
and an impressive subscription list headed by George Washington.

In the essay she had composed during the Revolution,
Judith had burst into verse to introduce her plea for the
"Equality of the Sexes."

> THAT minds are not alike, full well I know,
> This truth each day's experience will show; . . . .
>     Yet I cannot their sentiments imbibe,
> Who this distinction to the sex ascribe,
> As if a woman's form must needs enrol,
> A weak, a servile, an inferiour soul;
> And that the guise of man must still proclaim,  66
> Greatness of mind, and him, to be the same. . . .

Ranging the intellectual powers under the four heads of imagination, memory, reason, and judgment, she had examined woman's
record. Even the oft-ridiculed feminine inventiveness in
fashion and scandal gave proof of lively imagination; "was this
activity properly directed, what beneficial effects would
follow." No one would question the quality of woman's memory,

---

66 "On the Equality of the Sexes," 59.

and any deficiencies in reason and judgment could be accounted
for by lack of education. In every family, from early childhood, "the sister must be wholly domesticated, while the
brother is led by the hand through all the flowery paths of
science. . . . The one is taught to aspire; . . . the other
early confined and limitted [sic]. . . . Grant that their
minds are by nature equal, yet who shall wonder at the apparent
superiority, if indeed custom becomes second nature. . . ."[67]

> At length arrived at womanhood, the uncul-
> tivated fair one feels a void, which the
> employments allotted her are by no means
> capable of filling. What can she do? to
> books she may not apply . . . , lest she
> merit the appellation of a learned lady;
> . . . . Is she single, she in vain seeks
> to fill up time from sexual employments or
> amusements. Is she united to a person whose
> soul nature hath made equal to her own, ed-
> ucation hath set him so far above her, that
> in those entertainments which are productive
> of . . . rational felicity, she is not qual-
> ified to accompany him. She experiences a
> mortifying consciousness of inferiority,
> which embitters every enjoyment.[68]

---

67 Ibid., 132-133.

68 Ibid., 133-134. Several of the remarks in this essay,
written in 1779, published in 1790, oddly anticipated Mary
Wollstonecraft's strictures, which could not have reached
America until 1792. Strikingly similar, for instance, is
Judith Murray's ironical description of the one department
in which the world did seem to accord the palm to the female mind. "And indeed, in one respect, the preminence
[sic] seems to be tacitly allowed us, for after an education which limits and confines, and employments and recreations which naturally tend to enervate the body, and de-
bilitate the mind; after we have from early youth been
adorned with ribbons, and other gewgaws, dressed out like
the ancient victims previous to a sacrifice, being taught
by . . . our parents . . . that the ornamenting of our

Some critics insisted that education would interfere with domestic duties. Housewifely skills, Mrs. Murray answered, were easily learned, and once mastered left the mind free for reflection. In any case,

> I would calmly ask, is it reasonable, that
> . . . an intelligent being, . . . a candi-
> date for immortality, . . . should at pres-
> ent be so degraded, as to be allowed no
> other ideas, than those which are suggested
> by the mechanism of a pudding, or the sew-
> ing the seams of a garment. Pity that all
> such censurers of female improvement do not
> go one step further, and deny their future
> existence; to be consistent they surely
> ought.[69]

Fifteen years later, however, she was joyously celebrating the "happy revolution" in the condition of her sex.

> In these infant republics, where, within
> my remembrance, the use of the needle was
> the principal attainment which was thought
> necessary for a woman, the lovely proficient
> is now permitted to appropriate a moiety of
> her time to studies of a more elevated and

exteriour ought to be the principal object of our attention; after, I say, fifteen years thus spent, we are introduced into the world, amid the united adulation of every
beholder. . . . We are immediately intoxicated by large
draughts of flattery. . . . It is expected that with the
other sex we should commence immediate war, and that we
should triumph over the machinations of the most artful.
We must be constantly upon our guard; prudence and discre-
tion must be our characteristicks; and we must rise superiour to, and obtain a complete victory over those who have
long been adding to the native strength of their minds, by
an unremitting study of men and books. . . . Thus unequal,
we are, notwithstanding, forced to the combat, and the
infamy which is consequent upon the smallest deviation in
our conduct, proclaims the high idea which was formed of
our native strength. . . . Ibid., 223.

69 Ibid., 134.

> elevating nature. Female academies are
> everywhere establishing, and right pleasant
> is the appellation to my ear.
>      Yes, in this younger world, "the Rights
> of Women" begin to be understood; we seem,
> at length, determined to do justice to THE
> SEX; and, improving on the opinions of a
> Wollstonecraft, we are ready to contend for
> the quantity, as well as quality of mind.[70]

She confidently looked forward to seeing this generation of

girls inaugurate "a new era in female history." Without sac-

rificing a single feminine charm, they would relinquish the

old frivolous pursuits for literary improvement and a cheer-

ful and efficient performance of maternal and wifely duties.

"A sensible and informed woman -- companionable and serious --

possessing also a facility of temper, and united to a con-

genial mind -- blest with competency -- and rearing to maturity

a promising family of children -- surely the wide globe cannot

produce a scene more truly interesting."[71]

Satisfied with the outlook for woman's education, Judith

Murray turned to the subject of marriage. Though this might

be woman's ideal role, a girl should not feel that she must

catch a husband at all costs. She was far more likely to make

a happy match if she learned first "to respect a single life,

and even to regard it as the most eligible, except a warm, mu-

tual and judicious attachment had gained the ascendancy in the

bosom." Young women, Mrs. Murray insisted, if brought up with

---

70 The Gleaner, III, 188.

71 Ibid., 189, 190, 191.

habits of industry and order, were fully capable of earning their own living. Once having gained "that independence, for which a Wollstonecraft hath so energetically contended," a girl could choose a suitor with a deliberation "calculated to give a more rational prospect of tranquility"; if her husband had reverses or she was left a widow, she could contribute to the family support, thus avoiding "that kind of dependence" on relatives or friends "against which the freeborn mind so naturally revolts."[72]

For upperclass females of the eighteenth century, this was a startling idea, and Judith Sargent Murray had stated it almost as uncompromisingly as Mary Wollstonecraft herself. She was vague, however, about ways and means, suggesting only that girls "be taught with precision the art economical" (domestic science), and make themselves familiar with "some particular branch of business."[73] Indeed, in the circles in which Judith Murray moved, there were few opportunities for women to earn money, and she would not have condoned any departure from the standard decorum. She always thought Clarissa Harlowe "the best model for the sex, that I have ever . . . seen pourtrayed,"[74] and her only attempt at fiction, a sentimental serial loaded with moral lessons which filled most of

---

72 Ibid., I, 168, III, 220, 223.

73 Ibid., I, 168, III, 223.

74 Ibid., II, 66.

the first volume of The Gleaner, pictured a perfectly conventional heroine of such unsteady judgment that she barely escaped falling prey to a seducer.

Some of Mary Wollstonecraft's other American readers took a more defiant tone. A Philadelphia schoolgirl named Priscilla Mason argued woman's qualifications for public speaking at the annual examination in Poor's academy in 1793. In "volubility of expression" and powers of persuasion, Miss Mason staunchly claimed, women obviously equaled men, lacking only knowledge to become accomplished orators.

> Our high and mighty Lords . . . have denied
> us the means of knowledge, and then reproached
> us for the want of it. Being the stronger
> party they early seized the sceptre and the
> sword; with these they gave laws to society.
> . . . They doom'd the sex to servile or
> frivolous employments, on purpose to degrade
> their minds, that they themselves might hold
> unrivall'd, the power and pre-eminence they
> had usurped. Happily, a more liberal way of
> thinking begins to prevail.[75]

And an anonymous lady contributed this spirited song to the Philadelphia Minerva in 1795.

---

75 Benson, Woman in Eighteenth-Century America, 140-141; The Rise and Progress of the Young Ladies' Academy of Philadelphia, 90-92, quoted in Woody, History of Women's Education, I, 338-339. When this flurry of radicalism had died down a few years later, one Boston magazinist was pleased to observe that "Our boarding-school misses have become less eloquent, and more obedient." Monthly Anthology III (August, 1806), 438.

Man boasts the noble cause
Nor yields supine to laws
Tyrants ordain;
Let Woman have a sphere
Nor yield to slavish fear,
Her equal rights declare,
And well maintain.

. . . . . . .

Let snarling critics frown,
Their maxims I disown,
Their ways detest;
By Man, your tyrant lord,
Females, no more be aw'd
Let Freedom's sacred word
Inspire your breast.

Woman aloud rejoice,
Exalt thy feeble voice
In cheerful strain,
See Wollstonecraft, a friend,
Your injured rights defend,
Wisdom her step attend,
The cause maintain.[76]

The most notable convert to Mary's doctrines was the earnest young author Charles Brockden Brown.[77] A Philadelphian of
Quaker extraction, novelist, essayist, and editor, whose

---

76 Quoted in Stearns, "Early Philadelphia Magazines for Ladies,"
   483. The verses were apparently written to the tune of
   "God Save the King," which accounts for the curious meter.

77 William Dunlap, The Life of Charles Brockden Brown (Philadelphia, 1815), is the basic source, though inaccurate,
   for details of Brown's life. Carl van Doren has a good
   short account in the Dictionary of American Biography. See
   also David L. Clark's Brockden Brown and the Rights of
   Women (Austin, Tex., 1922) and his Charles Brockden Brown
   (Durham, 1952), and Harry R. Warfel, Charles Brockden Brown
   (Gainesville, Fla., 1949).

pioneering attempt to live by his pen was to earn him the
title of America's first professional man of letters, Brown
during the 1790's became an ardent exponent of the revolutionary philosophy. His reading of the Vindication and the works
of William Godwin led him at twenty-five to compose an essay
on "The Rights of Women," which he published in the Philadelphia Weekly Magazine in 1798, and at the same time in pamphlet
form under the title Alcuin; A Dialogue. A continuation of
the work, found among Brown's manuscripts after his death,
appeared in William Dunlap's biography of his friend in 1815.

Brown, whose nature united an inquiring, skeptical mind
with an ardently romantic temperament, was constitutionally
inclined towards idealistic enthusiasms. An omnivorous reader
from childhood, he had studied all the liberal thought of the
eighteenth century, from Locke to Godwin, from Rousseau and
Voltaire to Condorcet. His Quaker upbringing had taught him
to take equality of the sexes for granted. He often visited
Benjamin Franklin's house, probably meeting many of the political refugees from Europe who were entertained there. His boon
companions, however, were young intellectuals like himself.
Each of the cosmopolitan seaboard cities during these early
years of the new republic had its group of such kindred spirits, meeting together in clubs to discuss the new political
and social theories of the day and criticize each other's
literary efforts. In this society Brown doubtless argued,

defended and clarified the ideas that he was to advance in his dialogue on women's rights.[78]

This tract in fictional guise described the visit of Alcuin, an awkward young schoolmaster, to the salon of the widowed Mrs. Carter, "the favorite resort of the liberal and ingenious"[79] in Philadelphia. In lengthy, stilted conversation Alcuin and his hostess discussed every phase of the woman problem, the question of intellectual equality, education, occupations, political rights, and marriage. The opinions expressed varied from middle of the road to radical, growing more extreme as the dialogue progressed.

Alcuin and Mrs. Carter agreed that the sexes were essentially equal in mind, the schoolteacher quoting Locke's dictum that "human beings are moulded by the circumstances in which they are placed. . . . The differences that flow from the sexual distinction, are as nothing in the balance."[80] If no women had won distinction as statesmen or thinkers, lack of opportunity and education, rather than incapacity, was to blame. Mrs. Carter vigorously protested her sex's exclusion from the liberal professions like law, medicine, and the ministry and from the higher branches of learning. She favored Mary

---

78 For articles possibly written at the time, see above, pp. 102-103 and note 56.

79 Charles Brockden Brown, Alcuin (New Haven, 1935), 6.

80 Ibid., 21.

Wollstonecraft's plan for coeducation, deploring in language very reminiscent of the Vindication the custom of segregating the sexes and the double standard of morality and behavior it engendered. Her bitterest grievance, however, was the bar against woman suffrage, in her eyes a complete negation of democracy.

For the most part these views went far beyond Mary Wollstonecraft's conception of woman's rights, and were even less likely to appeal to popular taste. Such proved to be the case, though in a way Brown hardly anticipated. The vitality of Mary's book, written out of the anguish of personal experience in a concrete social situation, fairly forced it upon the public notice; Brown's Alcuin, an academic exercise in abstract idealism, was totally ignored. No contemporary reference to it has been found, and it is today one of the rarest American books, with only eight copies known to exist.[81]

In the second, posthumously published, section of the dialogue, devoted to a discussion of marriage, Brown's speculations carried him even further from reality. He pictured Mrs. Carter objecting violently to the existing system "because it renders the female a slave to the man" by depriving her of her property, enforcing promises of obedience and lifelong affection, and requiring cohabitation. To make matrimony a fit state for free individuals she proposed to limit its duties

---

81 LeRoy Elwood Kimball, preface to ibid., x.

to "occasional interviews and personal fidelity"[82] and allow
unlimited freedom of divorce. Alcuin went a step beyond,
questioning the utility of any form of marriage.

For these ultra notions, Brown was indebted to William
Godwin, England's leading exponent of the revolutionary
philosophy and an absolute individualist whose ideal society
would have abolished all authority but the promptings of pure
reason. How far they represented the young American's true
convictions, the dialogue gave no hint. His novels of the
next two years, however, revealed that while he continued to
be fascinated by Godwin's outlandish theories, Brown's own
ideas about marriage were more realistic, though far in advance
of current opinion.

Ormond, in the novel of that name, a sort of sinister
superman who flouted law and convention at will, considered
marriage "hateful and absurd."[83] Acting on this principle he
wrecked the lives of the women who crossed his path, in the
end encompassing his own destruction. Constantia Dudley, who
finally stabbed Ormond to preserve her virtue, was Brown's
prototype of womanly perfection. Far from regarding matrimony

---

82 Dunlap, Life of Brown, I, 93, 98. Godwin and Mary Wollstonecraft maintained separate establishments during their
brief alliance, Godwin insisting that cohabitation was a
major cause of marital discord. The wife's individuality,
he held, was inevitably compromised by the constant thwart-
ings of her will in petty disputes of the daily routine.

83 Charles Brockden Brown, Ormond; or, the Secret Witness
(Philadelphia, 1887), 174.

as the sole end of female existence, she determined at sixteen not to marry for seven years, when her character and that of any prospective suitor should be fully matured, enabling her to make a truly felicitous choice. The course of events reduced her to poverty, but she nevertheless refused a wealthy but uninspired citizen whom she did not love, feeling "homely liberty . . . better than splendid servitude."[84] When her fortunes improved she remained contentedly single, preferring the pleasures of study and friendship to an alliance without common interests and sympathies. Her parents had more conventional ideas about marriage, but allowed Constantia to decide for herself. Modest and unassuming enough to suit the most exacting eighteenth-century taste, and often afflicted with the overwrought emotions fashionable at the time, Constantia was nevertheless responsible, resourceful, and self-possessed, a thorough classical education having fortified her character and taught her to regulate her conduct by reason. None of Brown's other heroines were so fully delineated, but the most attractive of them shared some of her qualities.

These sterling virtues, however, left most novel readers of 1799 cold, and they pointedly neglected Brown's tales for stories which combined sensation and sentimentality according to the Richardson formula. As for Alcuin, Brown's little tract retains a certain historical interest as the first

---

84 Ibid., 82.

American appeal for woman's rights, but it exerted no influence whatever on the broad development of ideas about women. The customs and conventions ruling the lives of the sex were too firmly rooted in economic conditions to be shaken by a single headlong assault; Alcuin survives merely as a lonely reminder of the free and rational speculative spirit of the Revolutionary generation.

Chapter Three

THE RELIGIOUS REVIVAL AND THE NEW CONSERVATISM:

MARRIAGE AND THE HOME, 1800-1825

## Chapter Three

## THE RELIGIOUS REVIVAL AND THE NEW CONSERVATISM:
## MARRIAGE AND THE HOME, 1800-1825

Almost as soon as it reached its high-water mark, the tide of French Revolutionary enthusiasm began to recede  by the end of the decade it had gone underground. Even the most ardent idealists realized in the early years of the new century that society was hardly ready for Utopia and began to look back at their excitement of the 'nineties as a youthful aberration. When Charles Brockden Brown inaugurated a new magazine in 1803, _Alcuin_ was evidently weighing on his conscience. In the editor's address to the public, he expressed the fear that "my readers should judge of my exertions by my former ones," deploring the world's habit of forming its estimate of a man's "principles at fifty, from what he has written at fifteen." "I have written much," he added, "but take much blame to myself for something which I have written, and take no praise for any thing," and promised that "in the conduct of this work, a supreme regard will be paid to the interests of religion and morality."[1]

Thus did Brown in effect slam the door on radical speculative theory and step into a new intellectual milieu. By

---

1 _Literary Magazine and American Register_, I (October, 1803), 4-5.

1803 the interests of religion and morality had indeed risen paramount in America. From the slump in piety and morals which had followed the strain of the Revolutionary War, from the fashionable freethought of the Francophile 'nineties, the nation had been reclaimed for orthodoxy by a great religious revival.

The American revival had its counterpart in the mother country, where a religious awakening, begun some years earlier in reaction against the riotous living and spiritual torpor of the eighteenth century, had been enormously accelerated by hysterical fear of the French Revolution and especially of the Reign of Terror and which mounted with each perilous year of the Napoleonic wars.

Under energetic and dedicated leaders the two revivals pursued their common goal of spreading evangelical Protestantism through techniques worked out in the British movement: Sunday Schools, and societies for the distribution of Bibles and tracts and the support of missionaries. Rigidly moralistic, both preached duty and decorum in personal conduct with driving insistence, organizing public campaigns for temperance and the outlawry of dueling. In supplying the literature for these purposes as well as the technique of organization England took the lead, finding an eager market for books and pamphlets in her erstwhile colonies. The fact that these productions in some respects hardly suited American conditions seldom affected their popularity among the religiously minded.

The two revivals differed most sharply in their social and political orientation. Though its first practitioners in England had been the Wesleyan Methodists and their lower-class followers, the revival there came to be dominated and directed by the Evangelicals, a group of wealthy laymen within the Anglican church, genuinely reform-minded but congenitally anti-democratic. Horrified by events in France -- where, in Edmund Burke's words, they observed a "ferocious dissoluteness in manners" and "insolent irreligion" hand and glove with democracy rampant, the crown overturned, and "the principle of property . . . systematically subverted"[2] -- the Evangelicals used the religious excitement to divert English attention to the reform of manners and morals, while ruthlessly suppressing all movements for the reform of English institutions.

Nowhere in the United States did the revival develop such political overtones, though in New England for a brief period arch-Federalist clergymen of the established church attempted to arouse religious prejudice against the Jefferson party. But the majority of revivalists in all sections, so far as they had political sympathies, sided with the Jeffersonians, for the revival in America was predominatly lower-class, rural, and democratic. Its most sensational manifestations occurred in the raw West, where thousands joined in the emotional debauch of the

---

2 Reflections on the Revolution in France (New York, 1791), 29, 30.

great camp meetings. The relatively stable society of the Eastern seaboard, more receptive to English ideas, found its outlet rather in reform and good works.

Concerned as the revival was to an unusual degree with manners and morals, it inevitably devoted much attention to women. English writers concentrated their fire on the female profligates, the ladies whom Mary Wollstonecraft had denounced for their wasteful, frivolous existence, their useless ornamental education and extreme sensibility, their ceaseless pursuit of amusement and neglect of home duties. The United States, having in the large towns and cities its small share of this species, readily accepted English writings in this vein.

For the most part, however, Anglo-American womankind was above criticism on moral grounds. As we have seen, high standards of behavior for the well-bred Englishwoman had been established early in the eighteenth century, in revulsion against the loose living of the Restoration period, and the American colonies had automatically adopted these standards. Gradually there had grown up an ideal of womanhood best typified in the genteel heroine of the sentimental novel, a literary genre which had itself arisen in answer to a demand from the new class of women readers for entertaining reading matter which should be morally beyond reproach. Generations of girls since 1748 had dissolved into tears over the scene where Richardson's Clarissa Harlowe expired, a monument to outraged virtue. Ever since 1778 they had breathlessly followed the more prosperous fortunes of the

Evelina of Fanny Burney's immensely popular novel, a charming young lady of unspoiled beauty, disarming in innocence and simplicity, modest to the point of bashfulness and quite helpless in an emergency, but full of unaffected goodness of heart, discriminating taste, and high principle.

For those bred in this tradition in either country the revival and its rigorous new moral climate made little immediate difference. The newly pious put the old code of behavior on a firmer basis of religious authority, while Englishmen and Americans who remained aloof from the revival retained as a matter of course the social and intellectual outlook of the eighteenth century, including its attitudes toward women. Yet even among the latter group, the times were working a subtle change in values. A favorite heroine of this generation was the Belinda of Maria Edgeworth's novel of 1801, fully the equal of her famous literary ancestresses in beauty, virtue, and taste, but easily their superior in prudence and self-control.

To all appearances, however, the young lady or the well-bred matron of 1800 was the replica of her mother and grandmother in her ideas of what the world expected of her, and no more likely than her forbears to question them. Ladies seeking guides to conduct continued to consult the familiar manuals of Drs. Gregory and Fordyce and Mrs. Chapone, now over thirty years old. In the first quarter of the new century American printers issued at least six editions of Mrs. Chapone's Letters on the Improvement of the Mind besides one of her complete works, while

bookstores regularly imported additional copies from England.
One critic recommended the Letters as "perhaps the most unexceptionable treatise that can be put into the hands of female
youth."[3]

But the aroused religious conscience could not be content
with Mrs. Chapone's gentle piety, much less with the smooth
formalism of Gregory and Fordyce. It demanded a vigorous reas-
sertion of the conservative credo in a more emphatic moral con-
text. The new manuals of advice set out to crush the Wollstonecraft heresy and establish standards for "the strict performance
of every domestic, moral, and religious duty."[4] With this
message they began to reach a receptive new audience, "females
in the middle ranks of society" who, as they acquired unaccustomed wealth with the rise of industry, were eagerly seeking
instruction in the manners and customs of the best people. In
this expanding market handbooks for young ladies multiplied.
"If the rising generation be not the nearest to perfection of
any that have existed since the golden age," wrote one American

---

3 "It is distinguished by sound sense, a liberal . . . spirit
of piety, and a philosophy applied to its best use, the culture of the heart and affections. It has no shining eccen-
tricities of thought, no peculiarities of system; it follows
experience as its guide, and is content to produce effects
of acknowledged utility, by known and approved means."
"Memoirs of Mrs. Chapone," Literary Magazine and American
Register, II (June, 1804), 204-205; Boston Weekly Magazine,
III (May 25, 1805), 121.

4 Mrs. Jane West, Letters to a Young Lady (Troy and New York,
1806), 111.

reviewer, "it will certainly not be for want of information and advice in every shape."[5]

Thus with precept upon precept was the character of the American girl and her English cousin formed to fit their function in society. In 1800 wedlock was still woman's appointed destination, with the home her only theater of action unless she chose to pass her time in "the festive haunts of fashionable life."[6] Roundly condemning any such dereliction from household duty, however, the manuals undertook to inculcate the proper attitudes and conduct for the married state in all its phases from courtship through motherhood.

Americans could find the best thought of the period mirrored also in the light literature which native authors were beginning to produce. Popular magazines alternated satires on frivolity, vanity, and the other classic feminine foibles with paeans to the domestic virtues and "woman's influence" ("like the dew of heaven, gentle, silent, and unseen; yet pervading and efficient").[7] Magazine stories and novels alike knew only two

5 Mrs. Ann Taylor, Practical Hints to Young Females (Boston, 1816), v; Analectic Magazine, VII (March, 1816), 277; ibid., XI (April, 1818), 351.

6 Hannah Webster Foster, The Coquette [1797] (Boston, 1833), 80.

7 "The cynic, when he has nothing else to snarl at, and the wit when he is at a loss for a laugh, turns to the foibles of women as a never-failing source of gratification," one reader

stock feminine types: the model heroine, a gentle, high-minded, home-loving maiden, and her foil the flighty flirt, interested only in gossip, gadding, and attracting masculine attention.[8]

The modern reader is apt to dismiss with a smile these paltry efforts of the first American novelists. Devoid of literary merit, bound (like the third-rate English fiction on which they were modeled) to a sterile literary convention derived from Richardson, one and all rehearsed the tale of a young girl proceeding helplessly from sensibility to seduction and then to suicide. But under the layers of sensationalism and sentimentality he who looks may find a substratum of fact from which to reconstruct the woman of the period in her man-centered universe.

The authors themselves laid claim to realism, advertising in title page and preface that their plots were "Founded on Incidents in Real Life," or "Based upon Recent Facts." Such assurances, designed primarily to disarm popular prejudice

---

of the Port Folio complained sourly. "They there feast their vanity as authors and their spleen as men." Port Folio, V (January 12, 1805), 2. "Female Influence," New York Mirror, V (April 19, 1828), 327.

[8] By combining these two types into a character of real conflict, Mrs. Hannah Foster created in The Coquette the only convincing heroine in the sentimental novel. Well-bred but wayward Eliza Wharton, prodded by the voices of convention (her conscience and friends) to accept a tiresomely faultless suitor and settle down into matrimony, yields instead to an innocent desire for gaiety and pleasure which according to the sentimental formula duly leads her to seduction and ruin.

against fiction (still widely condemned on moral grounds),[9] were nevertheless more than window-dressing. For these novices in the novelist's art lacked the skill or imagination to stray far from reality.[10] Most of them women, writing for a female audience, they filled in backgrounds with detail from their own experience in the circumscribed woman's world of that day, leaving beneath the literary convention a picture of the habits and habitudes of the weaker sex which has real authenticity.

Further to allay public fears that fiction implanted "false ideas of life" in impressionable readers,[11] the sentimental novelists seized every opportunity "to afford moral instruction to the youthful mind," ballasting their volumes with preachments similar to the advice offered by the manuals.[12] Like

---

9 Herbert Ross Brown, The Sentimental Novel in America, 1789-1860 (Durham, 1940), ch. 1.

10 Tremaine McDowell, "Sensibility in the Eighteenth Century American Novel," Studies in Philology, XXIV (July, 1927), 401.

11 The historian Hannah Adams was one of those who criticized novels on these grounds. A Memoir of Miss Hannah Adams, Written by Herself (Boston, 1832), 4. Chapter 5 deals more fully with popular attitudes toward novels in connection with the rise of the woman author.

12 "Novel writing as an art," wrote Samuel L. Knapp of his friend Mrs. Susanna Rowson, "she seems to have considered a secondary object. Her main design was to instruct the growing minds and elevate the moral nature of her own sex. Fiction was one of the instruments which she employed for this laudable purpose." Rowson, Charlotte's Daughter (Boston, 1828), 11-12. The quotation in the text is from Eliza Vicery's Emily Hamilton (Worcester, 1803), iv, quoted in Brown, Sentimental Novel, 12.

Mrs. Rowson in her Charlotte Temple, they insisted that their
dearest wish was to "be of service to some who are so unfortunate as to have neither friends to advise nor understanding to
direct them through the various and unexpected evils that
attend a young and inexperienced woman in her first entrance
into life."[13]

The sentimental novel's preoccupation with the love life
of the young girl was only natural.  Courtship was still the
one exciting episode in a woman's career, as well as the most
momentous, since her existence thenceforth revolved around her
husband, and her choice was final.[14]  With early marriage the
custom, the schoolgirl became a bride after only a short sojourn
in society.  During this period courtship was every young lady's
dominating concern.

---

13 Charlotte Temple (New York, 1905), 4.  This famous novel,
first American "best-seller," which has gone through over
two hundred editions in the hundred and fifty years since
its first publication (in England) in 1791, described the
misfortunes of an English girl of fifteen, lured from her
boarding school by a dashing army officer with the aid of
her wicked French governess, taken by him to America and
there deserted, to die in a hovel after giving birth to his
child.  Mrs. Rowson based the story on "a series of authen-
tic events in the life of a relative. . . ."  R. W. G. Vail,
"Susanna Haswell Rowson," American Antiquarian Society,
Proceedings, XLII (1932), 62-63.

14 Though divorces could be obtained in most states, either
through a special act of the state legislature (the procedure
in colonial times) or through the courts (see George Elliott
Howard, A History of Matrimonial Institutions [Chicago, 1904],
III), they occurred very seldom.  To most women, if they
considered it at all, being left socially and economically
stranded by divorce must have seemed a worse evil than enduring an unfortunate marriage.

She must marry; for society made no provision for the single woman's livelihood other than as family helper in the home of a male relative, and most girls agreed with the heroine who cried, "I would not be an old maid for all the world."[15] In 1800 as in 1700 that epithet evoked in the popular mind a picture of a scrawny female of uncertain age, vainly trying every expedient to catch a man, until like the Miss Norcliffe of Helena Wells's Constantia Neville she ended "a virago disappointed in the accomplishment of her favorite wish." Mrs. Jane West in her Letters to a Young Lady found it necessary to reprove old maids' "propensity to relate their early conquests." They should also, she continued severely, avoid "all ridiculous affectation of youth, all 'hoisting the flag of distress,' as a witty author provokingly terms the pink ribband when it waves over the wrinkled brow of faded beauty."[16]

---

15 Tabitha Tenney, Female Quixotism [1801] (Boston, 1841), II, 141. The Rev. Thomas Gisborne, a leader in the Evangelical revival in England, laid down rules for the humane treatment of the female dependent in his Enquiry into the Duties of the Female Sex [1797] (London, 1798). "Pretend not to call her a friend, while you treat her as a drudge. . . . ," he instructed the young wife. "Remember the awkwardness of her situation, and consult her comfort. Is she to look for friends in the kitchen. . . . ? Assuredly not. . . . Admit her then," he urged, "not merely to the formalities, but to the freedom, and genuine satisfactions" of family life. 203-204.

16 Herbert R. Brown quotes Mrs. Wells in The Sentimental Novel, 107. Mrs. West, zealous churchwoman and a prolific writer of novels, poems and advice books of a strong moral cast, published the Letters to a Young Lady in London in 1806. Reprinted in New York in the same year, it deals with the conduct of the single sisterhood on pp. 374ff.

Humane writers, however, were increasingly protesting the ridicule heaped on these lone ladies. "This is a species of cruelty . . . which . . . merits unqualified censure," admonished Mrs. Ann Taylor in her Practical Hints to Young Females.

> Perhaps, ladies, some of these traduced and persecuted beings have been only more delicate in their choice than you have been; or circumstances may have arisen in this mutable world to prevent their entering a state which they were qualified to adorn. . . . It does not invariably happen that persons remain single because they are not worth having, or that others are married because they are. . . .[17]

The spinster's chief problem, as the Rev. John Bennett discerned, was that she lacked "objects of consequence enough to occupy the mind." A solitary being, "she wanders through a wide bustling world, uncomfortable in herself, uninteresting to others. . . ."[18] Mrs. West, however, reminded her readers that a spinster did not necessarily have to give herself up to restless indolence. "It is a false and dangerous assertion," she declared, "that single women must . . . pass their lives in a dull mediocrity, . . . unacquainted with real enjoyment." They could be daughters, sisters, aunts, and friends, even though not wives and mothers. "Let them but endeavour to be as useful to others as their limited means allow, and pursue

---

17 The Practical Hints was first published in London in 1815. The quotation is from the first American edition (Boston, 1816), 114-115.

18 Bennett, Letters to a Young Lady [1789] (Philadelphia, 1818), 261, 260.

every source of virtuous employment which their bounded sphere permits," and she ventured to predict that they would find themselves as respected and happy as many a wife.[19]

Such remonstrances, however, would make little headway until the world could give the spinster work to do which would bring prestige and economic independence in its train. As Jane Austen's heroine Emma Woodhouse observed acutely, "it is poverty only that makes celibacy contemptible to a generous public! A single woman, with a very narrow income, must be a ridiculous, disagreeable old maid! but a single woman, of good fortune, is always respectable, and may be as sensible and pleasant as anybody else." And there was some reason in the distinction, Emma thought, "for a very narrow income has a tendency to contract the mind, and sour the temper."[20]

In young America, however, the old maid was a freak of nature seldom met with, and her much maligned fate hardly a serious possibility. Yet to obtain a settlement in life required

---

19 West, Letters to a Young Lady, 375, 376. Other protests against the ignominy heaped on spinsterhood were voiced by the young Maine belle Eliza Southgate (A Girl's Life Eighty Years Ago [New York, 1887], 38) and Hannah Foster in The Boarding School [1798] (Boston, 1829), 122. An enthusiast for the doctrines of Malthus even dared to argue in the columns of the Literary Magazine and American Register the question, "Is Marriage or Celibacy Most Eligible?" II (September, 1804), 468-470.

20 Austen, Emma [1816] (Modern Library edition), 814.

circumspection.  In acquiring that piece of valuable property, a wife, the middle-class male demanded unsullied purity,
and the elaborate propriety which hedged about the young girl
of marriageable age was intended in large measure to preserve
this one indispensable asset in the marriage market.  Chastity
once lost, marriage was impossible, and life held nothing but
disgrace.  Chastity under the shadow of a doubt might as well
be lost.  "Reputation undoubtedly is of great importance to
all, but to a female 'tis every thing," the young Portland
debutante Eliza Southgate wrote to her cousin, adding, "I have
ever thought that to be conscious of doing right was insufficient; but that it must appear so to the world."[21]  Eliza
Wharton, vivacious heroine of Hannah Foster's The Coquette,
found this out the hard way.  By flirting with the profligate
Major Sanford, headstrong Miss Wharton so damaged her chances
of securing a husband that Sanford's conquest of her virtue
was almost anti-climactic.

---

21 A Girl's Life, 50-51.  Mrs. Rowson issued a fervent warning
on this point.  "A girl just entering the state of womanhood, especially if she is possessed of any personal or
mental accomplishments, and of an open ingenuous temper is
surrounded with innumerable dangers; her reputation is of
as delicate a texture, and may be as easily injured, as the
fairest blossom; the malignant whisperings of envy, or the
pestiferous breath of slander, may in an instant blast it;
it will droop under the keen eye of suspicion. . . ."  Mentoria; or the Young Lady's Friend (Philadelphia, 1794), I,
31.  Fortunately we have the traveler Adam Hodgson's observation that American girls, while "rather gay and social in
their dispositions," were at the same time "very observant
of the rules of female propriety. . . ."  Letters from North
America (London, 1824), II, 27.

Regarded in this light, the constant dwelling on the dangers of seduction in novels, magazines,[22] and even in handbooks seems more reasonable than ridiculous, especially in view of the extreme youth and inexperience of the innocent victims, and the dissolute lives led by many men in this heyday of the double standard. The genus rake was perhaps more at home in roisterous eighteenth-century England than in provincial America. Yet the Russian traveler Petr Poletika, an intelligent and rational observer, reported as late as 1823 "that in maritime cities, and even in the metropolis, libertinism is carried to a great length by the young men."[23]

"If I was called upon to write the history of a woman's trials and sorrows," wrote the English curate John Bennett, "I would date it from the moment when nature has pronounced her marriageable. . . . If I had a girl of my own, at this critical age, I should be full of the keenest apprehensions for her safety. . . ." With her catch-as-catch-can education, which had done nothing to discipline the reason and everything to encourage the excessive emotionalism demanded by the vogue of sensibility, the young girl emerged from her sheltered home, perhaps into a fashionable whirl where flattery might easily turn her

---

22 Herbert R. Brown deals with the magazines' obsession with this theme in his article, "Elements of Sensibility in The Massachusetts Magazine," American Literature, I (November, 1929), 287-290.

23 Petr Ivanovitch Poletika, A Sketch of the Internal Condition of the United States of America (Baltimore, 1826), 129.

head. "Never . . . believe any man in _earnest_," warned the
Rev. Mr. Bennett, "till he makes the most _pointed_ declarations
in your favour." "Not possessing that quick precision and
force of intellect which is the peculiar prerogative of man,"
Caroline Matilda Warren explained in her novel The Gamesters,
the young maiden "too often listens to the plighted vow, and
listening, is undone."[24]

Upon the fallen woman the respectable world coldly turned
its back, unless, perhaps, the sinner were a member of the
lower class who, once reformed, might be useful as a servant.
A pupil in Hannah Foster's Boarding School reclaimed an Irish
girl found sitting by the road "in a pensive attitude, with an
infant in her lap," but Mrs. Foster hastened to make it plain
that, "though I advocate the principles of philanthropy and
Christian charity, as extending to some very special cases, I
am far from supposing this fault generally capable of the least
extenuation."[25]

In the novels these outcasts quickly came to a distraught
and repentant death via suicide or a swift "decline," a fate

24 Bennett, Letters to a Young Lady, 259, 265; The Gamesters
[1805] (Boston, 1828), 281.

25 The Boarding School [1798] (Boston, 1829), 204, 207-208.
Times had changed since Dr. Gregory had advised his
daughters to "Show a compassionate sympathy to unfortunate
women, especially to those who are rendered so by the villainy of men. Indulge a secret pleasure, I may say pride,
in being the friends and refuge of the unhappy. . . ."
A Father's Legacy to His Daughters (New York, 1775), 16.

which can hardly have been the fixed rule in real life. The
overwhelming success of Richardson's Clarissa Harlowehad made
the lovebed-to-childbed-to-deathbed formula[26] into a literary
convention, worn threadbare by lesser artists in the next
seventy-five years. Nevertheless it was an indubitable element
of realism that won for the seduction theme the long life which
sex and sensation alone could not have purchased.

Not that the popularity of the theme was any gauge of the
actual extent of illicit love in the United States. In fact,
almost every traveler commented upon the high level of morality
among American women,[27] and the Massachusetts Magazine's estimate

---

26 Clarissa herself, of course, skipped the middle step.

27 "Licentious manners," the Marquis de Chastellux had written
in 1787, ". . . are so foreign in America, that communication with young women, leads to nothing bad. . . ." His
countryman Brissot de Warville echoed this verdict: "Their
frank and tender hearts have nothing to fear from the perfidy of men. Examples of this perfidy are rare. . . ."
And Petr Poletika capped these assertions in 1823 when he
asserted that "Women in the United States enjoy a reputation for morality which the most violent defamers of that
country have never dared assail." Poletika, however, observed signs of deterioration in public morals. "Within a
few years only, those mercenary dispensers ['dispensatrices']
of debauchery, who swarm in the large towns of Europe, have
here made their appearance in places of public resort; and
the time is but lately past, when prostitutes were obliged
to hide themselves from public view, and dared not expose
their infamous profession in the streets, for fear of being
hooted at and grossly insulted. But it must be confessed,
that this horror of incontinence has already undergone some
change, and the aspect of the cities of America, is not always, in this particular, very favorable to good morals."
Brown quotes Chastellux and Brissot in his Sentimental Novel,
49-50. Poletika's statements appear on pp. 128 and 129 of
his Sketch of the Internal Condition of the United States of
America.

that "Every town and village affords some example of a ruined female," was surely exaggerated. If a girl fell, it was not for lack of warning. "So often, my dear Maria, has the pen of the divine, the moralist, and the novelist been employed on the subject of female fraility [sic] and seduction," wrote Mrs. Foster, "that I am astonished when I see those, who have the best means of information, heedlessly sacrificing their reputation, peace and happiness to the specious arts of the libertine!"[28]

Conceivably, the young girl might live through the period of courtship without ever encountering a "libertine," receiving the overtures of bona-fide suitors. She would probably not have a very wide selection. Eliza Southgate declared that

> the inequality of privilege is very sensibly felt by us females, and in no instance is it greater than in the liberty of choosing a partner in marriage; true, we have the liberty of refusing those we don't like, but not of selecting those we do. . . . A woman of taste and sentiment will surely see but a very few whom she could love, and it is altogether uncertain whether either of them will particularly distinguish her. If they should, surely she is very fortunate, but it would be one of fortune's random favors and such as we have no right to expect.[29]

---

28 Brown quotes The Massachusetts Magazine (1791) in The Sentimental Novel, 287. Mrs. Foster commented on seduction in The Boarding School, 162.

29 A Girl's Life, 37-38. Mrs. West put her authority as an eminent moralist behind similar statements in Letters to a Young Lady, 378.

In making even this restricted choice, she must be wholly guided by her parents, particularly her father, whose knowledge of the world presumably made him the better counselor. "Let his judgment have an entire ascendancy over your mind and actions, especially in your intercourse and society with the other sex," Hannah Foster advised. "Consider him as better acquainted with their merit, circumstances, and views, than you can be; and, should you contemplate a connexion for life, let his opinion determine your choice." "Oh my dear girls," implored Mrs. Rowson in Charlotte Temple, "listen not to the voice of love, unless sanctioned by paternal approbation."[30]

Few fathers exerted their authority so harshly as old Van Rough in Royall Tyler's rollicking play The Contrast, who, determined that his daughter marry a wastrel with "the quit-rent of twenty miles square," addressed her, "I'd have you to know, Mary, if you won't make young Van Dumpling the man of your choice, you shall marry him as the man of my choice."[31] But families, anxious to have daughters "settled," and fearing for their helplessness if once deprived of masculine support, did tend to lean heavily on the side of security, thus giving the convention of the tyrannical and avaricious parent (patterned after Clarissa Harlowe's father and a favorite among the sentimental novelists) a basis in reality. Mrs. Foster, for instance,

---

30 The Boarding School, 228; Charlotte Temple, 53.

31 The Contrast [1790] (Boston, 1920), 35, 36.

shrank from the thought of marrying for money, yet counseled
her pupils that "A proper regard should always be had to a
comfortable subsistence in life." No grand passion was worth
risking "those embarrassing distresses of want, which will
elude the remedies of love itself, and prove fatal to the
peace and happiness at which you aim."[32]

Romantic love was hence not the primary consideration. "I
may be censured for declaring it as my opinion that not one
woman in a hundred marries for love," wrote Eliza Southgate.
"Gratitude is undoubtedly the foundation of the esteem we commonly feel for a husband. One that has preferred us to all
the world . . . surely merits our gratitude. If his character
is good -- if he is not displeasing in his person or manners --
what objection can we make that will not be thought frivolous.
. . .?" Romantic love was even suspect in some quarters. Mrs.
Foster thought "a passion of this origin tends not to substantial and durable happiness. To secure this, it must be of
quite another kind, enkindled by esteem, founded on merit,
strengthened by congenial dispositions and corresponding virtues, and terminating in the most pure and refined affection."[33]

Sometimes, however, inclination, duty, and interest might
go pleasantly hand in hand. Eliza Southgate's own courtship

32 The Boarding School, 91-92.

33 A Girl's Life, 37-38; The Boarding School, 88-89. Eliza
Southgate must have been reading Dr. Gregory's discussion
of marriage in A Father's Legacy to his Daughters, for
many of her phrases echo his.

was a case in point. Falling in love while visiting at Balls-
ton Spa in 1802, Eliza found herself at first "in a situation
truly embarrassing," hundreds of miles away from her Portland
home, "my Father and Mother a perfect stranger to the person."
Her suitor's conduct, however, "was such as I shall ever reflect on with the greatest pleasure, -- open, candid, generous,
and delicate."

> He knew I was not at liberty to encourage
> his addresses without the approbation of
> my Parents, and appeared as solicitous
> that I should act with strict propriety as
> one of my most disinterested friends. . . .
> He only required that I would not discour-
> age his addresses till he had an opportunity
> of making known to my Parents his character
> and wishes. . . . That I feel deeply inter-
> ested in Mr. Bowne I candidly acknowledge,
> and from the knowledge I have of his heart
> and character I think him better calculated
> to promote my happiness than any person I
> have yet seen. . . . I have referred him
> wholly to you, and you, my dearest Parents,
> must decide.

Inquiries quickly satisfied Dr. and Mrs. Southgate of Walter
Bowne's reputation as "a man of business, uniform in his conduct and very much respected." The marriage took place, and
from her new home in New York Eliza wrote her mother, "I realize
all the happiness you can wish me."[34]

---

34 A Girl's Life, 140-141, 164. She lived only six years after
her marriage, falling victim to tuberculosis at twenty-five.

The average young lady was not delivered to her husband without a generous portion of advice on the conduct becoming a wife. A female contributor to the Port Folio summed it up succinctly: "Our state in society is a dependent one, and it is ours to be good and amiable, whatever may be the conduct of the men, to whom we are subjected." Among the more inspired of Mrs. Ann Taylor's Practical Hints to Young Females was the suggestion: "accustom yourself, in the contemplation of your husband's character, to dwell on the bright side. . . ."[35] "You must bear with calmness," instructed Mrs. Foster, "every thing that the sincerest desire of peace can dictate; and studiously avoid every expression, and even look, which may irritate and offend."[36] "The colour of our lives," Mrs. West declared, "is so influenced by the propensities of our wedded partners," that in perhaps the majority of marriages "the business of the wife is to control her own inclinations, instead of projecting how she may gratify them."

---

35 "The American Lounger," Port Folio, II (May 8, 1802), 137; Practical Hints, 17.

36 The Boarding School, 200. In the same vein a distinguished Virginian admonished his newly wed daughter: "A man of sense, of prudence, of warm feelings, cannot and will not bear an opposition of any kind, which is attended with an angry look or expression. The current of his affections is suddenly stopped; his attachment is weakened; he begins to feel a mortification the most pungent; he is lessened even in his own eyes: and be assured, the wife who once excites those sentiments in the breast of her husband, will never regain the high ground which she might and ought to have retained." "Letter of Advice from a Father to His Only Daughter," New York Mirror, VII (August 29, 1829), 62.

> This subservience [she continued] is not
> solely confined to the conjugal tie, nor
> does it only revert backward to the conse-
> crated claims of paternity; our brothers,
> nay even our sons, will reap the privilege
> of Adam; and whenever we fix with them in
> a domestic residence, we must conform to
> their humours, anticipate their wishes, and
> alleviate their misfortunes, or else forfeit
> their affections and forego their society.[37]

Nor did the prospective husband escape without his share of advice. The English physician and literary scholar John Aiken offered sensible counsel on the choice of a wife, urging his son not to be swayed by "external charms and ornamental accomplishments." "No man ever married a fool without severely repenting it; for though the pretty trifler may have served well enough for the hour of dalliance and gaiety, yet when folly assumes the reins of domestic, and especially of parental, control, she will give a perpetual heart-ache to a considerate partner." Aiken emphasized the importance of housewifely skills. "A clean and quiet fireside, regular and agreeable meals, decent apparel, a house managed with order and economy, . . . --

---

37 Letters to a Young Lady, 30-31. The sentimental novelists delighted in portraits of long-suffering, uncomplaining wives. (Brown, Sentimental Novel, 108-109.) Despite the submission expected of her, however, the dutiful wife was not wholly without recourse in the battle between the sexes. "Without in the least derogating from the superiority of the other sex," remarked Mrs. Taylor, "she must be a very superficial observer who has not discovered, that they are deficient in that species of minute discernment, of intuitive penetration, which enables women . . . often successfully to combat superiour strength. . . . The woman who has gained complete ascendancy over her husband's affections, in general requires nothing but address to possess a proportionate influence upon his conduct." Practical Hints, 139.

all these things compose a very considerable part of what the
nuptial state was intended to afford us; and without them, no
charms of person or understanding will long continue to bestow delight."

Marriage also demanded "a certain energy of both body and
mind which is less frequently met with among the females of
the present age than might be wished." Delicate health in a
female might be appealing, but it was hardly desirable for a
lifelong connection since, as any close observer of society
would note, "occasions of alarm, suffering and disgust come
much more frequently in the way of women than of men. To them
belong all offices about the weak, the sick, and the dying.
When the house becomes a scene of wretchedness from any cause,
the man often runs abroad, the woman must stay at home and
face the worst."[38]

All writers found it necessary to remind the roving male
of his duty to seek his pleasures at home in his wife's society,
and to preserve an amiable, affectionate, and attentive de-
meanor towards her.[39] Many husbands, wrote Mrs. Taylor,

---

[38] Aiken, Letters from a Father to his Son [1794] (Philadelphia,
1796), 251-255.

[39] The Rev. William Jay of Bath, England, prominent dissenting
clergyman whose homilies were popular in America for half
a century, suggested as motives for the performance of this
duty the weakness of womankind ("A rose, a lily, allows of
no rough usages") and her dignity "as a mutual partaker of
the privileges of the gospel." "The Mutual Duties of Husbands and Wives," [1801] in Thoughts on Marriage (Boston,
1833), 90-94.

assumed that, if they were good providers, "if their conduct
is moral; if they neither beat, starve, nor imprison their
wives," they were everything needed to make a good husband,
"and they pass for such among the crowd: but as their domestick
virtues," she commented, "are chiefly of the negative kind,
the happiness of her whose lot it is to be united to such a
one for life, must be of the same description." The husband
was repeatedly urged to take his wife into his confidence on
money matters, informing her of his income and expenses and
assisting her to manage economically. The common habit of
keeping her in the dark as to his resources and doling out
money for household expenses with a reluctant and niggardly
hand was roundly condemned as often compelling women "to shel-
ter themselves under mean contrivances and low arts, equally
injurious to their husband's [sic] happiness, as to their own
characters."[40]


These concepts of woman as a dependent being, wholly subordinate to her masculine protector, had of course enjoyed a
long vogue. The nineteenth century, while giving the old doctrines a wider circulation than ever before, proceeded to

40 Taylor, Practical Hints, 152, 151. Hester Thrale in her
often-reprinted "Letter to a Young Gentleman on his Marriage" gave the same advice (The American Spectator or
Matrimonial Preceptor [Boston, 1797], 266-269), as did
William Jay in his Thoughts on Marriage, 88.

reinforce them with a new dogma of domesticity. The importance
of women's staying home and centering all activities there
became a favorite theme of the rising generation of writers.
In a day when the average woman was calmly taking this disposition of her life for granted, such concern may hardly seem
to have been warranted. Yet a general impression persisted
that the sex were preparing to fly the coop, some to flutter
about amid scenes of idle diversion, others to swoop down upon
the world of men claiming the rights demanded by Mary Wollstonecraft. To correct these tendencies moralists of every shade
bent their efforts.

The attack on gadding, as we have seen, was not without
provocation. Every city and town had its world of fashion,
whose female members attracted attention out of all proportion
to their actual numbers. These were mostly "women, who, having
nothing to do, or choosing to do nothing of a useful nature,"
found time heavy on their hands. In an effort to escape ennui,
observed Timothy Dwight, erstwhile president of Yale College
and pillar of New England Congregationalism,

> women of this description crowd to the the-
> atre, the assembly-room, the card-table,
> routs, and squeezes; flutter from door to
> door on ceremonious visits, and from shop
> to shop to purchase what they do not want,
> and to look at what they do not intend to
> purchase; hurry to watering places, to re-
> cover health which they have not lost; and
> hurry back again in pursuit of pleasure
> which they cannot find.

"Happily," Dwight concluded, "the number of these is not very great, even in our cities."[41]  England produced more such

giddy lilies of the field, its social life throughout the cen-

tury having been marked by extravagance and dissipation in all

classes, a legacy from the dissolute days of the Restoration.

It was this sort of female that had so disgusted Mary Woll-

stonecraft.  An irrepressible feminine type, perennial target

for moralists in every age and nation, the eighteenth century

had been unusually indulgent with her.

The religious revival, however, was rapidly tightening

standards of behavior.  For their campaign for domesticity,

its adherents found powerful sanction in St. Paul's injunction

that young women be "keepers at home."  The Rev. Thomas Gisborne,

whose Enquiry into the Duties of the Female Sex was one of the

textbooks of the Evangelical movement, expounded Paul's words

---

41 Dwight, Travels in New-England and New-York (New Haven,
   1821), IV, 477.  A Dartmouth College undergraduate named
   Samuel Lorenzo Knapp (later to become a literary figure of
   some minor note) wrote a satire on American society in
   1802 in which he luridly pictured city women of the fashionable upper class as wastrels, dissipated, profane, and
   unchaste, blaming their low moral tone upon the influence
   of Mary Wollstonecraft's doctrines. (Letters of Shahcoolen,
   A Hindu Philosopher [Boston, 1802], a clumsy imitation of
   Montesquieu and Goldsmith's famous satires on European society by imaginary travelers from the Orient.)  The book
   received considerable attention in the fledgling American
   periodicals of the day, but all reviewers agreed that his
   remarks on the degeneration of female moral and social life
   were exaggerated to the point of absurdity, declaring that
   "the publications of Miss Wollstonecraft have had little
   effect, comparatively, with the author's statement."
   [Winthrop Sargent], "Letters of Shahcoolen," Monthly Anthology, II (February, 1805), 85-88; "Letters of Shahcoolen,
   a Hindu Philosopher," American Review and Literary Journal,
   II (April-May-June, 1802), 209-212.

at length.  When a woman frittered away her days in social
activities, "domestic business is interrupted, vigilance as
to family concerns is suspended, industry, reflection, mental
and religious improvement are deserted and forgotten."  Furthermore, the home was woman's principal theater for doing
good, by setting a pattern for her neighbors "in personal
manners, in domestic arrangements, and in every branch of her
private conduct."  In her own neighborhood, too, where she
was known and respected, were her best opportunities to attend
to the wants of "the humbler classes of society."[42]

Even sophisticated high society conceded that many of its
women had turned the pursuit of pleasure into a marathon, for-
getting home and family responsibilities in their "extravagant
fondness for company and public resorts."[43]  Maria Edgeworth,
an expert observer of fashionable life, took for the central
theme of her novel Belinda the conversion of one Lady Delacour
from a career of headlong dissipation to sobriety and domestic
happiness, and the book, which a noted contemporary critic described as "highly entertaining,"[44] became one of her most
popular works.  America's ablest woman novelist of the period,

---

42 Gisborne, Duties of the Female Sex, 210-213.  Paul laid down
this rule in his letter to Titus, 2:5.

43 Foster, The Boarding School, 70.

44 Anna Laetitia Barbauld, ed., The British Novelists (London,
1810), XLIX, foreword, quoted in Bertha Coolidge Slade,
Maria Edgeworth (London, 1937), 93.

Mrs. Hannah Foster, who like Miss Edgeworth moved in the best circles, attempted to teach the same lesson in The Boarding School. The "preceptress" of this establishment "particularly endeavored to domesticate" her young charges and "turn their thoughts to the beneficial and necessary qualifications of private life," approvingly quoting Milton's

> nothing lovelier can be found
> In woman, than to study household good,

while she stressed "the utter insignificance and uselessness of that part of the sex"

> Bred only and completed to the taste
> Of lustful appetence, to sing, to dance,
> To dress, and troll the tongue, and roll the eye.

The girls whom she received in her "mansion" learned both fancy and plain sewing, even though "many, I am aware, suppose this last . . . beneath the attention of a lady." Needlework, too, they were told, would help pass the time at home when books and music palled, thus preventing recourse to "frivolous amusements" out of pure boredom.[45]

The mentors of the rising middle class sought anxiously to prevent their readers from aping the fashionable follies of their social superiors. The worthy Taylors ("a family which has . . . done more for Domestic Education . . . than perhaps any other in Great Britain"[46]) -- husband, Isaac, wife Ann,

---

45 The Boarding School, 7, 11, 14. Milton delivered these dicta in Paradise Lost, IX, 232-233, XI, 618-620.

46 Christopher Anderson, Book for Parents [1826] (Boston, 1834), 394.

and daughters Ann and Jane -- turned out dozens of improving
books for young people, designed "to promote domestick virtue,
and preserve the happiness of the fire side." Mrs. Ann Taylor
particularly warned young females against the "dangerous passion" for gadding, cautioning them to build up a happy home
life by efficient household management, harmonious family relationships, and simple home recreations.[47]

The reproofs administered the sex for their addiction to
pleasure, however, were as nothing compared to the consterna-
tion aroused by the notion that woman, having picked up wild
notions about equal rights, might stage an invasion into the
occupations so long regarded as men's exclusive province.
Thoroughly alarmed, the guardians of morals and manners now
for the first time felt impelled to make an exact definition
of woman's sphere and insist on her staying within it.

Behind this sphere propaganda lay a curious psychology.
Warning women away from men's pursuits at a time when most
females were utterly indifferent to them, emphasizing the all-
engrossing importance of home and home duties which few would
have thought to question, society's mentors and their readers
to all appearances were aggressively reaffirming the old values
at a time when society's familiar patterns were quite undisturbe

---

[47] Practical Hints, vii, 120ff.

Yet the vague fears which preyed upon them were not entirely
groundless. Already frightened by the radical ideas of the
French Revolution and aghast at the career of their leading
female exponent, they had begun to feel the first tremors of a
gigantic economic revolution which would soon crack the walls
of woman's sphere, opening the way to challenging work in the
outside world, but at the same time making her life a far less
comfortable one.

This first raising of the sphere question marked the onset of the modern era in woman's history, inaugurating for
better or for worse the tension between "home" and "career"
for which each succeeding generation has since sought easement.
No one had thought it necessary before to press the issue of
home because in previous economic eras all her activities had
naturally centered there. In the halcyon days before the
growth of industrial capitalism, when most men were farmers,
craftsmen, or traders, earning their livelihood at home, a
woman's life had happily combined the jobs of raising a family
and contributing towards its support as her husband's right
hand in his business. Corporations, swallowing up family enterprises in the course of the seventeenth and eighteenth centuries, drew the head of the family and his trade from home,
leaving his wife alone with the children in a more secluded
and monotonous household, no longer his partner but an economic
parasite.[48] Under these conditions, the energetic, confident

---

[48] Alice Clark developed this thesis in The Working Life of
Women in the Seventeenth Century (London, 1919), a work of
the first importance in women's history.

woman of Elizabethan and Puritan times had dwindled into the
dependent, helpless female of the eighteenth century, devoted
according to her taste and means either to domestic routine or
the pursuit of pleasure.[49]

The Industrial Revolution in its infinite complexity and
insatiable demand for workers was once again to provide an
outlet for woman's non-domestic talents. The new jobs, however, meant working as men did, outside the home, and to com-
bine them with home-making required adroit strategy. So novel
was the situation that most observers could not conceive of a
practical amalgamation of the two and, fearing for the future
of the family, evolved the philosophy of sphere to keep home
fires burning.

Recurring at intervals in the generations to follow, this
dogma of woman's sphere reflected in every instance a fresh
shock to the social body. The attending circumstances were always the same: a bold attack by left-wing thinkers on the status
quo, staged at a time when further economic change was threat-
ening society's hard-won stability. Since the guardians of the
old order lacked the prescience to probe to the basic sources

---

[49] Woman's role in agricultural communities, to be sure, would
hardly change until in the twentieth century modern industry
reached out to mechanize the farm, releasing the prosperous
farm wife from her chores to face some of the city woman's
problems like the employment of leisure. The farm wife in
any period held up her end of her family's livelihood,
though too often at the cost of overwork and stultifying
isolation.

of their distress, they inevitably made scapegoats of the offending radicals who, themselves suffering the same feelings of dislocation, thus bore both the discomfort and the blame for it.

The first act of this tragicomedy featured Mary Wollstonecraft in the leading role of public enemy. With every stroke of the pen the sphere definers of the turn of the century were battling the set of principles they associated with the author of the Rights of Woman, that "female lunatic" who wished to strip her sex "of every thing feminine, and to assimilate them, as fast as possible, to the masculine character."[50]

Mary's reputation had now been thoroughly blackened. Only rarely did some dispassionate observer protest the injustice of the verdict against her, pleading her genius and "the purity of her heart" in partial extenuation of her irreligion and her "error of eagerly hastening forward to the untimely practice of an abstract speculative theory of morals, incompatible with her own, and the general interests of society."[51] To read her book was now an act of some daring; to criticize any aspect of woman's status made one immediately suspect of the Wollstonecraft heresy. "I am aware of the censure that will ever await the female that

---

50 Knapp, Letters of Shahcoolen, 24, 23.

51 "Reflections on the Character of Mary Wollstonecraft Godwin," in Charles Brockden Brown's Monthly Magazine and American Review, I (August, 1799), 332, 333; "Mrs. Wollstonecraft," Boston Weekly Magazine, I (February 5, 1803), 61.

attempts the vindication of her sex," wrote Eliza Southgate, "yet I dare to brave that censure that I know to be undeserved. It does not follow . . . that every female who vindicates the capacity of the sex is a disciple of Mary Wolstoncraft [sic]."[52]

The general public had now forgotten, if it had ever realized, that Mary had demanded only spiritual, not temporal, equality for her sex; that her primary objective had been to make better wives and mothers by giving women self-respect and a sense of responsibility; that, though her philosophy implied women's freedom to undertake the same work as men, she had actually only suggested improving the social and economic status of the existing women's occupations, so that girls would not have to marry for a livelihood. People had forgotten, too, that her one reference to political rights for females had occupied a scant half-dozen words, spoken as if they were a goal to be attained in a dim, Utopian future. The mere connotations of the term "rights of woman," smacking of Tom Paine and violent republicanism, were sufficient grounds for denouncing Mary Wollstonecraft as a deep-dyed radical, a verdict easily confirmed

---

52 "Prejudice set aside," Eliza continued, "I confess I admire many of her sentiments, notwithstanding I believe should any one adopt her principles, they would conduct in the same manner, and upon the whole her life is the best comment on her writings." A Girl's Life, 61-62. "I know Mary Wollstonecraft is held in general abhorrence," wrote another New England girl in 1803, proceeding nevertheless to protest that her ideas were no more harmful to her sex than those of writers like Gregory and Fordyce who considered women "the mere baubles of an hour." Elizabeth A. Dwight, Memorials of Mary Wilder White, Mary Wilder Tileston, ed. (Boston, 1903), 111.

by her personal history and a glance at her book to sample
its inflammatory phraseology and bold arraignment of social
convention, aristocracy, and wealth.

Against this "champion of her sex's rights" the Reverend
John Thornton Kirkland, later president of Harvard College,
appealed to American females in 1798 to decide

> whether they are not as free, as lovely,
> as respectable, and happy, in their pres-
> ent situation in society, as they would
> be if their sexuality of character and
> employments were done away, and law and
> custom allowed them to exchange the dis-
> taff for the plough, the needle and the
> pencil for the axe and the hammer; and
> their stations as mistresses of their
> families, companions of their husbands,
> guides and protectors of their children,
> . . . to be lawyers, legislators, and
> town-meeting patriots.[53]

A pupil of Mrs. Susanna Rowson's school alarmed the assemblage
of parents and friends at the annual "exhibition" in 1802 by
reciting a poem which began in truculent vein,

> While Patriots on wide Philosophic plan,
> Declaim upon the wond'rous Rights of Man;
> May I presume to speak? and tho' uncommon,
> Stand forth the champion of the Rights of Woman.
> Nay start not gentle sirs, indeed 'tis true
> That Woman has her rights, as well as you,
> And if she's wise, she will assert them too.

Her listeners soon relaxed, however, when she defined these
"rights" as those of presiding over domestic matters, sharing
the grief of fathers, brothers, and friends oppressed with care,

---

53 "An Oration, delivered at the request of the Society of ΦBK,
in the Chapel of Harvard College, . . . July 9, 1798,"
Monthly Magazine and American Review, II (January, 1800),
57-59.

and helping victims of sickness and affliction.  Clinching the
argument were lines declaring,

> But know you not that Womans proper sphere
> Is the domestic walk?  To interfere
> With politics, divinity, or law,
> As much deserved ridicule would draw
> On Woman, -- as the learned grave divine
> Cooking the soup on which he means to dine. . . .[54]

In a heavily didactic boarding-school tale of 1817, Mrs.
Ann Taylor described a mother's advice to her daughter, about
to return home.  "It is chiefly there that the lustre of the
female character is discernible; because home is its proper
sphere.  Men have much to do with the world without; our field
of action is circumscribed; yet, to confine ourselves within
its humble bounds, and to discharge our duties there, may produce effects equally beneficial . . . with their wider range."[55]

It was Mrs. Jane West, however, who worked out the most
elaborate rationale of sphere.  Her sex, she declared, lacked
the physical and emotional stamina to handle men's work.  "The
slighter construction of our bodily organs, our sedentary habits, and the inconveniences and sufferings attached to materni-
ty" rendered females liable to "lingering decay and protracted
suffering."  Their tender hearts too often overpowered their
reason and judgment.  Conceivably they might possess the necessary intellectual equipment, yet "substantial moral reasons"

---

54 Boston Weekly Magazine, I (October 30, 1802), 2.

55 Mrs. Ann Taylor and Jane Taylor, Correspondence between a
Mother and her Daughter at School [c. 1815] (The Writings
of Jane Taylor [Boston, 1832], V), 120-121.

forbade their engaging in "business in which labours of the head are principally required."

> Could meekness [she questioned] preserve
> her olive wand unbroken amid the noisy con-
> tention of the bar; could delicacy escape
> uninjured through the initiatory studies of
> medicine; . . . could melting compassion be
> the proper agent of impartial justice; or,
> would gentleness dictate those severe but
> wholesome restraints, which often preserve
> a nation from ruin?

The few women who had acquitted themselves well in such pursuits, like Queen Elizabeth, owed their success, Mrs. West insisted, either to a total lack of really feminine qualities, to the aid of astute men advisers, or to special grace granted them for their difficult calling -- an assistance "we cannot hope to possess, if we rush madly from our sphere, . . . to venture on untried and forbidden paths."

Besides, domestic seclusion had positive advantages. It protected women from many vices like intemperance, profanity, treachery, and cruelty. Nor should their subjection be con-sidered degrading; it was ordained for the sake of family peace and was actually more pleasant and easy than the inde-pendence and self-control that seemed so inviting to the young-er generation. In short, Jane West concluded, "Providence has withdrawn us from the turmoil of worldly contention; and it is only some peculiar circumstances, or the improper encouragement of a busy disposition, which removes us from our proper sphere, domestic retirement."[56]

---

56 West, _Letters to a Young Lady_, 34-36, 40-41, 43ff, 47-48, 40.

No transgression of their appointed bounds horrified the average citizen more than women's taking an interest in politics. Mrs. Hannah Foster showed herself to be unusually broadminded on this subject in her novel The Coquette, when at a party where the conversation turned on politics she had her heroine "judiciously, yet modestly" enter in. Most people, however, felt that "There are certain subjects of conversation adapted to each sex; politics belong to the men, and to hear women declaim with the virulence of party is as unbecoming as to hear men declaim against the cut of a pair of ruffles."[57]

One Boston gentleman founded a ladies' weekly in 1806 with the avowed purpose of giving "the female part of the community" a paper of its own because "the devotion of the public prints of the day to political discussion and party debates" was "such as to render them uninteresting to the circle of the Fair." He promised that his pages would be "closed against politics and obscenity," including "every thing which might cause the crimson fluid to stain the cheek of unaffected modesty."[58]

Laughable as it seems today, this prejudice had some justification at a time when the battles between Federalists and

---

57 The Coquette, 65; "On Female Behaviour and Conversation," Boston Weekly Magazine, III (April 20, 1805), 101. The writer of the latter article borrowed several of his effects from a Spectator essay on female partisans.

58 Ladies' Visitor (December 4, 1806), quoted in Bertha M. Stearns, "Early New England Magazines for Ladies," New England Quarterly, II (July, 1929), 437-438.

Jeffersonian Republicans had exacerbated partisan feeling to
a point where politics and obscenity were familiar bedfellows.
At the height of the party rancor, Charles Brockden Brown
gave considerable space in his New York Monthly Magazine to
some strictures from a lady contributor. A woman was foolish,
wrote "Miss M.," to allow herself to be "agitated by every
movement of political affairs, which we are unable to understand or controul. . . . Who is president to-day or to-morrow,
whether he be a federalist or a democrat, is of no moment to
us, if he be wise and virtuous." Besides, "A female who assumes the character of a politician, lays aside her feminine
attractions." A better outlet for patriotic feeling was charitable work, since "whatever tends to private good, must, in
the order of events, give stability to government and new
strength to the public welfare." She who was "united to a man
. . . eminent in politics" had the special duty "to tranquil-
lize his passions" rather than aggravating them by echoing
his enthusiasms and resentments, thereby destroying "that
solace to which every man flies -- domestic repose."[59]

---

59 "Remarks on Female Politicians," Monthly Magazine and American Review, III (December, 1800), 417-418.

Chapter Four

CHARITY WORK AND EDUCATION, 1800-1825

## Chapter Four

## CHARITY WORK AND EDUCATION, 1800-1825

Wholly agreeing with these maxims, the genteel female
shrank from the mere thought of equality and pursued her accustomed ways. The hand that rocked the cradle did not stray
from its appointed task; no general exodus took place from
the home into the world of men. No new firebrand appeared to
challenge the old assumptions or threaten the settled habits
of family life. The insistence on sphere therefore subsided,
and the new century reached its quarter mark with the traditional code still officially in force.

Beneath the surface of convention, however, the old order
was weakening. By 1800, as the structure of society slowly
yielded to the pressure of economic change, there had already
begun a readjustment of women's life which, gathering speed
with succeeding generations, would mold their daughters and
granddaughters into the many-sided women of the modern industrial state. The beginnings of this historic process were
necessarily slow and hesitating. Working as it did upon a body
of mores almost sanctified in the popular mind by their intimate connection with family life, all change had first to be
fitted carefully into the framework of familiar habit. Nevertheless, the American woman, hitherto ignorant of business

161

matters, insulated from the intellectual and political concerns of the day in a world of home cares, social entertainment, light reading and fancy work, would come to take a more and more active interest in public affairs. No dereliction of domestic duty would be tolerated, but women who could manage their homes and other activities too had increasing opportunities to do so.

Tokens of progress toward a wider life were first evident in England. There the industrial revolution had begun well before 1800; by 1825 there were clear signs of the pattern of life it would impose on women. No respecter of sex, it increasingly demanded their efforts both to fill its working force, and to alleviate the sore spots and maintain the moral and cultural tone of society. The United States would not face the Industrial Age until the next generation; still, England remaining their guide on social and intellectual questions, Americans drew their ideas from writings shaped in an industrial milieu, sometimes even reproducing English institutions for which they had relatively little need.

Somewhat paradoxically, women began their adjustment to this new order under the aegis of the religious revival, which in its social and political thinking was so often the bulwark of the status quo and the sworn foe of all things revolutionary. Enforcing with one hand a straitlaced and unyielding canon of conduct for woman's domestic relations, the revival with the other hand gave organized religion's unimpeachable sanction to certain activities outside the domestic realm.

Pricked by a rudimentary sense of social responsibility, the revival in effect enlisted women's aid in dealing with problems raised by the industrial revolution, in dosing the poor with charity as well as tracts, instructing the rising middle class in manners and morals, and providing them and the coming generation with harmless or improving reading matter. Thus women moved towards the professions of philanthropy, reform, and authorship. The education of girls also benefited from the new atmosphere of moral purpose. Little progress was made along institutional lines, but the subject was frequently discussed, and able arguments presented for a solid course of study, presumably still to be pursued by upper-class girls in the privacy of home or a select school.

Foremost among woman's new roles was that of lady bountiful, bringing succor to society's unfortunates. Women, of course, had always dispensed charity from their homes as occasion arose, sheltering the homeless, feeding beggars at the door, carrying comforts to the village poor and sick. Now, however, private almsgiving was beginning to give way to organized public relief, and the well-bred female went on her errands of mercy as directress or lady manager of a charitable society which might command funds of several thousand dollars.

It was an age peculiarly susceptible to benevolent impulses
and possessed of ample means to implement them. To the Enlightenment's legacy of humanitarian concern for the dignity
of man, the religious revival had added an insistence on
good works, while in the expanding cities of both old and new
worlds poverty and vice waited to be reclaimed.

England led the way with a host of organizations which
Americans faithfully copied, freely inventing others for every
conceivable need with the irrepressible instinct of a nation
of joiners.[1] The religious outlook of the age strongly tincture
all these benevolent endeavors. In the eyes of the pious, the
moral and spiritual defects of the needy loomed larger than
their physical wants, easily ascribed to God's Providence or
man's improvidence; the public accordingly took rather more
lively interest in restoring the soul than the body. Sunday
Schools, tract, Bible, and missionary societies spread spiritual sustenance, while other beneficent associations strove to
ease the terrestrial lot and raise the moral standards of the
indigent, the insane, the handicapped, the enslaved, and the
imprisoned.

Simply assuming from long habit that where the church
moved they would follow, women quickly learned the new mode
of operations and set to work, little realizing the significance

---

1 The phrase is Arthur M. Schlesinger's, from Paths to the
  Present (New York, 1949), 23-50.

of these small experiments in group action. In nearly every community a Female Society for the Promotion of Christian Knowledge had tracts printed and gave them away, a Female Mite Society supported foreign missions by prayer and contributions of a cent a week, a Female Education Society raised money and collected clothing for poor but deserving youths studying for the ministry. Women gave furnishings for the Hartford Retreat for the Insane, and formed their own associations "for the Support and Instruction of the Indigent Deaf and Dumb."[2]

In the field of poor relief, propriety dictated that ladies confine their efforts to their own sex. Destitute women and children, moreover, had a clear title to charity, being obviously unable to fend for themselves. They were not sturdy loafers seeking to avoid an honest day's toil. By 1805 every large city and town had societies supplying soup, sewing, and firewood to "Respectable and Aged Indigent Females," "Poor Widows with Small Children," and "Single Women," under the direction of ladies from the leading families, and sometimes even a school to teach "the female children of poor people, reading,

---

2 The Rev. Daniel Dana, A Sermon Delivered before the Gloucester Female Society for Promoting Christian Knowledge (Newburyport, 1815); Dixon Ryan Fox, "The Protestant Counter-Reformation in America," New York History, XVI (January, 1935), 26; Charles R. Keller, The Second Great Awakening in Connecticut (New Haven, 1942), 124-126, 234; United States Literary Gazette, IV (July, 1826), 317.

writing, and plain sewing."[3]

The plight of orphan girls particularly stirred the sensibilities of an age ever-conscious of the dangers besetting the unprotected female. To rescue these waifs "from want, from sufferings, from temptation, and from vice; and by proper instruction . . . , to prepare them for . . . respectable situations in life, and by the aid of divine grace, for happiness in the world to come," energetic ladies in dozens of towns set up female asylums. There, under the supervision of a "governess," a score of little girls from three to ten would be taught cleanliness, good manners, domestic skills, and a little reading and writing, and at ten, placed as servants in "virtuous families."[4]

The public watched these efforts with benign interest. Magazines frequently printed statistics of funds received and aid rendered by the societies, and reports of the public meetings which yearly marked the anniversary of their founding. For these affairs the ladies organized an elaborate program including the singing of hymns and odes on charity (written especially for the occasion), prayers, and a sermon by a local

---

3 John B. McMaster, A History of the People of the United States (New York, 1913), IV, 535; "Free School," Port Folio, III (July 30, 1803), 243. Mrs. Susanna Rowson was president of the Boston Fatherless and Widows Society, Mrs. Martha Laurens Ramsay of the Charleston society of the same name.

4 The Rev. John Lathrop, A Discourse Delivered before the Members of the Boston Female Asylum (Boston, 1804), II, 16.

minister extolling their efforts as "a work in which angels would rejoice to be employed."[5]

A few die-hards had at first frowned upon these under-takings, some prophetically raising doubts as to where it all would end, some claiming that almshouses already met the need. Others felt "that distributions to the poor, and especially that plans and establishments for their permanent relief and support, belong exclusively to men." At the least it seemed "improper that women in the conjugal relation should employ themselves in such designs." But such objections quickly subsided before a barrage of Biblical references -- to the virtuous woman of Proverbs, stretching out her hand to the poor; to Mary and Martha and the women who labored with Paul in the gospel. "How plain, how inevitable," exclaimed the Rev. Daniel Dana of Newburyport, "is the inference that virtuous and amiable women are acting in character, and moving in their proper sphere, while actively patronizing the indigent. . . ."[6]

Other proofs that charity "is peculiarly incumbent on

---

5 Ibid., 12. The Rev. William Bentley of Salem, who was frequently called upon for this duty, left descriptions of a number of such meetings. (The Diary of William Bentley, D.D. [Salem, 1905-1914]).

6 Rev. Thomas Gray, "Emerson's Discourse before the Female Asylum," Monthly Anthology, III (February, 1806), 102; Dana, A Discourse Delivered . . . before the Members of the Female Charitable Society of Newburyport (Newburyport, 1804), 19n., 14, 15.

the sex, as well as one of its brightest ornaments" were
quickly forthcoming. "The soft emotions of the female heart"
were evidently designed for the comfort of the afflicted.
They were peculiarly qualified to aid other women -- "To
whom shall the friendless orphan girl repair, but to one who
knows the feelings, the distresses, the dangers of the sex.
. . .?" They had more time and opportunity than men for
benevolence, while their unselfish exertions would set their
menfolk an example of superior moral excellence. The propriety of charitable work once granted, the advantages of
organization and system over individual effort would surely
be obvious.[7]

Most people, however, hardly waited to be convinced, but,
like Charles Brockden Brown, hailed "the establishment of
female charitable associations . . . [as] an oera in our social and moral history. . . . We can only say," he wrote in
his American Review and Literary Journal, "that while some
affect to view these societies as ephemeral trifles, we can
never cease to regard . . . them, with the highest respect,
and to anticipate an augmentation of human happiness by their
means."[8] The religious press was no less enthusiastic, the

---

7 Ibid., 16, 17, 18, 19; Rev. William Bentley, A Discourse
Delivered . . . at the Annual Meeting of the Salem Female
Charitable Society (Salem, 1807).

8 American Review and Literary Journal, II (July-August-
September, 1802), 347.

Connecticut Religious Intelligencer, leading organ of the revival in that state, proclaiming it "a peculiar honor to our age, that, as a sex, women have discovered, and extensively entered . . . the great work of doing good."[9]

The hard times that followed the War of 1812 subdued this bounding optimism. In the seaboard cities poverty and suffering appeared to an extent never imagined before. New Yorkers in 1817 estimated that one out of every seven citizens was living on charity. In this crisis, the causes and cure of pauperism became a topic of absorbing interest. Committees appointed to study the problem laid the blame chiefly on drink and indiscriminate charity, and for the latter, it was generally felt, the ladies must bear part responsibility. The naive generosity of Philadelphia's numerous benevolent associations, for instance, was reported to have made that city a veritable mecca for beggars.[10]

The ladies, too, had apparently made nuisances of themselves in their zeal for collecting funds.[11] A satirical friend of James Kirke Paulding complained "that there was

---

9 Religious Intelligencer, I (1816), 210, quoted in Keller, Second Great Awakening, 234.

10 American Monthly Magazine and Critical Review, II (February, 1818), 252; "Society for Industry," American Monthly Magazine and Critical Review, II (April, 1818), 470; McMaster, History of the People of the United States, IV, 524ff.

11 "Progress of Useful Institutions," Port Folio, ser. 5, XVII (April, 1824), 338.

hardly a day in which he was not called on for charitable
contributions, either to relieve somebody, or to convert
the Hindoos, or Hottentots." Paulding himself had conceived
"a confirmed antipathy to charitable institutions, and especially to those venerable ladies, and thrice venerable spinsters, who go about our cities like roaring lions, doing good."[12]
Sentimental apostrophes to "Mercy's gentle sprite" sent "to
lull the throes of keen distress"[13] now died away as new
writers resuscitated the sphere issue to launch a back-to-
the-home drive. "Women," Paulding continued sourly,

> have always duties to perform at home, if
> they choose to attend to them; and . . .
> ought to leave public charities to men, who
> are acquainted with the innumerable masks
> under which idleness and vice levy contri-
> butions on society.
> In truth, I have no opinion of this
> gadding benevolence in woman. She is a
> gentle household divinity. . . . She
> reigns over the happiness of man, not by
> leading armies, . . . or vindicating the
> right of women to be as vicious and immodest
> as men, -- or by enlisting in a blue-stock-
> ing club, -- or by diving into stews and
> beer-cellars, to acquire views of vice,
> which the most virtuous woman cannot witness
> without soiling the purity of her heart. No,
> . . . it is not by such means that women be-
> come the source and sacred fountain of our
> happiness. It is by the exercise of those
> gentle female virtues that pass unheeded by
> the world; . . . but which meet their reward

---

12 American Monthly Magazine and Critical Review, II (January,
   1818), 234.

13 Joseph Story, "Ode," sung before the Salem Female Charitable
   Society, July 11, 1804, Monthly Anthology, I (July, 1804),
   426.

in the gratitude of children, the smiling
happiness of the domestic circle, the lofty
and affectionate estimation of the husband,
and the blessing of Heaven.[14]

Out of their depth in the complicated problems of urban

relief, the female charitable societies gradually disbanded.

The benevolent spirit, however, was not so easily squelched.

Women continued to bustle about in the pious work of spread-

ing the Gospel at home and abroad, serving a valuable appren-

ticeship for the greater humanitarian endeavors of the next

generation.

The interest in education aroused by Rousseau and other

apostles of the Enlightenment continued unflaggingly into

the new century. The concepts of democracy and human per-

fectibility which had furnished its original inspiration had

indeed fallen from favor, but to take their place the revival

supplied an equally compelling concern for the forming of

moral character and religious feelings in youth. As Mrs.

Jane West wrote, "A rage for education is one of the marked

features of the great world; and it has been much increased by

the labour of writers who belong to the new school of morals."[15]

No aspect of the question was so tirelessly canvassed as

---

14 Paulding, Letters from the South (New York, 1817), II, 56-
57.

15 Letters to a Young Lady, 102.

female education. With the times beginning to demand more of
woman, her training had assumed new significance. The novel-
ty of the idea was intriguing. Furthermore, women's education was a subject upon which every man and his neighbor felt
qualified to speak. Homilies, witticisms, and old saws about
the female mind and how to form it became a staple of magazines, novels, plays, and polite conversation, while the
pious and learned discoursed at length in weightier essays
and books. Women writers, who had personal reasons to be
concerned with it, took the field for their special province,
nearly every authoress of note concocting an elaborate apologia.

All this commotion produced surprisingly little that was
new in ideas for either theory or practice. The discussion
invariably followed a set formula, centering on the elementary
question of whether women should be educated or not. The relative mental capacity of the sexes was the most popular issue,
perenially fascinating since it was impossible really to
prove it either way. The arguments against female education,
most of them already hoary with age, were regularly rehearsed
and rebutted. There usually followed some effort to define
the intellectual level on which young women should pursue
their studies, fixing it at some point between the rigors of
classical or scientific learning reserved for men and the
enervating culture of ornamental accomplishments.

No more daring in pedagogical practice, this generation

was content to contemplate the quiet progress of the academy movement initiated a decade before. Ample facilities for educating upper-class young women now existed, quite satisfying this aristocratic age's sense of its own needs.[16] The well-bred girl, destined for a life of domestic seclusion or conspicuous leisure, would use intellectual resources only for personal solace or to enhance the pleasures of select company. She could be guided in every accomplishment or serious study by relatives or tutors in the sheltered privacy of her home. In the select boarding school or academy she received much the same sort of personalized instruction for as long as her parents cared to keep her there. The graded school course and standardized curriculum that would become necessary when women had to be educated in large numbers and for responsible positions in the world outside the home waited for the vision of the educational reformers of the next generation.

Despite such limitations, however, the discussion was far from futile. The shrewd onlooker might have observed that the progressive side now tended to get the better of the old

16 "In our principal cities and great towns," Joseph Dennie observed complacently in 1819, "systems of education . . . are admirably calculated to form accomplished daughters, and good wives . . . .; and in all the useful and in many of the ornamental branches of instruction, the ladies, particularly of the upper and more opulent classes, need not shrink from any comparison." "On Female Education," Port Folio, ser. 3, I (May, 1809), 383-384.

argument, thanks partly to the atmosphere of serious moral
purpose introduced by the religious revival. "The claim
which society has upon you is of the most awful nature," the
Rev. James Gray informed the young ladies finishing at the
Philadelphia academy in 1810. For them "to promote the
polish of social manners, and contribute largely to the amount
of social pleasures" was no longer enough. In addition it
was woman's high prerogative "to pour balm into the wounds
of bleeding humanity, to still the storm of social passions,
to impart popularity and confidence to virtue" by her own
bright example.[17] For this new function women clearly needed
stronger minds and firmer character than for their old role
of mere passive goodness. Dr. Gregory's famous dictum, for
instance ("if you happen to have any learning, keep it a
profound secret, especially from the men, who generally look
with a jealous and malignant eye on a woman of . . . cultivated understanding"), was now generally deprecated. "Let
talents be graced with simplicity, with good humour, and with
feminine modesty," the Rev. Thomas Gisborne assured the sex,
"and there is scarcely an husband's heart which they will not
warm with delight."[18]

---

17 "Female Education," Port Folio, ser. 3, IV (July, 1810),
    101.

18 John Gregory, A Father's Legacy to his Daughters (New
    York, 1775), 15; Gisborne, An Enquiry into the Duties of
    the Female Sex (London, 1798), 196.

The volume and insistence of the discussion, moreover, brought the point home to greater numbers of people than ever before, softening prejudice against the "literary lady" and accustoming the public to the idea that women might be educated without damage to the home, the family, or masculine comfort. Thus was smoothed the way for the rapid educational advances of the years ahead.

No respectable debate on women's education could get underway until the vexed question of male versus female mentality was disposed of. One protagonist might try to evade the issue, by asserting the Creator had bestowed upon the sexes "an abundance of genius for the discharge of their respective duties"; another might blandly assume that it had all been settled long ago; a third casually dismiss it as much ado about nothing; a fourth protest impatiently that "the argument on the comparative strength of male and female capacities for literature and science, which was never edifying, useful, or liberal, is now by repetition become vapid and wearisome in the greatest degree."[19] But as long as the

---

19 "Female Education," Port Folio, ser. 3, IV (July, 1810), 93; Foster, The Boarding School, 135; James Milnor, "On Female Education," Port Folio, ser. 3, I (May, 1809), 387; "A Literary Lady," Literary Magazine and American Register, III (April, 1805), 255-256; Sydney Smith, "Female Education," Port Folio, ser. 3, IV (July, 1810), 101; "De l'Influence des Femmes," Analectic Magazine, I (February, 1813), 105.

general level of female attainments remained so low as to
cast a shadow of doubt, the public refused to abandon the
argument.

Nobody observing the women he met every day, their minds
running the gamut from vacancy to mediocrity, could, however,
argue with any conviction for present equality.[20] The dispute therefore turned largely on the potentialities of the
female intelligence, skeptics assuming that nature had cast
the feminine mind irrevocably in its present mold, optimists
claiming that better education would foster abilities rivaling
those of men.[21]

---

20 Cultivated men, for instance, were continually exasperated
   with female conversation which, confined to the two topics
   of fashion and domestic incident ("chit chat," one gentleman declared, "that might have disgraced the nursery"),
   made mixed parties extremely dull. Francis Hall, Travels
   in Canada, and the United States, in 1816 and 1817 (London,
   1819), 232; "On the Puerile Amusements and Insipid Manners
   of Young Women in General," Boston Weekly Magazine, II
   (May 19, 1804), 118. Travelers noted that American women
   could not compare either in intellectual culture or ornamental accomplishments with European ladies, evidently
   because they married before they had been in society long
   enough to acquire polish. Henry Bradshaw Fearon, A Narrative of a Journey . . . through . . . America (London,
   1818), 380; Hall, Travels, 231; Frances Wright, Views of
   Society and Manners in America (New York, 1821), 26; Adam
   Hodgson, Letters from North America (London, 1824), II, 27-
   28; Isaac Candler, A Summary View of America (London, 1824),
   71; Godfrey T. Vigne, Six Months in America (London, 1832),
   II, 243-244.

21 As their trump card, the optimists had always pointed to
   famous women of the past and present for proof of brain-
   power parity, regularly reviewing a parade of ladies from
   Semiramis, legendary founder of Babylon, Sappho, and
   Cleopatra to Queen Elizabeth, Catharine the Great, and
   Madame de Staël. Since most of these women, however,

Since they were reasoning from facts rather than faith, the skeptics on the whole got the better of the dispute. Enthusiasts for education like the Rev. John S. J. Gardiner, rector of Boston's Trinity Church and a shining light in the city's literary circles, might inveigh against the double standard for the training of the sexes. While boys, he pointed out, were gaining "a deep and broad foundation of intellectual vigour . . . in the study of the dead languages" (Mr. Gardiner spoke here with authority, for on the side he conducted a classical school for boys),

> Girls . . . , of the same age, are employed in the mere manual exercise of sprigging muslin, painting flowers, and fingering a musical instrument; employments comparatively frivolous, and little connected with intellectual improvement. If to these trifling attainments, they can dance gracefully and prattle French, they are deemed by their injudicious friends all-accomplished, and are the envy and admiration of their companions.[22]

Little wonder then that they were weak in judgment and reason.

---

were vulnerable to criticism on grounds of morality or femininity or both, they were quickly discredited by this upright generation. Early-nineteenth-century fashion was to dismiss the great queens as unfeminine freaks or the puppets of men councilors. Thus the Elizabeths and Catharines, too amazonian for the taste of a day which glorified modesty and self-effacement (the virtues of domestic retirement), were relegated to the background; in their stead Mary Queen of Scots, who for all her faults lived as a woman should by her emotions rather than her brain, became the historical heroine of the hour.

22 A Sermon, Delivered before the . . . Boston Female Asylum (Boston, 1809), 15. See also the piece "On Female Acquirements," Boston Weekly Magazine, I (May 21, 1803), 121.

But, the opposite camp would rejoin, how did it happen that
"there should be no instance of a Burns, or a . . . John
Bunyan . . . in petticoats? We find many such illiterate
geniuses among men, and very few geniuses, literate or illiterate, amongst women."[23] Evidently education alone could not
account for the difference.

Eliza Southgate, whose private thoughts at eighteen would
have astounded the friends and relatives who knew her as a
gay belle of Maine society, hit closer to the truth. "The
business and pursuits of men require deep thinking, judgment,
and moderation. . . . Women who have no such incentives to
action suffer all the strong energetic qualities of the mind
to sleep in obscurity. . . . In this dormant state they become enervated and impaired, and at last die for want of exercise."[24]

A few perspicacious social critics nearly realized that
it was the repressive standards of behavior, so rigidly enforced, which, tyrannizing over women's minds, most effectually
stifled independent thought and intellectual vigor. "Ladies
cannot consistently be charged with wanting education," remarked
one intelligent young Bostonian, "when it is considered out of

23 Richard Chatterton, "On the Difference between the Sexes,"
Port Folio, ser. 5, XVIII (July, 1824), 28, 29-30; "A Lit-
erary Lady," Literary Magazine and American Register, III
(May, 1805), 359.

24 A Girl's Life Eighty Years Ago, 59.

their sphere to give an opinion beyond the fashions of the day, or the amusements of the season. . . ."[25] Eliza Southgate's own experience was a case in point. Her young cousin Moses Porter, to whom, venturing for once to be serious, she confided her ideas on woman's mind and sphere, was scandalized at her bold presumption. Eliza, shocked and hurt, replied to his letter,

> I hardly know what to say to you,
> Cousin, you have attacked my system with
> a kind of fury that has entirely obscured
> your judgment. . . . You beg me to drop
> this crazy scheme and say no more about en-
> larging the mind, as it is disagreeable, and
> you are too much prejudiced ever to listen
> with composure to me when I write on the sub-
> ject. I quit it forever. . . . On what sub-
> jects shall I write you? I shall either
> fatigue and disgust you with female trifles,
> or shock you by stepping beyond the limits
> you have prescribed.[26]

Forcing a gay tone, Eliza finished her letter with a lively description of a ball she had attended in Portland. So far

---

25 Yet this same young man, while deploring the insipid conversation prevailing at mixed parties, hesitated to encourage the ladies to converse on a higher level for fear
that they might become too "familiar" with the opposite
sex, losing "that natural dignity of character, which is
the best support of female worth." [Robert Hallowell Gar-
diner], "Remarker, No. 26," Monthly Anthology, IV (October, 1807), 534-535. See also [Arthur Maynard Walter],
"Blue Stocking Club," Monthly Anthology, III (November,
1806), 579-580; "The Ladies Vindicated," Boston Weekly
Magazine, I (December 11, 1802), 26; "On the Puerile
Amusements and Insipid Manners of Young Women in General,"
Boston Weekly Magazine, II (May 19, 1804), 117-118; "Female Conversation," Boston Weekly Magazine, III (August
24, 1805), 174; Gisborne, Enquiry into the Duties of the
Female Sex, 73.

26 A Girl's Life, 104-105.

as we know from her surviving letters, she never attempted
again to think out of her sphere.

The conservative Moses Porters, having won their point,
proceeded to erect a rationale for the inferiority of the
female intellect. A favorite method was to draw elaborate
analogies between the physical and mental endowments of the
sexes, and their proper spheres.

> The mind of man, like his body [rea-
> soned one English writer], is cast in a
> grander mould than that of his more deli-
> cate companion, and is composed of a firmer
> material. . . . It is to him that the
> difficult and important duties of life are
> committed, -- women are physically incapable
> of exerting them. Man, therefore, must be
> endowed with the faculties which . . . these
> offices require, that is, . . . superior
> vigour, strength, boldness, and sagacity of
> mind.

Woman having less need for these qualities in discharging "the
inactive, peaceful, and domestic offices, adapted to the
softer and more delicate sex," God had imparted them to her
"with a more sparing hand."[27]   "A woman's form," in fine, was
"the metaphor of her mind; weak, elegant, beautiful, but not
sublime."[28]

---

27. Chatterton, "On the Difference between the Sexes," Port
    Folio, ser. 5, XVIII (July, 1824), 28; Gisborne, Duties
    of the Female Sex, 15; Hannah More, Strictures on the
    Modern System of Female Education (The Works of Hannah
    More [New York, 1835], VI), 89; [Sarah Ewing Hall], "On
    Female Education," Port Folio, ser. 5, XX (November,
    1825), 414-415.

28 Chatterton, "On the Difference between the Sexes," 31.
    Also Boston Weekly Magazine, III (November 10, 1804), 10;
    "Dialogue on Female Education," Portico, II (September,
    1816), 211.

The next step was to define the sexual differences of the mind more carefully. Hannah More, apostle of the Evangelical revival in England and leading authority on the training of girls, worked out the classic statement in her "Comparative View of the Sexes," a chapter from her best-selling Strictures on the Modern System of Female Education which was widely reprinted and plagiarized for years afterward.

The sex in general, Hannah More declared, though possessing quicker and more acute powers of observation and discernment than men, tended to be encumbered by details and hence inferior in broad understanding. While women often equaled men in particular ways such as the qualities of memory and imagination, "they seem not to possess, in equal measure, the faculty of comparing, combining, analyzing, and separating . . . ideas; that deep and patient thinking which goes to the bottom of a subject; nor that power of arrangement which knows how to link a thousand connected ideas in one dependent train. . . ." Their warm feeling, natural taste, and abundant fancy clearly marked the field of polite letters for their province, but they lacked the steadiness requisite for profound scholarship. Hannah admitted, however, that no final estimate of women's mental capacity could be made until they received a more reasonable education. "When we see (and who will deny that we see it frequently?) so many women nobly rising from under all the pressure of a disadvantageous

education and a defective system of society, and exhibiting
the most unambiguous marks of a vigorous understanding, a
correct judgment, and a sterling piety,"[29] it was impossible
not to believe that under more favorable conditions woman's
intellect would grow in stature.

The best-reputed writers in the field joined Hannah More
in this sensible and fair-minded stand. The happiness of the
sexes was so closely connected, wrote Maria Edgeworth, popular
British novelist and practical educator, "that it seems to me
absurd . . . to set [them] . . . at variance by vain contention
for superiority. It ought [rather] . . . to be our object . . .
to determine what is most for our general advantage."[30] One
could be certain that nature had gifted woman with the intellect sufficient for her needs; the important thing, as the
Scotswoman Elizabeth Hamilton put it in her treatise on educational psychology, was to see that she used it.[31]

---

29 Strictures on Female Education, 146-148. Similar ideas
were voiced by: [John Adams], Sketches of the History,
Genius, Disposition, Accomplishments, Employments, Customs,
Virtues, and Vices, of the Fair Sex, in all Parts of the
World (Philadelphia, 1796), 119ff; Gisborne, Duties of the
Female Sex, 14-16; Elizabeth Hamilton, Letters on the Ele-
mentary Principles of Education (Boston, 1825), I, 12;
[John S. J. Gardiner], "To Cornelia," Monthly Anthology,
I (August, 1804), 453; "Woman," New York Mirror, I (August
16, 1823), 19.

30 Letters for Literary Ladies (Works of Maria Edgeworth
[Boston, 1824], II), 30.

31 Hamilton, Letters on the Elementary Principles of Education
(Boston, 1825), I, 12, II, 19, 23; Sydney Smith, "Female
Education," 102; "The Female Sex," Literary Magazine and
American Register, III (April, 1805), 255-256.

Despite such modest claims and aspirations, the advocates of better training for girls had uphill work, contending at every turn with "the mean notions entertained by men of narrow minds,"[32] who pictured as the product of a sound education a generation of female pedants, literary slatterns, and ambitious Amazons bent on a struggle for power with men.

The female pedant, a stock character in eighteenth-century literature, seems to have been in real life most often a tiresome young woman who from addiction to reading had come to fancy herself an intellectual giant. "Of all women," the Rev. Mr. Gardiner remarked in one of his charity sermons, "I have generally observed that your great readers are the most insufferable, who repeat whole passages of prose and poetry, in season and out season, and who, instead of obtaining the admiration they aim at, disgust all who hear them with their vanity and impertinence."[33] Such absurd pretensions to erudition, Hannah More declared bluntly, derived not from too much learning but from too little sense. The true remedy was more education, not less. "Diffuse knowledge generally among women," advised Sydney Smith, "and you will

32 Hamilton, Letters on Education, II, 210.

33 John S. J. Gardiner, A Sermon, Delivered before the . . . Boston Female Asylum, 16; "Remarker, No. 36," Monthly Anthology, V (September, 1808), 489; "De l'Influence des Femmes," Analectic Magazine, I (February, 1813), 110-112; Hannah More, Strictures, 137, 91.

at once cure the conceit which knowledge occasions while it
is rare."[34]

An even more persistent objection to women's pursuit of
learning was that study would spoil them for domestic tasks.
On the contrary, progressives asserted, a woman of cultivated
mind would realize more fully the importance of these duties,
and discharge them with greater skill and efficiency. Religious writers found this allegation particularly annoying,
pointing out that fashionable dissipation was far more likely
to distract females from the duties of their sphere than a
passion for books. ("The time nightly expended in late female

---

[34] Ibid., 196-197; Smith, "Female Education," 104. Nothing
better has ever been written on the subject than this
latter essay (first published in the Edinburgh Review of
January, 1810) by Sydney Smith, Anglican cleric, critic,
and wit who later became a bête noir to Americans for his
scathing exposure (1820) of their cultural limitations
("In the four quarters of the globe, who reads an American
book?"). For similar remarks on the pedantry question, see
"Dialogue on Female Education," Portico, II (September,
1816), 211; Gisborne, Duties of the Female Sex, 195; Maria
Edgeworth, Letters for Literary Ladies, 20; Elizabeth
Hamilton, Letters on Education, II, 224-225. Most studious
girls, of course, were brought up to be so impeccably
feminine in other respects as wholly to disarm criticism.
Elizabeth Hamilton's aunt, for instance, on discovering
that her niece was reading "many books by stealth. . . . ,
expressed neither praise nor blame, but quietly advised
her to avoid any display of superior knowledge, by which
she might be subjected to the imputation of pedantry."
Looking back on her girlhood in after years, Miss Hamilton
remembered "hiding Kaims's [sic] Elements of Criticism,
under the cover of an easy chair, whenever I heard the
approach of a footstep, well knowing that ridicule to
which I should have been exposed, had I been detected
in the act of looking into such a book." Elizabeth Ogilvy
Benger, Memoirs of the Late Mrs. Elizabeth Hamilton (London, 1818), I, 50, II, 31.

vigils is expended by the light of far other lamps than those
which are fed by the student's oil. . . . And for one literary slattern, who now manifests her indifference to her
husband by the neglect of her person, there are scores of
elegant spendthrifts who ruin theirs by excess of decoration."[35]) Besides, said Sydney Smith, nature presumably had
some voice in the matter; could anyone picture a mother deserting her infant for a quadratic equation?[36]

The conduct of certain female intellectuals in the past
(Mary Wollstonecraft's history was always in the back of
everyone's mind) had encouraged a belief that women would im-
bibe "a daring spirit," proceed to flout custom and opinion --
even transgress the moral code -- and engage in a furious
rivalry with the opposite sex. In stubborn Moses Porter's
words, "the enlargement of the mind will inevitably produce
superciliousness and a desire of ascendancy." Careful early
training, patiently reasoned the Edgeworths and Hamiltons,
would obviate this danger. Further (Sydney Smith again had

35 More,Strictures, 196, 137-139; also Ann Taylor, Reciprocal
Duties of Parents and Children (Boston, 1825), 74-79.

36 "Female Education," 105. Also Maria Edgeworth, Letters
for Literary Ladies, 16, 23; Elizabeth Hamilton, Letters
on Education, II, 152, 221; Gisborne, Duties of the Female
Sex, 198; "Female Learning," Literary Magazine and American
Register, I (January, 1804), 245; "A Literary Wife," Literary Magazine and American Register, III (March, 1805),
195; "Mrs. E. Montagu's Letters," Analectic Magazine, III
(March, 1814), 217-218; "Dialogue on Female Education,"
Portico, II (September, 1816), 214.

the last word), the natural desire of the sexes to please each other "would guarantee the preservation of "all that delicacy and reserve which are of such inestimable value to women."

> It would appear [he continued sarcastically], from the tenor of such objections, that ignorance had been the great civilizer of the world. Women are delicate and refined, only because they are ignorant; -- they manage their household, only because they are ignorant; -- they attend to their children, only because they know no better. Now, we must really confess, we have all our lives been so ignorant as not to know the value of ignorance. We have always attributed the modesty and the refined manner of women, to their being well taught in moral and religious duty, -- to the hazardous situation in which they are placed, -- to that perpetual vigilance which it is their duty to exercise over thought, word, and action. . . .37

The proponents of women's education, having done their logical best to rout the opposition, offered some positive arguments of their own. A cultivated mind would provide resources for old age and solace in times of trouble. It would enable the once isolated and forlorn old maid to become useful and self-respecting. Maria Edgeworth, who lived to an alert and busy old age in single blessedness, secure in the affectionate regard of her large family circle and the literary

---

37 Edgeworth, Letters for Literary Ladies, 10-12, 13, 23-24, 26, 30-32; A Girl's Life Eighty Years Ago, 104; Hamilton, Letters on Education, I, 152, II, 219ff; Smith, "Female Education," 108; Literary Magazine and American Register, VIII (July, 1807), 4; "Dialogue on Female Education," 215; [Theophilus Parsons], "Life and Writings of Madame de Stael," North American Review, XI (July, 1820), 128-129.

public, knew from experience that "unmarried women, who have stored their minds with knowledge, who have various tastes and literary occupations, who can amuse and be amused in the conversation of well informed people, are in no danger of becoming burthensome to their friends or to society. . . ."[38] Cultivated women would elevate the tone of their homes and of social life. "Manners would be improved; . . . morals might receive additional strength, and literature . . . be adorned with new fascinations."[39]

Most important of all was the influence which an educated mother might exert upon her children. To idealists the prospect of indoctrinating the future mothers of the race opened up a practically limitless vista of human improvement. So far, however, this vision had been manifested to only a few. It had no relevance for the upper-class homes of the eighteenth century, where mothers seldom assumed the physical care or

38 Letters for Literary Ladies, 19; Taylor, Reciprocal Duties, 79; West, Letters to a Young Lady, 375; Smith, "Female Education," 109, 118; "Dialogue on Female Education," 214.

39 [A. M. Walter], "Blue Stocking Club," Monthly Anthology, II (November, 1806), 580; Edgeworth, Letters for Literary Ladies, 35-36, Practical Education (New York, 1801), II, 142-143; [Susanna Rowson], "Influence of the Female Character on Society in General," Boston Weekly Magazine, I (October 30, 1802), 2-3; [Susanna Rowson], "Female Seminary," Boston Weekly Magazine, II (October 29, 1803), 2-3; "Influence of Women," New York Mirror, V (January, 1828), 211; Ladies Museum (Providence), July 16, 1825, quoted in Stearns, "Early New England Magazines for Ladies," New England Quarterly, II (July, 1829), 442.

guidance of their children, entrusting them to nurses and governesses until they should be old enough for boarding school. Educational enthusiasts, however, gradually coming to realize the importance of early childhood training, were challenging this long-established custom. The Edgeworth family's system, for instance, was built upon Mr. Edgeworth's belief in household or "private" education, and disapproval of "public" schools.[40] He, his successive wives, and his eldest daughter Maria themselves educated the seventeen younger children on the family's Irish estate, shielding them with elaborate care from the influence of servants. As the new century opened, this practice was spreading. "Ladies have become ambitious to superintend the education of their children," Maria Edgeworth testified, "and hence they have been induced to instruct themselves, that they may be able to direct and inform their pupils."[41]

This subject lay especially close to the heart of Elizabeth Hamilton, a worthy spinster much esteemed by contemporaries for her works on education,[42] since wholly forgotten. (As was

---

40 He criticized the latter (which had reached their nadir in this period) for the rigidly classical course of study and their inability to furnish individual attention or moral guidance.

41 Letters for Literary Ladies, 22.

42 See, for example, Port Folio, I (September 26, 1801), 312; Mrs. Anne Grant to Mrs. _____ Smith, May 13, 1913, Memoir and Correspondence to Mrs. Grant of Laggan, J. P. Grant, ed. (London, 1845), II, 16; "Miss Hamilton's Popular

customary in England among single women of literary note,
she adopted the title of "Mrs." in middle life.) An object
of respectful wonder in her lifetime because she took for
her province the abstruse masculine study of philosophy,
Mrs. Hamilton made her reputation by popularizing the re-
searches of Locke, David Hartley, and the Scottish common-
sense philosophers in the psychology of learning, applying
their theories on the human mind to the training of youth.

> She has shown, for instance [wrote Miss
> Edgeworth], how the doctrine of the asso-
> ciation of ideas may be applied in early
> education to the formation of habits of
> temper, and of the principles of taste
> and of morals: she has considered how all
> that metaphysicians know of sensation and
> abstraction can be applied to the cultiva-
> tion of the attention, the judgment, and
> the imagination of children.[43]

Since the exacting work of directing this "development
of the infant faculties" clearly devolved upon the mother,
Elizabeth Hamilton urgently wished to awaken women to the importance of this duty and for them to be equipped to discharge
it. In no way, she felt, could she "plead the cause of my
sex more effectually, than by explaining the influence of

Essays," Analectic Magazine, V (February, 1815), 122;
American Monthly Magazine and Critical Review, I (June,
1817), 154-155.

43 Benger, Memoirs of the Late Mrs. Elizabeth Hamilton, I,
208-209, 133; Lord Woodhouselee, Memoirs of . . . the
Honourable Henry Home of Kames (Edinburgh, 1814), II,
282n; Hamilton, Letters Addressed to the Daughter of a
Nobleman, on the Formation of Religious and Moral Principle (Salem, 1821), vii-viii, xii-xiii.

early education; and thus rendering it evident to every un-
prejudiced mind, that if women were so educated as to qualify them for the proper performance of this momentous duty;
it would do more towards the progressive improvement of the
species, than all the discoveries of science, and the re-
searches of philosophy." She had no intention, she insisted,
of involving females "in the nice subtleties of logic or metaphysics." She only wished them to learn to reflect and observe, to reason, judge, and generalize like rational creatures. "To be an humble instrument in rousing my sex from
the lethargy of quiescent indolence, to the exertion of those
faculties which the bounty of a kind Providence has conferred
. . . is a species of glory to which . . . [she confessed], I
am not indifferent."[44]

The faintly feminist tone of these remarks was no accident. For all her correct principles and faultless deportment (she moved in the best Edinburgh society, taking an active part in women's charities[45]), Mrs. Hamilton was more
independent in her thinking than any woman since Mary Wollstonecraft. Indeed, she owed some of her opinions to the

[44] Letters on Education, II, 10, I, 12-13, II, 9, 213, I,
21-22, II, 23.

[45] Benger, Memoirs of Mrs. Hamilton, I, 177-179, 211-212;
Mrs. Anne Grant to Mrs. ___ Hook, October 1, 1816, Memoir
of Mrs. Grant of Laggan, II, 129-130; Maria Edgeworth to
Mrs. Margaret Ruxton, August 9, 1813, The Life and Letters
of Maria Edgeworth, Augustus J. C. Hare, ed. (Boston,
1895), I, 231.

<u>Vindication of the Rights of Woman</u>, expressing distaste for the prudential morality enforced upon women,[46] condemning the double standard of virtues,[47] and branding the men who opposed the cultivation of the female mind while encouraging over-sensibility as "voluptuaries." ("A dear creature crying for she does not know why, or palpitating with terror at she does not know what, excites . . . associations . . . that produce emotions, which, though very foreign to those of esteem, are nearly allied to passion."[48])

These flaws in orthodoxy, however, detracted in no wise from Elizabeth Hamilton's influence upon the reading public of her day. A royal pension supported her declining years in "acknowledgment that her literary talents had been meritorious-ly exerted in the cause of religion and virtue." At her death Maria Edgeworth could write that she had "opened a new field

---

46 Under present conditions, she wrote, "girls learn to place the virtues recommended to their practice on an improper basis; not founded on immutable truth, but on worldly no-tions of prudence and propriety. . . . Far am I from considering the preservation of female delicacy as a matter of slight importance; but it is in the purity of the heart, and not in deference to public opinion, that I would fix its basis." <u>Letters on Education</u>, I, 152-153.

47 "By the early distinction that is made between the sexes, the idea of a . . . separate code of morality is inevitably inspired." For instance, she continued, "modesty has been, with much truth and propriety, represented as the first ornament of the female mind; but it may be questioned, whether both sexes have not been injured by considering it as a <u>sexual</u> virtue." <u>Ibid.</u>, 153-155.

48 <u>Letters on Education</u>, II, 212.

of investigation to women . . . by exciting them to reflect upon their own minds, and to observe what passes in the minds of their children. . . ."[49] The oblivion which settled upon her works within a decade was in some part at least a tribute to their impact; by the second quarter of the century the mother's role as she understood it was beginning to be taken for granted, and her books seemed merely to be elaborating the obvious.

On the question of what the educational process itself should be a persistent confusion reigned. The one point of agreement was that it could not be entirely devoted, as boys' training was, to furnishing the mind. So long as most women remained in domestic seclusion, the virtues, graces, and mental attitudes developed over the century past for this way of life had still to be inculcated. To these requirements the religious revival added insistence on a thorough indoctrination in Christian principles.

In the apportionment of time to these several departments the pursuit of knowledge came off a poor third. The Rev. Thomas Gisborne pronounced "the dictates of sober judgment" to be "palpably abandoned" when "improving and ornamental acquisitions" were allowed to interfere with the teaching of

---

49 Benger, Memoirs of Mrs. Hamilton, I, 165, 210.

principles which would insure a girl's happiness both in this world and the next. His friend Hannah More devoted the major part of her Strictures on Female Education to careful directions for the spiritual and moral training of the young.[50] Even the Edgeworths -- correct Anglicans who, classing religion with politics as personal matters, stood apart from the revival[51] -- viewed the upbringing of females with the same intense concern over morals and manners.

All agreed that too much could not be said on the importance of forming "those early habits of reserve and modesty which constitute the female character."[52] It was particularly necessary that girls acquire a sweet temper and submissive spirit. They should be early accustomed to restraint, to bearing reproofs and enduring opposition without protest. "It is a lesson which the world will not fail to furnish them," remarked Hannah More, "and they will not practice it the worse for having learnt it the sooner." Besides her peace of mind, a woman's influence in domestic life also depended upon gentleness and good nature; reason and wit without them could avail her nothing.

---

50 Gisborne, Duties of the Female Sex, 26-27; More, Strictures, 36.

51 Their educational works contained no religious teaching, for which they were widely criticized.

52 Edgeworth, Letters for Literary Ladies, 24; More, Strictures, 68ff.

> A man, in a furious passion [Miss
> Edgeworth explained], is terrible to his
> enemies; but a woman in a passion, is dis-
> gusting to her friends; she loses the re-
> spect due to her sex, and she has not mas-
> culine strength and courage to enforce any
> other species of respect. These circum-
> stances should be considered by writers who
> advise that no difference should be made
> in the education of the two sexes. We
> cannot help thinking that their happiness
> is of more consequence than their specula-
> tive rights, and we wish to educate women
> so that they may be happy in the situations
> in which they are most likely to be placed.[53]

Girls must also be taught greater caution and prudence

than boys. The latter might learn by experience; females,

unable to "rectify the material mistakes in their conduct,"

could not afford this luxury. Miss Edgeworth warned that

parents should "even, in trifles, avoid every circumstance

which can tend to make girls venturesome." They should be

"discouraged from hazarding opinions in general conversation,"

-- even, counseled Hannah More, "led to distrust their own

judgment." "Timidity, a certain tardiness of decision, and

reluctance to act in public situations," Miss Edgeworth re-

sumed, were not considered defects in a woman, but rather a

"graceful, auspicious" token of feminine virtue.[54]

In this atmosphere of perpetual solicitude for the fe-

male character the idea of serious intellectual training was

first admitted to respectable status as a handmaid to piety

---

53 Ibid., 78-79; Edgeworths, Practical Education, II, 274, I, 147.

54 Ibid., II, 273-275; More, Strictures, 79.

and morals. Zealous religionists like Hannah More, for instance, justified serious study for the young lady because "it abstracts her from the world and its vanities; it fixes a wandering spirit, and fortifies a weak one; . . . it concentrates her attention, assists her in a habit of excluding trivial thoughts, and thus even helps to qualify her for religious pursuits."[55]

With study for its own sake hardly considered ladylike, the cultivation of the mind had further to compete with the training in the arts and graces which identified the woman of means and leisure. To resolve this conflict was apparently beyond the powers of this generation, who, while aware that the old order was passing, could not yet clearly sight the wave of the future. With no one philosophy in the ascendant, educational practices varied widely from school to school. At one extreme, a few of the New England academies added to the standard curriculum instruction in Latin, "higher branches of mathematics" (probably algebra and plane geometry), and "moral science" (philosophy, more particularly ethics). A number of travelers singled out New England girls for their unusually "solid acquirements."[56] At the opposite pole were

---

55 Ibid., 90.

56 Timothy Dwight, Travels in New-England and New-York (New Haven, 1821), IV, 475; [William Tudor], Letters on the Eastern States (New York, 1820), 186; Frances Wright, Views of Society and Manners in America (New York, 1821), 311; Isaac Candler, A Summary View of America (London, 1824), 72; Adam Hodgson, Letters from North America (London, 1824), II, 28.

the many schools, both in America and England, on the order
of Mrs. Goddard's establishment in Jane Austen's Emma, "where
a reasonable quantity of accomplishments were sold at a reasonable price, and where girls might be sent to be out of the
way, and scramble themselves into a little education, without any danger of coming back prodigies." Significantly
enough, the fictitious institutions which figured in two notable boarding-school stories of this period, Hannah Foster's
The Boarding School and Ann and Jane Taylor's Correspondence
between a Mother and Her Daughter at School, were of this
same type, chiefly devoted to instilling principle and applying polish in varying proportions.

In the middle of the road were seminaries like Mrs.
Rivardi's in Philadelphia, whose "plan of education" Joseph
Dennie, urbane editor of the Port Folio, advertised as "finely
calculated to nourish the best qualities of the female mind."
Mrs. Rivardi's prospectus offered

> Reading, Writing, Orthography, Grammar,
> . . . Epistolary Style, Arithmetic, Geog-
> raphy, System of the Universe with the use
> of Maps and Globes, Ancient and Modern
> History, with their application to Chron-
> ological Charts; . . . Drawing and Painting,
> Vocal and Instrumental Music (Harp or Piano-
> Forte) the French . . . Language; Embroidery
> of all kinds; Artificial Flowers, with every
> other fashionable Fancy-work, Plain Sewing,
> Marking.

Her school kept in continuous session twelve months of the
year, with some eighty girls in attendance for longer or

shorter periods, promoted individually according to their progress.[57]

Public opinion on the state of female education and what should be done about it displayed similar variations.  Many observers, contemplating the progress made since the start of the academy movement in the 1780's, were well satisfied with the status quo.  "Indeed," Joseph Dennie wrote in 1810, "an astonishing revolution of sentiment and practice with respect to the education of women has, of late, been accomplished in America."  He could recall "when a girl of the brightest talents had no other discipline than what the narrowest school could bestow.  To read and spell without much hesitation; to trace a character in penmanship, which if not absolutely cramp, was almost unintelligible, and to cipher, God knows how, through the first four rules of no ambitious arithmetic, constituted once the sum total of female education in America."[58] Similarly reflecting upon times past, the Rev. Dr. James Gray was lost in admiration as he addressed the pupils of the Philadelphia academy at the close of their public examination:

> When we behold before us a number of
> young ladies who have scarcely attained their

57 "Education," Port Folio, V (December 14, 1805), 389.  Also describing schools of this kind are the articles on "Education," Port Folio, n.s. I (February 8, 1806), 74; "Mrs. Rowson's Academy," Boston Weekly Magazine, I (October 30, 1802), 2; and [William Tudor's] "Silva, No. 47," Monthly Anthology, VI (January, 1809), 22-23.

58 "Female Education," Port Folio, ser. 3, IV (July, 1810), 85.

full stature, capable of reading their
native language, and of relishing the
beauties of its authors; possessed of the
enviable talent of recording their own
thoughts, and supporting a literary correspondence with propriety and elegance;
acquainted with the geography of this
globe . . .; not strangers to the general laws of this planetary system; qualified, if necessity should require, to
manage pecuniary transactions with mer-
cantile correctness; at the same time that
they . . . understand most of the leading
principles of the true religion, and have
already acquired many of its practical virtues; we cannot help exclaiming, What a
prodigy! In many parts of the world a
thousand women have not so much information as one of our girls![59]

Some of New England's clergymen, however, were less well

satisfied. The Rev. John S. J. Gardiner of Boston's Trinity

Church thought there was something to be said for former cus-

toms. Mr. Gardiner disclaimed any desire to return to the day

"when the mistress was little more than an upper servant in

her own house, and her ideas not raised above that condition."

But he questioned whether the "solid qualities" of those times

"had not been exchanged for mere tinsel to catch the eye";

whether substituting a knowledge of fashions for skill in

domestic economy had made women "more useful members of the

community than formerly." And Timothy Dwight, erstwhile

---

59 Ibid. Comments in this vein appeared in many of the magazines, for example, "Thoughts on Religion, as a Branch
of Female Education," Literary Magazine and American Register, II (June, 1804), 166; Boston Magazine, I (December
21, 1805), 35; "On Female Education," Port Folio, ser. 3,
I (May, 1809), 387; "Mrs. E. Montagu's Letters," Analectic
Magazine, III (March, 1814), 215ff.

president of Yale College, regarded Americans as "seriously defective" in female education. "Efforts of a higher nature than any which we make," he stated in 1822, "are due to their daughters, from all persons who are possessed of wealth."[60]

The most persistent criticism was directed at the ornamental accomplishments. Very fashionable parents allowed training in the arts of painting, music, and dancing to engross nearly all of a girl's schooldays. A young lady's skill at the piano and her ballroom graces served as a measure of social prestige and were generally supposed also to enhance her charms in the eyes of suitors. An easy target for the reform-minded, this custom particularly outraged the religious conscience and Hannah More, its most insistent voice. Her Strictures on the Modern System of Female Education was a fully mounted assault on the prevailing "frenzy of accomplishments."[61]

Hannah did not wish to be understood as wholly condemning these pursuits. "The customs which fashion has established, when they are not in opposition to what is right, when they are not hostile to virtue, should unquestionably be pursued in the education of ladies. . . . But the admiration bestowed, the sums expended, and the time lavished on arts, which add

---

60 Gardiner, "Female Education," Monthly Anthology, III (March, 1806), 130; Dwight, Travels, IV, 475.

61 More, Strictures, 38.

little to the intrinsic value of life, should have limitations."[62]

Her objections were based on both moral and practical
grounds.  The principal faults fixed in the feminine nature
she identified as vanity and selfishness.  Instead of chasten-
ing or uprooting these evils, however, the ornamental system
of female education actually fostered them, focusing a girl's
attention upon her person to the tragic neglect of her intellect, moral character, and spiritual welfare.  Nor did this
type of training prepare woman for her function as wife and
mother.  "When a man of sense comes to marry, . . . it is not
merely a creature who can paint, and play, and sing, and draw,
and dress, and dance" that he wanted; "it is a being who can
. . . reason, and reflect . . .; one who can assist him in
his affairs, lighten his cares, soothe his sorrows, purify his
joys, strengthen his principles, and educate his children."[63]

In the thousands of copies of the Strictures circulated
on both sides of the Atlantic and as echoed in scores of magazines, these sentiments reached a wide audience.[64]  They

---

62 Ibid., 46.

63 Ibid., 36, 52-53.

64 For example, see "Letter . . . on Mental Improvement,"
Boston Weekly Magazine, II (December 17, 1803), 29; "The
American Lounger," Port Folio, IV (March 10, 1804), 73;
"Settlement in Marriage," Literary Magazine and American
Register, III (June, 1805), 416-417; Gardiner, A Sermon,
Delivered before the . . . Boston Female Asylum (Boston,
1809), 16-17; "A Review of the Systems of elementary Ed-
ucation in the United States," Analectic Magazine, IX
(April, 1817), 290.

were reinforced by an able chapter in the Edgeworths' Practical Education, where Maria's common sense put all the conceivable arguments in favor of education by accomplishments
completely to rout.[65]

But even where schools and parents managed to resist the
rage for accomplishments, their methods, many felt, left much
to be desired. The usual pedagogy required the hasty cramming
of quantities of miscellaneous information, taxing the powers
of memory while leaving reason and judgment in a state of nature.[66] (Eliza Southgate, who had attended one of the best
schools of her day, Mrs. Susanna Rowson's academy near Boston, eagerly learning all that was offered her, was craving
food for thought a scant two years later. "I left school
with a head full of something, tumbled in without order or
connection," she wrote her young lawyer cousin. The "few
patchwork opinions" remaining were "now almost worn threadbare, and as I am about quilting a few more, I beg you will

---

65 With the plea that they enlivened the tedium of women's
   sedentary lives, Miss Edgeworth was tempted to be lenient.
   "Women are peculiarly restrained in their situation, and in
   their employments, by the customs of society: to diminish
   the number of these employments, therefore, would be cruel;
   they should rather be encouraged . . . to cultivate those
   tastes which can attach them to their home, and . . .
   preserve them from the miseries of dissipation." Unfortunately, however, experience proved that most girls let
   their artistic skills lapse as soon as they married, thus
   facing the long future with few resources either of hand
   or mind.

66 United States Review and Literary Gazette, II (July, 1827),
   267ff; Gardiner, "Female Education," Monthly Anthology,
   III (March, 1806), 130-131; Edgeworths, Practical Education, II, 143-144; More, Strictures, 86ff.

send me any spare ideas you may chance to have that will serve my turn."[67])

This unfruitful method was by no means confined to the education of girls. The strictly amateur status of female studies, however, tended to encourage the practice. Despite all Hannah More and others said of the moral value of serious study, the fact remained that with no professional use for learning, a woman had no need to delve very far into her studies nor to specialize. For her situation in life it was more practical to acquire that "general tincture of knowledge . . . which marks the cultivated mind," enabling her "to engage gracefully in general conversation"[68] in mixed company without rendering her an obnoxious femme savante.

In fact, a myriad of writers were constantly warning the sex against "any recondite study, or abstruse science," particularly such subjects as politics, metaphysics, mathematics, or the classical languages, the staples of men's education.[69]

---

67 A Girl's Life, 56-57.

68 Anna L. Barbauld, The Works of Anna Laetitia Barbauld (New York, 1826), I, 19, II, 242.

69 West, Letters to a Young Lady, 25, 310; Edgeworths, Practical Education, II, 143; "De l'Influence des Femmes," Analectic Magazine, I (February, 1813), 107; Merrimack Magazine and Ladies Literary Cabinet (December 21, 1805), quoted in Stearns, "Early New England Magazines for Ladies," 436-437; The American Lady's Preceptor (Baltimore and Philadelphia, 1811), 24-25; [Benjamin Welles], "Women," Monthly Anthology, IV (May, 1807), 253; [Nathaniel Appleton Haven, Jr.], "Memoirs of Mrs. Carter," Monthly Anthology, IX (September, 1810), 194-195; [Sarah Ewing Hall], "On Female

Instead, they were directed to the English classics; the Bible and works on morals ("that study in which alone both sexes have an equal interest"); the study of geography ("a vast body of interesting and amusing information") and history. The last was considered especially valuable as supplying the knowledge of human nature which women had no opportunity to acquire in the active walks of life, as well as "incontrovertible evidence of the justice of the ways of Providence."[70] From science likewise the young lady was expected rather to "take what belongs to sentiment and to utility" than to conduct experiments or make calculations; she should seek to understand "the great laws of the universe, the nature and properties of these objects which surround us" because such study would enhance her sense of gratitude to her Maker, teach her "not to despise common things" and give her an interest in everything around her.[71]

---

Education," Port Folio, ser. 5, XX (November, 1825), 413ff.; "On the Superiority of Women to Men, in the More Refined Feelings," Monthly Anthology, V (July, 1808), 372ff.

70 Anna Laetitia Barbauld, "On Female Studies," Works, II, 241; James Milnor, "On Female Education," Port Folio, ser. 3, I (May, 1809), 392; West, Letters to a Young Lady, 311; Foster, The Boarding School, 22ff.; [William Smith Shaw], "Picture of a Wife," Monthly Anthology, IV (July, 1807), 373; "On the Method of Reading for Female Improvement," Boston Weekly Magazine, III (December 15, 1804), 29.

71 Barbauld, "On Female Studies," 240-241; Edgeworth, Letters for Literary Ladies, 22-23; American Lady's Preceptor, 25; "Survey of the progress . . . of Natural Sciences in the United States," American Monthly Magazine and Critical Review, II (December, 1817), 87.

"In no subject is she required to be deep, -- of none ought she to be ignorant," declared Anna Laetitia Barbauld, and this dictum by "one of the most correct and elegant among the female writers of England,"[72] admired on both continents for her charming poetry and her moral readings for children, perfectly expressed the view of cultured people everywhere.

---

72 Barbauld, "On Female Studies," 242; "On Female Education," Port Folio, ser. 5, XVII (April, 1824), 340.

Chapter Five

THE RISE OF THE WOMAN AUTHOR

# Chapter Five
## THE RISE OF THE WOMAN AUTHOR

"The great number of females who at present . . . pursue
writing for a subsistence is a remarkable circumstance in the
picture of our own times," observed Charles Brockden Brown in
1805. His was but one of a chorus of voices proclaiming "the
age of female authors." "There have lived, within the past
twenty years," the London Quarterly Review declared in 1813,
"more women distinguished for their literary talents, . . .
whose works are likely to immortalize their names, than in the
twenty centuries . . . [since] the time of Sappho. . . ."[1]

Any literary dabbler could reel off the names of two
dozen or so of these immortals. England boasted the "most
brilliant constellation of female worthies,"[2] from stars of
the first magnitude like Hannah More and Maria Edgeworth to
lesser lights like Amelia Opie, who wrote melancholy verse,
Charlotte Smith, author of thirty-eight volumes of fiction, and

---

1 "Female Authorship," Literary Magazine and American Register,
IV (October, 1805), 254; [Nathaniel Appleton Haven, Jr.],
"Memoirs of Mrs. Carter," Monthly Anthology, IX (September,
1810), 194; "Mrs. E. Montagu's Letters," Quarterly Review,
X (October, 1813), 31. Washington Irving promptly reprinted
the Quarterly's remarks in the Philadelphia journal of which
he was then editor, the Analectic Magazine, III (March, 1814),
215.

2 "Memoirs of Miss Hannah More," Monthly Magazine and American
Review, III (December, 1800), 465.

many others since faded beyond recognition. But America, too, had its authoresses, a "brilliant addition to our national glory"[3]: versatile Susanna H. Rowson and a cluster of less inspired practitioners in the sentimental novel, the poetess Sarah Wentworth Morton, and even a historian or two.

The literary world, critics and reading public alike,was astonished but nonetheless highly gratified at the appearance of "these unaccustomed votaries of literature."[4] Hastily ascribing the phenomenon to the improvement in women's education, they hailed it as evidence of the rapid progress of society in general and of the sex in particular. As the Quarterly Review complacently pointed out, "A few great men may rise up in a comparatively rude and dark age, diffuse a sudden light, and give a new impulse to the world; but a distinguished female writer is the effect of civilization carried to a very high point -- of consideration already paid to her sex, and of knowledge widely spread."[5]

Women, to be sure, had been authors in the past but with few exceptions strictly in amateur standing. The seventeenth century had produced more than one lady of means and leisure, made articulate by wide reading, who, isolated in an English

3 Henry Sherburne, The Oriental Philanthropist, or True Republican (Portsmouth, N. H., 1800), 5.

4 [Brown], "Female Authorship," 254.

5 "Mrs. E. Montagu's Letters," Analectic Magazine, III (March, 1814), 217.

country house or even in a New England village, composed verses for her own pleasure. Popular opinion, however, frowned
upon serious literary effort on a woman's part. Feeling a
little guilty to be writing at all, therefore, these ladies
shrank from the public eye, and their works appeared in print
only posthumously, by piracy, or on the initiative of male
relatives.

Massachusetts' Anne Bradstreet was a case in point. As
a young wife living in the frontier town of Ipswich, Mrs.
Bradstreet turned to poetry for solace during her husband's
absences from home on colony business. She had no thought of
publication until an admiring brother-in-law took a sheaf of
her manuscript to London without her knowledge in 1650 and had
a small volume printed. For this Anne was hardly to blame,
yet more than one "carping tongue" seems to have taken her to
task for her presumption.[6]

---

6 In a spirited stanza (published only after her death) Anne
  protested this hostility.

> I am obnoxious to each carping tongue,
> Who says my hand a needle better fits.
> A Poets pen all scorn I should thus wrong,
> For such despite they cast on Female wits;
> If what I do prove well, it won't advance,
> They'l say it's stoln, or else it was by chance.

The Works of Anne Bradstreet, John Harvard Ellis, ed.
(Charlestown, 1867), 101.
    One other New England woman published a book in the
seventeenth century, Mrs. Mary Rowlandson, whose narrative
of her Indian captivity came out in 1682. Mrs. Rowlandson
had intended her account only for her own personal use, to
serve as "a memorandum of Gods dealing with her." Her

In the seventeenth century only a noblewoman could flout propriety and indulge literary ambitions freely. Margaret Cavendish, Duchess of Newcastle, let her recklessly active, wholly undisciplined mind burst out "in torrents of . . . poetry and philosophy" during the 1650's and 1660's. With her thirst for fame satisfied by the lavish praise of university

---

friends, however, were "so much affected with the many passages of working providence discovered therein, as to judge it worthy of publick view. . . . And therefore though this Gentlewomans modesty would not thrust it into the Press, yet her gratitude unto God made her not hardly perswadable to let it pass, that God might have his due glory, and others benefit by it as well as her self." This elaborate explanation was prefaced to the second edition of the book by "a friend" who hoped that "by this time none will cast any reflection upon this Gentlewoman, on the score of this publication of her affliction and deliverance." Evidently some criticism had greeted the first printing. The Soveraignty & Goodness of God, together with the Faithfulness of His Promises Displayed, Being a Narrative of the Captivity and Restauration of Mrs. Mary Rowlandson [Cambridge, 1682] (facsimile edition, Boston, 1937), preface. No copy of the first edition is known to exist.

When "Gentlewomen" like Mrs. Bradstreet and Mrs. Rowlandson, who enjoyed superior social standing and whose works themselves were perfectly unexceptionable, came under attack merely for writing, a female who flouted majority opinion in any way was inviting popular wrath. The Rev. Thomas Parker of Newbury, Massachusetts, was aghast when he heard in 1650 that his sister, back in England, had been converted to heretical doctrines and, even worse, had written a book about them. Addressing her in a public letter he declared that "Your affectation and writing of Assurance did not formerly so well savor, and your printing of a Book, beyond the custom of your Sex, doth rankly smell. . . ." He appealed to her to "Redeem your name and credit amongst Saints, . . . by protesting against that horrid Book, and humbling your self for an attempt above your gifts and Sex." The Copy of a Letter Written by Mr. Thomas Parker, Pastor of the Church of Newbury in New-England, to his Sister, Mrs. Elizabeth Avery, Sometimes of Newbury in the County of Berks, Touching Sundry Opinions by her Professed and Maintained (London, 1650), 13, 17.

scholars awed by her rank and wealth, the duchess from her
unassailable social position ignored the everyday world's
opinion. ("Sure the poore woman is a little distracted,"
Dorothy Osborne commented to Sir William Temple, "shee could
never bee soe rediculous else as to venture at writeing book's
and in verse too, if I should not sleep this fortnight I should
not come to that.")[7]

Other isolated cases of women emboldened by special circumstances to follow a literary bent in the face of popular
prejudice occurred occasionally in England during the Restoration period and through the generation following. In addition
several women, left in desperate economic straits without relatives to rescue them, now for the first time took the gamble
of earning a living by their literary talent and won. But
they succeeded at the price of their reputations, for the
literary world of that day was no place for a lady. Making a
living in it meant writing as men did, and the rowdy plays and
savage satire of the period lay outside the pale of virtuous
safety where the genteel female dwelt.

Indeed, Aphra Behn, England's first professional woman
writer, had little experience of the sheltered life. Her early
career included a visit to the West Indies as the mistress of

---

7 Virginia Woolf restores the Duchess of Newcastle to life in
A Room of One's Own (New York, 1929), describing her "wild
generous, untutored intelligence" on p. 106, quoting Dorothy
Osborne on p. 107. See also Mrs. Woolf's The Common Reader
(New York, 1948), 101-112.

a shady politician in bad odor at home, adventures as a spy during the Dutch wars, and a term in debtor's prison. About 1670 she turned to playwriting and thereafter held her own among the wits and rakes of Restoration drama for some twenty years. ("The stage how loosely does _Astraea_ tread, Who fairly puts all characters to bed" was Alexander Pope's characterization of Mrs. Behn.)[8]

Between such hardy dames and the Mores and Edgeworths of a century later profound changes occurred in English life and literature which metamorphosed the female author from a laughing stock or social outcast into a pillar of respectability. The solid burghers whom Britain's commercial prosperity raised to wealth and influence in the course of the eighteenth century had moral standards and literary values quite different from those of the careless aristocracy of Aphra Behn's day. Shocked by the bawdry and cynical wit of the Restoration stage, bored by the formal accents of poetry in classical style, they craved a realistic rendering of everyday life. For their taste the novel was invented in mid-century, a plain and straightforward fiction dealing in recognizable scenes and characters. If novels could also inculcate a moral lesson, so much the better, for the empire's matter-of-fact merchants were

---

8 V. Sackville-West describes Mrs. Behn's career in _Aphra Behn, The Incomparable Astraea_ (London, 1927); Harrison Gray Platt, Jr., sheds new light on her early life in "Astraea and Celadon: An Untouched Portrait of Aphra Behn," _PMLA_, XLIX (June, 1934), 544-559.

earnestly interested in problems of conduct and eager to buy
books which would serve as guides in self-improvement.

The novel was a natural instrument for the female writer:
an indeterminate form, apparently requiring no classical education, no rigorous literary apprenticeship, only a keen eye
for manners and mores and a fertile imagination.[9] Such a concept of the art was likely to produce third-rate fiction and
too often did. But third-rate fiction perfectly answered the
needs of the new reading public. No longer did a select group
of literati serve as arbiters of taste; a larger, less cultivated, less critical audience was now thronging the market.

A numerous and influential portion of this audience belonged to the weaker sex. As we have seen, prosperity had
bestowed upon the middle-class woman the troublesome gift of
leisure. A genteel female could while away many an hour by
reading, and by 1800 nearly every English and American town had
its circulating library, crowded with ladies and their maids

---

9 "Indeed it is a task for which women appear to be particularly well qualified," wrote Lord Dudley in the Quarterly
Review in 1814. "They are, generally speaking, gifted with
a nice perception of the various shades of character and
manners. This faculty is cultivated by constant habit.
Private life is everything to them. The laws of society
confine them within its sphere, and they are therefore
likely to observe it with care and to describe it with
precision." ("Miss Edgeworth's Patronage," X (January,
1814), 303.) Francis Jeffrey of the rival Edinburgh Review
made similar observations in an article on "Standard Novels
and Romances," XXIV (February, 1815), 336-337. See also
J. M. S. Tompkins, The Popular Novel in England, 1770-1800
(1932), 19.

borrowing the "soft, simp'ring tales of amorous pain"[10] spun
out by the woman novelists.  By 1825 there were enough female
readers to provide some uncertain support for women's magazines as well, and even to encourage a few of the fair to become editors of such publications.

The latter-eighteenth-century interest in education, and
particularly in the training of children, opened up another
field to aspiring authoresses.  Woman's maternal function presumably gave her an instinctive understanding of the child
mind; it seemed clearly her prescriptive right, therefore, to
entertain and instruct it.  By the same token women were mani-
festly the appropriate monitors of their sex on all matters
pertaining to conduct and education.

The most popular woman writers practiced in two or three
of these fields at once, most often, like Maria Edgeworth,
combining novels with works on education or stories for children.  The English Taylor family wrote manuals of advice for
the rising middle class alternately with nursery rhymes.  American Hannah Foster turned from seduction in her Coquette to instruction in The Boarding School; Susanna Rowson applied her
boundless energy impartially to composing novels, patriotic
plays and songs, and schoolbooks for her pupils.  The ladies
wrote easily, rapidly, and constantly.

---

10 John Trumbull, "The Progress of Dulness," The Poetical
   Works of John Trumbull (Hartford, 1820), II, 44.

Before this wave of literary success, the long hostility
to the female author subsided with hardly more than token resistance.  A few die-hards might still protest that "a woman
has no business with a pen in her hand, unless it be to com-
pute the expences of her housekeeping."[11]  But when women like
Elizabeth Hamilton and Anna Laetitia Barbauld, Judith Murray
and Sarah Wentworth Morton combined an exemplary performance
of their feminine duties with the writing of literature pure
in sentiment and earnestly moral, criticism was quickly dis-
armed.  As one reviewer candidly remarked, "This is certainly
not the age in which those who speak slightingly of female
talent should expect to be listened to with much attention."[12]

When one looks at the bulk of the women writers' output
in this period, however, he wonders whether the fanfare which
greeted their entrance into the literary world was not a tribute more generous than just.

The lady poets of the day are a case in point.  Most of
them struck off verses in the Della Cruscan manner, imitating
a school of English poetasters who encrusted their lines with
extravagant adjectives and far-fetched metaphors, almost

---

11 John Davis, Travels of Four Years and a Half in the United
   States of America [1803] (New York, 1909), 215.

12 [John Taylor Coleridge], "Mrs. Hemans's Poems," Quarterly
   Review, XXIV (October, 1820), 130.

obscuring what little meaning lay beneath. Mrs. Sarah Wentworth Morton of Boston, America's leading poetess of the post-Revolutionary generation, was adept at this sort of fancy work. Witness Mrs. Morton addressing the summer moon:

> Thou silent traveller, of the glance benign,
>     Who from yon crystal car on high,
>     Shedds't the full lustre of thy moving eye. . . .[13]

The Della Cruscans had some competition from songstresses like England's Amelia Opie. "The verses of this amiable woman," the Port Folio's Joseph Dennie observed, "are remarkable for a certain plaintive cast. Her Muse is often in tears." No parlor with pretensions of elegance was complete without a mournful volume by Mrs. Opie, "a great favorite with the ladies, and . . . those sighing swains, in whose estimation nothing in poetry is comparable to the serious and the sentimental."[14]

Dennie did not always achieve such restraint in his comments. A man of sensitive taste, he lived in a state of suppressed irritation at the "authours in petticoats" whose productions he had to scrutinize in the line of duty. Exploding one day in 1808, he pointed to a passage by the pert young Irishwoman Sydney Owenson dedicating a volume of poems to her patron. "At some distant day," Miss Owenson had written, "I might solicit your attention to some less idle vision; but the

---

13 Morton, My Mind and Its Thoughts (Boston, 1823), 141.

14 "Literary Intelligence," Port Folio, n.s. VI (October 22, 1808), 271.

ardour of gratitude spurns the cold delay of protracted intention, while its feelings call for an immediate avowal."
"This," pronounced Dennie, "is a splendid specimen of the
superfine style, and yet so perfectly feminine in its character, that of one hundred letters, or essays, which we might,
in any . . . year, receive from writing women, . . . upwards
of ninety . . . would contain divers periods after the same
pretty pattern."[15]

In the field of poetry the author in petticoats cut no
very wide swath. Verse was still little more than the pastime
of a few society ladies indulging a literary bent. Most would-
be authoresses were now choosing a more popular genre. This
was the heyday of the sentimental novel, and that "farrago of
love, and absurdity, and ignorance," as young Alexander Everett
contemptuously defined it,[16] was a feminine specialty. English
women got a head start in the manufacture of this commodity;
the author of the first American novel, The Power of Sympathy,
deplored the fact in 1789 that "American literature boasts so
few productions from the pens of the ladies."[17]

In a very few years, however, the American fair had followe
suit. By the turn of the century a highly respectable contingen

---

15 "Criticism," Port Folio, n.s. VI (November 12, 1808), 317.

16 "Corinna, or Italy," Monthly Anthology, V (Junek 1808), 336.

17 William Hill Brown, The Power of Sympathy [1789] (New York,
1937), II, 15.

could have been found with ink-stained fingers, concocting variations on Richardson's old theme of domestic misadvanture, or trying their hand at the imaginary horrors of the Gothic romance à la Mrs. Ann Radcliffe. Where the recipe came from, however, made little difference, since the ingredients were always the same: a feeble plot and insipid characters, embellished with gobs of stilted dialogue and gushing description. The stream of stories about incredibly beautiful maidens and their impossible trials with tyrannical parents, loathsome suitors and unsanctioned lovers, their abductions, seductions, rescues, and reunions discouraged even Charles Brockden Brown, who generally took a liberal view of women's literary efforts. Thinking back in 1799 over the output of novels in recent years, Brown was forced to admit that "the greater number of female productions, in this kind, are sadly wanting in proofs of good sense and the qualities of good writing."[18]

These simple virtues, however, were not in demand among "the ingenious frequenters of circulating libraries, . . . the lively inquirers after new books in duodecimo."[19] For this feminine audience the female novelist had exactly the right

---

18 Monthly Magazine and American Review, I (September-December, 1799), 447. Lively accounts of this fiction can be found in J. M. S. Tompkins, Popular Novel in England and Herbert Ross Brown, The Sentimental Novel in America, 1789-1860 (Durham, N.C., 1940).

19 [Francis Jeffrey], "Mad. de Staël -- Sur la Literature [sic],", Edinburgh Review, XXI (February, 1813), I.

formula, and the book trade was quick to take advantage of such a happy conjunction of circumstances. We are assured, for instance, that Hocquet Caritat, proprietor of New York's most fashionable lending library, "could tell a good book from a bad one. . . ." Nevertheless the astute Frenchman knew where his profits came from. "Place aux dames was his maxim, and all the ladies . . . declared that the Library of Mr. Caritat was charming."[20] From his shelves they could make a selection among some thousand novels bearing irresistible titles like Female Frailty, The Posthumous Daughter, and The Fatal Promise, or Mortimore Castle, The Devil in Love, and 'Twas Wrong to Marry Him. The "inland towns of consequence" also had their "social libraries," perhaps in a corner of the apothecary's shop, or at the milliner's, catering to feminine customers of all ages and stations.[21] To some disgusted observers it seemed

---

20 Davis, Travels in the United States, 204n.

21 Royall Tyler's description in The Algerine Captive (1797) of the novel mania in rural New England is quoted on p. 10 of George G. Raddin, An Early New York Library of Fiction (New York, 1940), which describes Caritat's establishment. See also C. K. Bolton, "Circulating Libraries in Boston, 1765-1865," Publications of the Colonial Society of Massachusetts, XI (Boston, 1910), 196-207, and Brown, Sentimental Novel in America, ch. 1. At her circulating library a lady might also read or borrow copies of female magazines like the Philadelphia Minerva (1795-1798), devoted "to the selection of the most admired and sentimental pieces in prose and verse, entertaining anecdotes, and affecting narratives," or the Boston Weekly Magazine and Ladies' Miscellany (1816-1818), "an amusing guide to innocent pleasure and useful knowledge." Bertha M. Stearns, "Early Philadelphia Magazines for Ladies," New England Quarterly, II (July, 1929), 439.

that "novel-mania" had seized the whole female population,
as they watched "servants, black and white, nursery maids,
young ladies -- alas! old ones too -- flitting impatiently
along" the streets carrying the tell-tale little half-bound
volumes with marbled covers. Proprietors made every effort
to build up their business. "The library is open from morn-
ing to eight at night," one New York bookseller advertised,
"and the readers may have a book exchanged, if they please,
every day."[22]

Most of this merchandise had to be imported, and houses
like the Minerva Press of London, England's leading publisher
of cheap fiction between 1790 and 1820, were hard pressed to
keep up with the demand at home and abroad. William Lane, the
Minerva's proprietor, printed anything he could lay his hands
on, reissuing old novels under new titles, pirating the works
of American writers, and even advertising in the newspapers for
new authors. "Genius and Taste," he promised, would find at
the Minerva Press not only "Fidelity in ushering their Productions to the World" but "Encouragement and Advantage in their
Literary Pursuits." These were the very words to embolden a
timid female to come forward with a package of manuscript. Her
pecuniary reward would be a mere ten or twenty pounds, but,
no matter how slipshod or silly, the book was almost certain to

---

22 "Patronage," Port Folio, ser. 4, IV (August, 1814), 165;
Brown, Sentimental Novel, 24.

be published and sent on its way to speed the turnover in the circulating libraries.[23]

As Lane and other publishers expanded production of cheap fiction to meet the demand from this exciting new market, a kind of literary Gresham's Law went into operation. Soon the mass-produced sentimental novel was driving better fiction from the field, and since men writers of talent could have no interest in a literary form so debased, the New Hampshire authoress Tabitha Tenney could truthfully observe by 1801 that "the ladies of late seem to have almost appropriated this department of writing." So completely effeminate did the novel become, in fact, that publishers' hacks commonly assumed the disguise of "A Lady" on the title page lest readers suspect any deviation from the sentimental formula.[24] Men readers who enjoyed fiction had to take circulating library fare or do without, and most preferr the latter alternative. (Novel-reading was "a singular taste for a man," Mrs. Tenney remarked.) Others no doubt shared the experience of Dr. John Aiken, who sometimes in a weak moment

---

23 Dorothy Blakey, The Minerva Press, 1790-1820 (London, 1939), 72, 73, and passim.

24 Tenney, Female Quixotism [1801] (Boston, 1841), I, 7; Blakey, Minerva Press, 51-52; B. G. MacCarthy, The Later Women Novelists, 1744-1818 (Oxford, 1948), 39. Actually it is hard to tell whether the onslaught of female fiction discouraged men who might have written good novels, or whether there simply happened to be no masculine talent in this period (from the death of Smollett in 1771 to the publication of Scott's Waverley in 1814) when the English novel reached its lowest ebb.

picked up a novel from the parlor table only to find curiosity
compelling him "through the most tedious and disgusting pages,"
which "like Pistol eating his leek, I have swallowed and exe-
crated to the end."[25]

The female reader therefore had the field to herself.
Nevertheless she persued her favorite pastime under some difficulty.  Young women, especially, had to submit to solemn lectures on the subject from all the good people who took seriously
their responsibilities as mentors of the sex.  A young lady
might be indulged in an occasional novel on an idle afternoon,
but when she developed a craving that consumed all her waking
hours it was a matter for serious concern.  Parents tried persuasion but to little avail.  "I have a family of three daughters, who are mad  upon reading novels, and I can seldom prevail
upon them to read anything else," wrote one worried mother.
Prohibition only drove the offending volumes under cover.  What
girl could resist the urging of a Mephistopheles like the author
of The Wanderings of William: "Avail yourself of the moment that

---

25 Tenney, Female Quixotism, I, 9.  Joseph Dennie was one of
   the few men who confessed a liking for fiction.  "Of the
   ordinary trash of a circulating library," he said, "my
   friends will easily acquit me of the suspicion of being
   studious."  (Port Folio, II [May 8, 1802], 138.)  But he
   could still enjoy Cervantes, Le Sage, and the eighteenth
   century English classics by Fielding, Smollett, and Fanny
   Burney, though he had no use for "the everlasting babblement
   of that prig, Richardson."  "The American Lounger," Port
   Folio, II (June 5, 1802), 169; "Criticism," n.s. VI (November 12, 1808), 316; and "An Author's Evenings," III (May
   28, 1803), 170-171, in which he quotes "the judicious Dr.
   Aikin, one of the most eminent living critics" and brother
   of the distinguished authoress Anna Laetitia Barbauld.

offers to indulge in the perusal of this book. Take it, read
it; there is nothing to fear. Your governess is gone out,
and your mamma is not yet risen. Do you hesitate? Werter has
been under your pillow, and the Monk has lain in your toilet."
At their wits' end, parents appealed to outside authority "to
caution the fair sex against reading improper books," and "to
be particularly severe against . . . novels."[26] Rallying to
their support, educators, philosophers, clergymen, and even
novelists themselves united as one voice to preach the dire
effects of a fictional diet.

Warnings against novels filled the magazines, found their
way into sermons and moral treatises, cropped up in travel
books and private letters. That these sentimental tales were
an utter waste of time was obvious. "A hundred volumes of
modern novels may be read, without acquiring a new idea," Noah
Webster declared in 1790. Worse, Thomas Jefferson was writing
some thirty years later, "when this poison infects the mind,
it destroys its tone and revolts it against wholesome reading."[2]

---

26 Ladies' Magazine and Repertory of Entertaining Knowledge
(Philadelphia), I (1792), 11, and John Davis, The Wanderings of William (Philadelphia, 1801), both quoted in
Brown, Sentimental Novel, 7, 14-15. Goethe's The Sorrows
of Young Werther (1774) and Matthew Gregory Lewis's The
Monk (1797) were possibly the most reprehensible novels in
circulation at the time, the former investing suicide and
illicit love with romantic glamor, the latter a Gothic
nightmare of sadistic horrors.

27 Webster, "On the Education of Youth in America," A Collection of Essays and Fugitiv [sic] Writings (Boston, 1790), 29;
Jefferson to Nathaniel Burwell, March 14, 1818, Thomas Jefferson and Education in a Republic, Charles F. Arrowood, ed.

Besides blocking intellectual progress, novel-reading was likely to cause emotional disturbances. A young lady's emotional balance was deemed to be delicate at best, since the cult of sensibility put a premium on sensitive feelings and encouraged giving way to them at the least opportunity. An impressionable girl would suffer agonies of distress as she thrilled and despaired with each harrowing turn of the heroine's fortunes, weeping copiously over the tiny, close-printed pages. In some cases, young women were warned, this overstimulation of the feelings had "introduced a train of the most painful nervous complaints"[28] and even a physical decline.

Most serious of all was the danger that a girl's "head [would be] . . . turned by the unrestrained perusal of Novels and Romances." Living in a dream world of "shady groves and purling streams, fashions, etiquette, and romantic scenes of love and high life,"[29] she was likely to acquire false expectations of life. In the crucial period of courtship, particularly, such notions could betray her into indiscreet or even

(New York, 1930), 178. For some other instances of anti-novel opinion, see Rev. James Gray, "Female Education," Port Folio, ser. 3, IV (July, 1810), and the Scottish moralist Dugald Stewart, Elements of the Philosophy of the Human Mind (Philadelphia, 1793), quoted in Raddin, Early New York Library of Fiction, 29-31. G. Harrison Orians says the last word on "Censure of Fiction in American Romances and Magazines, 1789-1810" in PMLA, LII (March, 1937), 195-214.

28 Hannah Adams, A Memoir of Miss Hannah Adams, Written by Herself (Boston, 1932), 16, 15.

29 Tenney, Female Quixotism, I, 4; Enos Hitchcock, Memoirs of the Bloomsgrove Family (Boston, 1790), II, 81.

immoral conduct which might wreck her chances for happiness.[30]
No authenticated records of such calamities seem to have survived. The novelists themselves, however, always willing to
turn traitor to their trade, seized eagerly on the idea as a
theme for fiction. "Many fine girls have been ruined by reading Novels," solemnly declared William Hill Brown in The Power
of Sympathy,[31] while Hannah Foster regaled her pupils in The
Boarding School with the hair-raising history of one Juliana.

Daughter of a wealthy merchant who was too busy to supervise her education, Juliana fed her romantic fancy on "every
light publication which a circulating library could furnish."
When it came time for her to marry, "a sober, rational courtship would not answer her ideas of love and gallantry." Re-
jecting with disdain a worthy but sedate gentleman selected by
her father, Juliana was swept off her feet by "a military captain, . . . . young, handsome, easy, bold and assuming." Her
worried friends "warmly remonstrated against her imprudent conduct in receiving the addresses of a man, destitute of property
to support her, and void of every kind of personal merit," and
her father forbade him the house, but to no avail. The deluded
girl eloped and married her captain, who promptly ran through

---

30 Tenney, Female Quixotism, I, 6, 9; Adams, Memoir, 4; Timothy
Dwight, Travels in New-England and New-York (New Haven,
1821), I, 517; Trumbull, "Progress of Dulness," Works, II,
76-77; Clara Reeve, The Progress of Romance [Colchester,
1785] (New York, 1930), I, 78.

31 The Power of Sympathy, I, 53.

her money and then returned to his regiment, leaving Juliana
to suffer "the dreadful effects of her folly, in the accumulated ills of poverty and neglect."[32]

Amid these excited warnings, however, a few calmer voices
could be heard. The much respected English writer Anna Laetitia
Barbauld regarded the novel mania with unruffled composure.
"Now and then," she admitted, "a girl perhaps may be led by
them to elope with a coxcomb; or, if she is handsome, to expect
the homage of a Sir Harry or My lord, instead of the plain tradesman suitable to her situation in life. . . ." But in general
novels would do little harm. They might even do good. Mrs.
Barbauld knew considerably more about women's life than most
of the sex's mentors, and she felt that, while the "scenes of
perpetual courtship" might make a woman's existence seem more
monotonous by contrast, novels on the other hand could do much
to relieve that monotony. "The humble novel is always ready to
enliven the gloom of solitude, to soothe the languor of debility
and disease, to win the attention from pain or vexatious oc-
currences. . . ." It was a diversion, too, which kept the

---

32 The Boarding School (Boston, 1798), 19-22. The most famous
example in fiction of a young lady led astray by novel-
reading is, of course, Jane Austen's Catherine Morland, who
got herself into an awkward situation by making furtive ex-
plorations in the manner of a Gothic heroine around the
corridors of Northanger Abbey (1803). With a clumsier pen
Tabitha Tenney burlesqued the novel mania in Female Quixotism
(1801), subjecting her heroine Dorcasina Sheldon to a series
of indignities and embarrassments arising from her expecting
life to conform to the sentimental novelists' pictures of
it.

young woman safely at home while at the same time giving her
some knowledge of the world -- a less dangerous way to learn
about it "than by mixing in real life."[33]

After all, Mrs. Barbauld sensibly concluded, preaching
against novels was largely wasted breath.  They might be "condemned by the grave, and despised by the fastidious; but . . .
they occupy the parlour and the dressing-room while productions
of higher name are often gathering dust upon the shelves."
And things could be worse.  No matter how trashy, English novels did maintain a decent moral tone.  A girl might be squander-
ing her time mooning over them, but at least "she will not have
her mind contaminated with such scenes and ideas as . . . have
[been] published in France."[34]

The comfort Mrs. Barbauld took in the purity of English
fiction was generally shared by the British and American public.
Self-appointed guardians of the weaker sex might preach against
novels until they were hoarse, but more easygoing citizens, satisfied that these stories offered no threat to religion, the
home, or female modesty, let their womenfolk read undisturbed.
Anyone could see that the language was perfectly chaste.  Virtue was always rewarded and vice held in abhorrence.  "Where

---

33 Barbauld, "On the Origin and Progress of Novel-Writing,"
The British Novelists (London, 1810), I, 58, 54, 47, 51.

34 Ibid., 1, 58.

can we behold finer models of heroic virtue, invincible chastity, and noble disinterestedness, than in the Julia's and in the Eliza's, the Henry's and the Edward's of the storied page?" queried one novelist proudly.[35] As if teaching by such examples were not enough, writers would frequently interrupt the narrative to deliver a moral lecture to their readers. This was particularly true of the American authoress, who, writing for a less sophisticated audience, often let the sermon crowd the story off the page altogether. (A giddy young lady in Mrs. Foster's The Boarding School had nothing but scorn for these home-made products. "An American novel is such a moral, sentimental thing, that it is enough to give any body the vapours to read one," she confided to a friend.[36])

To many twentieth-century readers this literature seems somewhat less pure than it pretended to be. Whether the moral dosage was strong or weak, theme and plot were lurid and sensational in the extreme. In every novel a tender maiden stood at bay for three volumes, besieged by experienced older men

---

35 "A General Defence of Modern Novels," in Monckton; or, The Fate of Eleanor (1802), quoted in Raddin, Early New York Library of Fiction, 24.

36 Miss Amelia Parr found imported fiction much more to her liking. "They have attained to a far greater degree of refinement in the old world, than we have in the new; and are so perfectly acquainted with the passions, that there is something extremely amusing and interesting in their plots and counter-plots, operating in various ways, till the dear creatures are jumbled into matrimony in the prettiest manner that can be conceived!" Boarding School, 156-157.

whose sole purpose was to possess her by fair means or foul.
Needless to say, her surrender was always deferred until the
last chapter. Then, as the story was ending either in capitu-
lation to the crafty seducer or in marriage to a virtuous
suitor, the authoress hastily brought down the curtain. Certainly the basic situation was suggestive enough. Nevertheless, in a thousand pages the novelist would not have depicted
one scene of passion, and though modern readers may find such
interludes the more conspicuous by their absence, the latter-
eighteenth-century female may well have been too innocent to
realize what she was missing.

At any rate, that generation was satisfied with its own
brand of moral veneer. Professional critics put an automatic
seal of approval on novels which made proper obeisance to the
proprieties. This "lively and instructive tale inculcates lessons of the greatest importance; such as piety, temperance,
moderation, patience and resignation" was a sample judgment.
"The hero and heroine in this work are virtuous characters; and
nothing can be perceived in it of an immoral tendency." "This
is an innocent and interesting novel."[37]

Such standards of criticism were hardly calculated to inspire the scribbling sisterhood to strenuous artistic effort.
But even if the critics had been exacting, the novelist had few
models to study. The mid-eighteenth century's masculine

---

37 Quoted in Raddin, Early New York Library, 28.

pioneers in the novel had left a rich storehouse of art and life, but the roisterous realism of Fielding and Smollett, their hearty vulgarity, were now distasteful. "Nobody now reads either but the school-boy," a critic declared in 1820, "and one of the earliest signs of an improved taste, and an advancement in Christian morality, is the rejection of both."[38] As to Richardson, opinion stood divided. Certainly his descriptions of "vice" were overly "luxuriant," and he had "laid open scenes, which it would have been safer to have kept concealed. . . ." ("By what unction of purity our great-grandmothers were preserved," exclaimed one horrified gentleman, "when they studied Pamela without danger or disgust, we know not.")[39] Still, Richardson's Clarissa Harlowe was incomparably the most perfect of women, her conduct under excruciating circumstances never wavering from the path of rectitude. The objectionable details could be easily omitted, and Richardson's settings and events lay within the female novelist's limited experience. Unfortunately the master's psychological insight, his overpowering emotional effects, remained his own secret. His bevy of followers merely used the immortal Clarissa as a pattern from which they snipped out shoddy copies without style or distinction.

---

38 "Sketch of the Progress of Novel-Writing" [from the British Review], Port Folio, ser. 4, IX (April [?], 1820), 269.

39 Hitchcock, Bloomsgrove Family, II, 87; "Sketch of the Progress of Novel-Writing, 268. For other strictures on the eighteenth-century realists, see Foster, Boarding School, 160-161, 181-182, and Mrs. Barbauld's essays on Fielding and Smollett in The British Novelists, XVIII, XXX.

Yet the female authors, in whose hands the novel had fallen to the lowest station in literature, were finally to redeem both it and themselves. There would always be popular trash, and much of it written by women, but by 1800 it was possible to distinguish a respectable body of better fiction.

As far back as 1778 Fanny Burney, a shy London miss of twenty-six, had invented a new kind of realism, deserting the Richardson formula to write, in Evelina, the history of a young girl's adventures as a clever comedy of manners without "a single line inconsistent . . . even with virgin delicacy."[40] In the 1790's Mrs. Ann Radcliffe had brought forth a new kind of romance in her Gothic novels, transplanting the familiar persecuted heroine into romantic settings somewhere in the antique past and conducting her through her trials with such mastery of terror and suspense, such feeling for the picturesque in nature, that the reader's emotions were irresistibly engaged.

For the generation of 1800, however, the literary heroine of the hour was Maria Edgeworth. Miss Edgeworth's convincing, realistic stories of everyday life, each firmly anchored to a moral, satisfied both literary taste and conscience, making her a household favorite in America as well as in England. "He, who even in an hour of the most yawning lassitude, begins one of these moral and entertaining narratives," declared the

---

40 T. B. Macaulay, "Madame D'Arblay," Critical and Miscellaneous Essays (Philadelphia, 1844), V, 81.

fastidious Joseph Dennie, "will scarcely close the volume, until it be finished."[41] Her work alone was enough to raise fiction to a respectable position in the literary world. "The writings of Miss Edgeworth," explained the Edinburgh Review, in an article promptly reprinted in a Philadelphia Magazine, "exhibit so singular an union of sober sense and inexhaustible invention -- so minute a knowledge of . . . manners . . . in every condition of human fortune -- . . . that it cannot be thought wonderful that we should separate her from the ordinary manufacturers of novels, and speak of her Tales of works of . . . serious importance."[42]

Indeed, by the end of the new century's first decade fiction was so generally approved that the chief publicist of England's Evangelical revival, the revered Hannah More, undertook an experiment in the field. At sixty-four Hannah had behind her three treatises dedicated to the moral improvement of her sex,[43] but these, she feared, had reached only the "good

41 Port Folio, IV (December 29, 1804), 414.

42 "Miss Edgeworth's Tales of Fashionable Life," XX (July, 1812), 100-101, reprinted in the Analectic Magazine (Philadelphia), I (January, 1813), 22.

43 Essays on Various Subjects, Principally Designed for Young Ladies (1777), a work of the era of Dr. Gregory and Mrs. Chapone, written before the rise of the Evangelical movement and Hannah's conversion to it; Strictures on the Modern System of Female Education (1799), described in ch. 4, above; and Hints towards Forming the Character of a Young Princess (1805), addressed to the tutors of Charlotte, heiress-presumptive to the throne, but "meant to be useful to all young persons of rank and liberal education." Even this last book was widely read in America, despite republican prejudices against royalty. (William Roberts, Memoirs of the Life and Correspondence of Mrs. Hannah More [New York, 1835], II, 125, 418.)

people," those already half-converted to her doctrines.  In an
effort to touch "a larger class of readers whose wants had not
been attended to, -- the subscribers to the circulating library,"[44] she published in 1809 a novel called <u>Coelebs in Search</u>
<u>of a Wife: Comprehending Observations on Domestic Habits and</u>
<u>Manners, Religion and Morals</u>.  This ponderous story conducts
the rich young bachelor Charles Coelebs on a tour of English
society, introducing him to a series of giddy young ladies of
fashion, from whom he piously recoils, and finally to a maiden
of retiring modesty and strict principle, whom he promptly takes
to wife.[45]  The book was immensely popular, particularly in the

---

[44] Hannah More to Sir William W. Pepys, <u>ibid</u>., 168.

[45] Lucilla Stanley was the embodiment of all the theories about
women's education which Hannah More had elaborated in her
<u>Strictures</u>.  She did not play, sing, or draw, spending her
time instead on useful pursuits: helping her mother with the
household management and the instruction of her younger
sisters, teaching the village children, and making visits
of charity to the neighborhood poor.  Her chief pleasure
was gardening, but she also found time for two hours of
improving reading before breakfast and a daily hour of
study with her father.  Mr. Stanley, early discovering her
"strong bent to whatever relates to intellectual taste," had
begun to teach Lucilla Latin at the age of nine and since
that time had "read over with her the most unexceptionable
parts of a few of the best Roman classics."  As a general
rule, however, he thought instruction in the dead languages
unwise for girls, and out of deference to popular prejudice
this accomplishment of Lucilla's was kept a strict secret
in the family.  When Coelebs and the other house guests ac-
cidentally discovered it one afternoon at tea, Lucilla
blushed excessively, and after putting "the sugar into the
cream-pot, and the tea into the sugar-basin," had to leave
the room in her confusion.  "How does that sweet girl manage to be so utterly devoid of pretension?" asked a lady
guest.  "So much softness and so much usefulness strip her
of all the terrors of learning."  Mr. Stanley assured the
company that a heart fortified with real Christianity was

United States, where it went through thirty editions in the next quarter-century.[46] One Massachusetts lady, herself an authority on female behavior, later remembered that around 1810 she "was constantly hearing the praises of Miss Hannah More. Everybody had read, or was reading, her religious novel of 'Coelebs in Search of a Wife'... . ."[47]

Besides entertaining and elevating the adult world, the female authors of this era were opening up new vistas to young people, giving them for the first time a literature of their own, cut to youthful patterns. To this experiment they brought their extensive experience with the novel and, equally important, a new attitude toward the child. In fact, the advent of books for juveniles was only one sign of a major change in ideas about child life and training, one of the revolutions in western

immune to pride of talents, and Coelebs rejoiced in the prospect of a wife who could share his intellectual pleasures. Coelebs in Search of a Wife (The Complete Works of Hannah More [New York, 1835], II), 257, 254. Hannah More's ablest biographer maintains that this portrait formed the Victorian ideal of womanhood. M. G. Jones, Hannah More (Cambridge, 1952), 195.

46 Ibid., 193. Hannah More wrote to friends in 1825 that she had "lately had a visit from the principal American bookseller of New-York, who told me that he had sold thirty thousand copies of 'Coelebs;' and he added, it did more good there than my decidedly religious writings, because it was read universally by worldly people, who might shrink from some of the others." Roberts, Memoirs, II, 394-395.

47 Eliza R. Farrar, Recollections of Seventy Years (Boston, 1866), 219.

thinking spurred by the turbulent genius of Jean Jacques Rousseau. Children, hitherto regarded as miniature adults with a special propensity to mischief and rigidly held to adult standards of conduct, were represented in the Émile as immature beings of unformed mind and heart whom education according to the laws of nature could mold into a higher order of humanity.

Rousseau's method was soon demonstrated to be impractical, [48] but his concept of child nature became the cornerstone of modern progressive thought about education and family relationships. Rationalist and religionist alike now began to regard the mind of youth as a vast new field of missionary endeavor and hence to take special interest in reading for boys and girls.

Children in previous eras, to be sure, had been well supplied with religious reading matter. Little Puritans in America had imbibed the elements of Calvinism from The New England Primer sundry shorter catechisms, and a lugubrious account of preternaturally pious babes entitled A Token for Children, being an Exact Account of the Conversion, Holy and Exemplary Lives and Joyful Deaths of Several Young Children. Written by an English clergyman, this last work was many times reprinted in the colonie

---

48 Notably in England by Richard Lovell Edgeworth (Maria's father) and his friend Thomas Day. Mr. Edgeworth's rearing of his eldest son literally by the precepts of the Émile proved a sad mistake; the eccentric Day's two attempts to train an orphan girl into an ideal wife for himself were an even more dismal failure. Day had better success producing an Émile in fiction: his History of Sandford and Merton (1789), which became a children's classic.

with an appendix by Cotton Mather providing some American examples.[49]

For story books, however, young Puritans as well as other children on both sides of the Atlantic had to resort to adult literature, adopting Pilgrim's Progress and Foxe's Book of Martyrs and later discovering Crusoe and Gulliver. Not until midway in the eighteenth century did anyone think of writing fiction especially for children. This was the inspiration of a London printer named John Newbery, who together with his hacks turned out dozens of tiny bright volumes of nursery rhymes and moral fables (including the famous History of Little Goody Two-Shoes), scoring a notable publishing success. Colonial booksellers regularly imported this line, and after the Revolution Isaiah Thomas, America's leading publishers, reprinted thousands of copies of the Newbery favorites at his press in Worcester, Massachusetts.[50]

Given a start in life by Newbery, juvenile literature nevertheless remained for some time a neglected stepchild in the literary family, the adult world content to leave it to the mercies of hack writers and printers so long as they maintained

49 Alice Morse Earle, Child Life in Colonial Days (New York, [1899] (1929), 128-132, chapter 13.

50 Ibid., chapter 14; Monica Kiefer, American Children through Their Books (Philadelphia, 1948), chapter 1; Cambridge History of English Literature (Cambridge, 1932), XI, chapter 16; Florence V. Barry, A Century of Children's Books (New York, 1923); Rosamond Bayne-Powell, The English Child in the Eighteenth Century (London, 1939).

a decent moral tone. Then near the close of the century it was adopted by the woman author, and by her sympathetic hand raised to a position of real importance and prestige.

The women took on this new responsibility quite unconscious that they were inaugurating what would come to be hailed as "a golden era, . . . deserving of a rank among the most glorious dates of improvement."[51] The first practitioners were conscientious mothers with a literary bent, responding to the new theories on child raising by an attempt to produce instructive reading matter for their own offspring. Dissatisfied with the tepid morality of Newbery's pieces, they developed a new kind of story, the didactic tale in a strictly realistic setting. Enthusiastic family and friends persuaded them to seek a wider audience, and the fireside story-tellers became popular favorites almost overnight. Children had never had reading so accurately pitched at their level of understanding, while other mothers and fathers, also feeling new and weighty responsibility for the upbringing of the young, welcomed this timely aid.

The ladies who wielded the pen in this minor literary revolution were all English; it would be another generation before women in the United States tried their hand at the new genre. But their names and their books were as familiar in American as in British homes. Precocious American toddlers learned to read

---

[51] F. W. P. Greenwood, "Hope Leslie," North American Review, XXVI (April, 1828), 408.

from Anna Laetitia Barbauld's Lessons for Children (1780),
written originally for her own three-year-old son, while older children enjoyed her Evenings at Home (1792), a collection
of instructive fables, dialogues, and poems which remained a
standard work in the United States for most of the following
century. Parents were attracted by the title of Mrs. Sarah
Trimmer's Fabulous Histories, Designed for the Amusement and
Instruction of Young Persons (1786), but inside the covers
their offspring found a lively and humorous story of a family
of robins from which they painlessly learned kindness to animals
and other "lessons of domestic virtue."[52]

The children's favorites, however, were the shorter tales
that Maria Edgeworth had first invented to entertain her flock
of small brothers and sisters. Put on the market as The
Parent's Assistant (1796) and Early Lessons (1801), they quickly
became juvenile classics. "There is scarcely an intelligent
child in America, who does not love her name," the pastor of
Springfield's Unitarian church wrote of Miss Edgeworth in
1834.[53] The first artist in fiction to write for young people,
Maria Edgeworth filled her stories with dramatic interest and
a fascinating set of stage properties. Impulsive Rosamond, who
learned that things are not what they seem by choosing the

52 Some Account of the Life and Writings of Mrs. Trimmer (London, 1825), 51.

53 W. B. O. Peabody, "Helen," North American Review, XXXIX
(July, 1834), 175.

purple jar in the apothecary's window in preference to a new
pair of shoes; Lazy Lawrence, led by indolence and boredom into petty crime; sensible Ben of "Waste Not, Want Not," whose
good fortune eventuated from the frugal habit of saving string,
were real companions to successive generations of children until their simple morality and way of life had become wholly
archaic.


With Barbaulds and Edgeworths and Hannah Mores winning
fresh literary laurels year by year, the public developed a
lively interest in female authors and their careers.  Here was
a new kind of celebrity.  Here also was a social phenomenon --
a considerable number of women making a startling departure from
woman's conventional role.  Curiosity was immediately aroused.
In this new combination of functions, what would happen to the
woman?  Would she be swallowed up in the author -- her femininity warped by ambitious competition for fame, money, professional eminence?  The question was in everyone's mind, and it
was frequently voiced.

The answer came from the women themselves.  It was a def-
inite no.  Far from being courageous trail blazers for their sex
into the new profession, they clung to old habits of mind and
in fact often seemed to be pushed into authorship against their
will.  It was hardly necessary for the critics, as representa-
tives of public opinion, to lay down standards of propriety; the

woman author had probably already stated them, and her adher-
ence to them, in her preface.

The first thing the public wanted to know about any authoress was how she discharged her domestic duties. Women's prefaces to their books overflowed with assurances that writing
was never permitted to impinge on home or family responsibilities. Hannah Foster informed her readers that she had "employed
a part of her leisure hours" only, "in collecting and arrang-
ing her ideas on the subject of female deportment" for The
Boarding School. Writing novels was not Caroline Matilda
Warren's main object in life but only her "principal amusement."
Mrs. Sarah Wood, Maine author of four novels, set her record
straight by stating, however ungrammatically, that "not one
social, or one domestic duty, have ever been sacrifieed or
postponed by her pen. . . ." "I hope no one will supppse,"
she explained in another work, "that I entertain ideas so fal-
lacious as to imagine it necessary for a female to be a writer:
far from it. I am sure 'That Woman's noblest station is retreat;' and that a female is never half so lovely, half so engaging or amiable, as when performing her domestic duties, and
cheering, with smiles of unaffected good humor, those about her.
But there are some, who, forgetful of those sacred duties, . . .
devote a large portion of time to dissipation. . . ." Surely
it was better for a woman to write than to indulge in "such
fashionable occupations as waste many hours. . . ."[54]

---

54 Foster, Boarding School, 3; Warren, The Gamesters; or Ruins

Mrs. Wood was generously willing to give character references for her sister authors also. She arranged for a figure in one of her novels to visit Mrs. Judith Sargent Murray at her home in Boston. "I have dined with this lady," he reported, "and was . . . pleased to find that her literary pursuits did not interfere with her domestic virtues; she is a most excellent wife, and one of the best of mothers, and the perfect order . . . of her house-hold declares her a complete housewife. . . ."[55]

The poetess Sarah Wentworth Morton couched her apologia in her best Della Cruscan style. She had heard criticisms of "application to literature in a female" but felt they were founded on misunderstanding. She herself could not spare time for poetry during the busy winter months. "It is only amid the leisure and retirement, to which the sultry season is devoted, that I permit myself to hold converse with the Muses; nor does their enchantment ever allure me from one personal occupation, which my station renders obligatory; but those hours, which might otherwise be lost in dissipation, or sunk in languor,

---

of Innocence [1805] (Boston, 1828), ii; Wood, Julia and the Illuminated Baron (Portsmouth, N.H., 1800), iv, and Dorval; or the Speculator (Portsmouth, 1801), iv. See also Mrs. Wood's Introduction to Ferdinand and Elmira (Baltimore, 1804), 3-4. This authoress took up writing during a long widowhood, after her children were grown. She remarried in 1804 and is usually known by her second husband's name though she ceased to write after she acquired it.

55 Julia, 82.

are alone resigned to the unoffending charms of Poetry and Science."[56]

Such evidence should have been more than enough to allay the fears of people who half expected to find a female pedant in every authoress. This popular stereotype -- an aggressive lady who neglected her person and her home for useless study -- had, as we have seen, long stood in the way of improvements in women's education. These first-generation professional writers were consciously trying to escape the taint. By 1829 we find the Irish Lady Morgan (Sydney Owenson) declaring the myth exploded. Author of forty volumes of poetry, novels, and travel, Sydney Morgan preened herself on the fussy feminine décor of her Dublin home. "What a disappointment to . . . visitors, who expect to find her in the midst of that . . . literary litter, intellectual disorder, and . . . neglect of all the elegancies of ordinary life, which marked the menages of the femmes-savantes of the late and preceding centuries! -- the broken tea-cup (substituted for a wine-glass) of Mary Wolstonecraft [sic]! or the Scotch mull and brown pocket-handkerchief of Catherine Macauley [sic]! . . . ."[57]

It was reassuring to learn that women authors led a normal

---

56 Introduction to Beacon Hill (1797), quoted in Emily Pendleton and Harold Milton Ellis, Philenia, The Life and Works of Sarah Wentworth Morton, 1759-1846 (University of Maine Studies, XXXIV, no. 4, Orono, 1931), 64.

57 The Book of the Boudoir (New York, 1829), I, 172-173. On Catharine Macaulay, see below, note 103.

family and social life, but what about the effect of fame on their character and conduct? One secret of Maria Edgeworth's enormous popularity was her perfect and happy conformity to the age's ideals of feminine behavior. Modest and self-effacing, she wrote not for personal aggrandizement but only to be useful. Fame sought her out, but it could not spoil her. Never, observed Willard Phillips of the North American Review, "has her brilliant success betrayed her into any display of the pride of authorship." "She never seems to pause to admire her own powers of composition, or to wait for the admiration of her readers" was high praise from an Edinburgh reviewer.[58]

The same could be said of Elizabeth Hamilton. When she came to live in Edinburgh, the force of her example dispelled conservative Scottish distrust of bluestockings. Mrs. Hamilton's "kind heart and unpretending manners . . . set the sneers of prejudice at defiance. . . . No one that ever knew her could discover that she founded any pretensions on authorship, or that she valued her literary reputation on any other ground but as a means of usefulness."[59]

---

58 [Francis Jeffrey], "Miss Edgeworth's Tales of Fashionable Life," Edinburgh Review, XX (July, 1812), reprinted in Analectic Magazine (Philadelphia), I (January, 1813), 24; [Willard Phillips], "Miss Edgeworth's Harrington and Ormond," North American Review, VI (January, 1818), 157; [Jeffrey], "Miss Edgeworth's Popular Tales," Edinburgh Review, IV (July, 1804), 331.

59 Elizabeth Benger, Memoirs of the Late Mrs. Elizabeth Hamilton (London, 1818), I, 176-177. Mrs.Hamilton herself made a point of declaring that "arrogance and ambition . . . are alike foreign to my heart." Letters on the Elementary Principles of Education (Boston, 1825), II, 23.

Far from feeling elated over their achievement, some authoresses found acutely painful the publicity it brought them. One's first experience of appearing in print could be a shocking ordeal, especially when taken unawares. This happened to Elizabeth Hamilton, whose journal of a tour in the Scottish highlands was sent by a friend "to a provincial magazine, in which it appeared to the unspeakable dismay of the youthful writer" who thus became "the object of curiosity and criticism to her neighbours. . . ." When sixteen-year-old Caroline Howard of Cambridge, Massachusetts, "learned that my verses had been surreptitiously printed in a newspaper, I wept bitterly, and was as alarmed as if I had been detected in man's apparel."[60]

Fanny Burney committed Evelina print voluntarily, though taking elaborate precautions to keep her identity secret. Nevertheless, when she heard that the novel was in demand at all the circulating libraries, she felt "an exceeding odd sensation." It was almost as if she herself were exposed on the shelf to the stares of the public.[61] Miss Burney in 1778 was

---

60 Benger, Memoirs, I, 52; Caroline Howard [Gilman] is quoted by Helen Grey Cone in "Woman in Literature," Woman's Work in America, Annie Nathan Meyer, ed. (New York, 1891), 110.

61 Frances Burney D'Arblay, Diary & Letters of Madame D'Arblay, Charlotte Barrett, ed. (London, 1904), I, 23. Even after Evelina had become the rage of London, Fanny tried desperately to conceal her authorship. When another guest at Mrs. Thrale's began to talk about the novel at supper, "My heart beat so quick against my stays that I almost panted with extreme agitation, from the dread either of hearing some horrible criticism, or of being betrayed: and I munched my biscuit as if I had not eaten for a fortnight." Diary, I, 93.

writing before female authorship had become commonplace. As
late as 1806, however, the Philadelphia Port Folio was publishing a disapproving letter "On Literary Women" which declared that a female "the finest of whose thoughts, and the
most delicate of whose sentiments, every bookseller will give
for a little silver" had forfeited all claims to privacy.[62]

Experienced writers, too, sometimes shrank from celebrity.
Even after the crashing success of her Gothic romances in the
1790's Mrs. Ann Radcliffe lived in such seclusion that the
public had assumed she was dead for years before she died in
1823. Mrs. Radcliffe would have been welcomed into the most
cultivated society, "but a scrupulous self-respect . . . induced her sedulously to avoid the appearance of reception, on
account of her literary fame. The very thought of appearing in
person as the author of her romances shocked the delicacy of
her mind." Having created a work of art, Ann Radcliffe, like
Fanny Burney, had yielded to an "odd inclination to see it in
print," but "nothing could tempt her to publish herself. . . ."[63]

62 "Fragment of a Letter of a Mother to her Daughter on the
  Education of Young Ladies, and on Literary Women," Port
  Folio, n.s., I (March 1, 1806), 122, reprinted in the
  Boston Magazine, I (March 15, 1806), 82.

63 [Thomas Noon Talfourd], "Memoir of the Life and Writings of
  Mrs. Radcliffe," in Ann Radcliffe, Gaston de Blondeville
  [1802] (London, 1826), 12-13; Charles Burney, Memoirs (1832),
  II, 129, quoted in Charlotte Barrett, "Editor's Introduction,"
  Diary & Letters of Madame D'Arblay, I, 16. Mrs. Radcliffe
  had no children, so "the duties of a family did not engross
  her attention," but she preferred her husband's companionship
  to other society. When she became famous "she chose at once
  the course she would pursue, and, finding that her views met
  the entire concurrence of Mr. Radcliffe, adhered to it
  though life." Talfourd, "Memoir," 13.

The shy or fastidious authoress could also take refuge in anonymity. For one's first venture into print this was the usual rule, especially in the field of fiction, since beginning novelists were most likely to be inexperienced females who not only lacked confidence but also, like Mrs. Sally Wood, knew "that writers of Romance are not highly estimated."[64] Writers of serious literature were less fearful of public criticism and probably realized also that a moral or educational treatise of uncertain authorship would win little attention. The successful authoress in any field, however, usually permitted her name to appear on the title page as soon as her reputation was established. Even Ann Radcliffe brought herself to sign her third novel. (Fanny Burney, on the other hand, even after she had become the pet of literary London and had written a second and, in 1796 at the age of fifty-four, a third novel, clung to the transparent disguise, "by the author of Evelina.")[65]

In general, among both the British and the American fair, the amateur hid behind her veil while the professional drew it aside. Ladies who wrote for a living could not afford to indulge

---

64 Julia, iii.

65 Elizabeth Hamilton signed her work from the beginning, though with misgivings. (Benger, Memoirs, I, 128-129.) Maria Edgeworth, after her first try, did likewise, except in the case of Castle Rackrent, which was a private project, written without her father's hand at her elbow. Hannah More and Laetitia Barbauld published the poems and plays of their youth anonymously, then signed their serious and improving works of later life. Jane Austen's novels appeared anonymously during her lifetime.

delicate scruples when their literary reputation was part of
their stock in trade. This no doubt was why "judicious friends"
insisted that the historian Hannah Adams steel herself to "pre-
fixing her name" to her first book.[66] The only other American
lady who was financially dependent on her pen, far from suffering qualms over the publicity, used her title pages for discreet
advertising. The famous Charlotte Temple was "By Mrs. Rowson,
of the New theatre, Philadelphia," while later books were la-
beled "by Susanna Rowson, preceptress of the Ladies' academy,
Newton, Mass."

Authoresses without this airtight excuse for writing were
more careful of appearances. Hannah Foster, well-to-do wife
of a prominent clergyman, identified herself only as "a Lady
of Massachusetts." As the granddaughter of a rich Maine trader
Sarah Wood could also dispense with what her generation euphe-
mistically liked to term "pecuniary emolument." Her four novels
therefore appeared under the same modest alias. (Social pressure rather than timidity seems to have determined Mrs. Wood's
decision, however. Her prefaces were so volubly personal that
one suspects she did not enjoy playing the part of the shrinking
authoress but in reality had a guilty hankering for fame.) In
sophisticated circles anonymity could become a mere stylish convention. Everybody who was anybody in Boston, for instance, knew

---

66 Adams, An Alphabetical Compendium of the Various Sects Which
Have Appeared in the World from the Beginning of the Christian
Æra to the Present Day (Boston, 1784), i.

that "the divine Philenia" was Sarah Wentworth Morton, "the laurelled Nymph," center of the city's most select literary coterie in the 1790's.[67]


Even those more assured women who could face print with reasonable equanimity, with their names emblazoned on the title page, found other ordeals in store for them. For one thing, the business dealings involved in getting a book out were "a peculiar trial" to the sheltered female who, instead of encountering the polished executive of a big modern publishing house, had to haggle with a local printer-bookseller who was oftentimes crude and unmannerly and perhaps a sharp operator as well.[68] Then once the book was safely through the press she

67 Pendleton and Ellis, Philenia, 48. "Philenia" and the other feminine aliases affected in this circle were imitations of the English poet Robert Merry and his friend Mrs. Hannah Cowley, who under the names "Della Crusca" and "Anna Matilda" carried on an effusive literary flirtation in verse which was reprinted in Boston papers.

68 Sarah Josepha Hale, then a rising literary lady of the younger generation, referred understandingly to these difficulties when reviewing A Memoir of Miss Hannah Adams for her Ladies' Magazine in 1832. (V [May, 1832], 239.) Miss Adams's own experiences were harrowing. She was "completely duped by the printer, in making the bargain" for her first book, receiving nothing but fifty copies in payment, while the book had a good sale. A clergyman friend handled the arrangements for her the next time, with better results, but in the case of two later books, "the printer failed while it was in the press, which deprived me of the profit I expected to derive from it." The agonies Miss Adams endured "in doing business out of the female line, which exposed me to public notice" were almost as painful as her financial losses. Memoir, 15, 21, 31, 33-34.
 English women also suffered embarrassment in their "attempts of trafficking with booksellers." (An article on

might be drawn into one of those public disputes common in a
day when vindictive feuds and jealousies were endemic in the
literary world.

Fortunately most authoresses were spared the necessity of
"doing business out of the female line." In nearly every case
a male relative was standing by, ready not only to take entire
responsibility for marketing her manuscripts but also to give
help and encouragement while she wrote. Elizabeth Hamilton took
up authorship at the behest of a beloved brother. Jane Austen's
family, all "great Novel-readers and not ashamed of being so,"
must have egged her on to write. Her father sent her first
story to a publisher, and after his death one of her brothers
took over all the arrangements. Richard Edgeworth had a paternal

---

"Female Authorship" in Charles Brockden Brown's Literary
Magazine and American Register, IV [October, 1805], 254-255,
thus refers to the trials of a British poetess who "looked
up to her pen for a resource.") A Minerva Press tale of 1789
contained a description of a young lady's attempt to sell
her novel to a publisher. "The politeness that passed at
the [first] interview, shall be buried in oblivion." She
then tried another establishment, only to discover that she
had strayed into a magazine house by mistake. "At this
period, disconcerted and distressed," she turned to William
Lane of the Minerva, and her troubles were over. Lane, she
discovered, "receives these kind of light airy readings" with
encouraging politeness. "Flattered by this, I informed him
I did not present the book from any pecuniary motives, as it
was the employment of my leisure hours; but if worthy of
being printed, a small compliment would not be unacceptable.
-- Have you, madam, ever favoured the public before? I had,
but my name must be concealed." In the upshot, "This work
[was] . . . presented to the shrine of public favour."
Beneath the advertising and obvious satire on the popular
feminine style this passage has a ring of authenticity.
Dorothy Blakey, The Minerva Press, 70-71.

finger in nearly all Maria's literary pies from start to finish.  Ann Radcliffe began writing at her husband's urging, to while away the lonely evenings when he had to work on his newspaper.  The "pecuniary advantages" she derived from her later novels, large sums then unprecedented for works of fiction, were no doubt Mr. Radcliffe's achievement.[69]

A husband or father, however, could not ward off malicious rumors or prevent a woman from becoming innocently involved in public controversy.  Mrs. Radcliffe, for instance, suffered severe pain when it was hinted that she had taken credit for the anonymous plays of another lady.[70]  Frequently masculine parties to a literary quarrel would not escape without having their politics and their religion flayed as well as their supposed literary offenses.  This state of affairs was sometimes alleged to be an insuperable barrier to female authorship.  Since such treatment was hard enough for men to take, "women, who have more susceptibility of temper, and less strength of

69 Benger, Memoirs of Mrs. Hamilton, I, 125; Jane to Cassandra Austen, December 18, 1798, Letters of Jane Austen, Edward, Lord Brabourne, ed. (London, 1884), I, 178; C. Linklater Thomson, Jane Austen, A Survey (London, 1929), 27, 15; Talfourd, "Memoir of Mrs. Radcliffe," 7-8, 12.  Hannah Adams's father tried to help her with her affairs, but being equally impractical he succeeded no better than she.

70 Talfourd, Memoir," 90.  "Women have no means of manifesting the truth, nor of explaining the particulars of their life: if any calumny is spread concerning them, the public hears it; but their intimate friends alone can judge of the truth."  This statement by Madame de Staël was reprinted from the English Universal Magazine by the Philadelphia Analectic Magazine, I (April, 1813), 362.

mind, and who, from the delicate nature of their reputation, are more exposed to attack," would hardly be able to endure it.

So argued a gentleman of the old school in Maria Edgeworth's dialogue "Letters for Literary Ladies."[71] The most notable case of this sort, in American annals at least, seems to prove that such fears were groundless. This dispute involved the Reverend Jedidiah Morse, Boston clergyman and writer of geography books, and Miss Hannah Adams, a worthy female of humble origins and humbler manners who had earned a modest reputation as a compiler of popular reference works on religious and historical subjects. The ostensible issue was the Rev. Mr. Morse's alleged invasion of Miss Adams's territory by publishing in 1804 a history of New England for schools just as Hannah Adams, who had previously produced a full-length history of the region, was on the point of making an abridgment of it for the same market. This was hard luck for Miss Adams, who needed the money to support herself and her aged father. The episode, however, would probably never have became a cause célèbre if she had not happened to know some Boston ministers of the Unitarian faction who were already battling Morse, a pillar of the old Con gregational orthodoxy, over the appointment of a liberal to the chair of theology at Harvard College. So pitiable was Miss Adams's need, and so bitter were their feelings against Morse,

71 Works of Maria Edgeworth (Boston, 1824), II, 14.

that the excited Unitarians immediately took up cudgels in her
defense.

The controversy raged for years in a newspaper, letter, and
pamphlet war that did not finallywear itself out until 1814.
It was a distressing experience for Miss Adams, who suffered
from an almost pathological shyness, but she survived it in
better shape than her opponent. Morse, a somewhat obtuse but
honorable man, found himself in an impossible position, for
Hannah Adams in all innocence was using lethal arguments against
which there was no defense. "Had I no reason to complain, that
. . . [Dr. Morse] should enter on a literary ground preoccupied
by me, a helpless woman, dependent on the scanty products of
my pen for subsistence?"[72] Then, as if this injustice were not
enough, "he now adds the cruel injury of dragging me before the
public. . . ." It did little good for Dr. Morse to reply that
Miss Adams "has suffered herself to be 'dragged before the
public,' as a shield to certain individuals, acting under the
influence of a party," when in return she could ask her fellow-
citizens "whether this . . . public attack, upon an unoffending
female, does not imply a want of the common feelings of a man
. . . ?[73]

Every crisis in the controversy reduced Hannah to a state

---

72 Adams, A Narrative of the Controversy between the Rev. Jedidiah Morse, D.D. and the Author (Boston, 1814), 8.

73 Morse, An Appeal to the Public (Charlestown, 1814), 10, 13-14.

of nervous and physical collapse. The worry and strain made
Morse ill, too, but that gave him no claim on public sympathies. He felt the whole thing was unfair. "The truth is,
gentlemen," he declared to the referees appointed at one stage
to judge the case, "Miss A. and her complaints, against me;
her sex, her merits, her bodily infirmities, her poverty, her
aged parents, &c. all together, furnished to my . . . adversarie
an admirable weapon with which they might wound me." Out of an
affair which "in its origin and design, was among the most innocent and laudable transactions of my life"[74] he had had nothing
but grief. One of his sons later wrote that Morse's "influence
in Boston and its vicinity was indeed, to a great extent, de-
stroyed by it."[75] The Unitarians won another battle, and timid,
helpless Hannah Adams emerged from the uproar in greatly improve
circumstances. In 1809 her Unitarian friends relieved her financial embarrassments permanently by raising an annuity for
her.[76] The controversy ruined the sale of Morse's ill-starred
history, while Miss Adams's abridgment became a standard school
text.[77] Her later books enjoyed flattering critical acclaim and

---

74 Ibid., 93, 131.

75 William B. Sprague, The Life of Jedidiah Morse (New York,
1874), 276-277; James King Morse, Jedidiah Morse (New York,
1939), 101.

76 Morse, Appeal, 120; Harris E. Starr, "Hannah Adams," Dictiona
of American Biography, I.

77 Sprague, Life of Morse, 276-277; [Sidney Willard], "Adams'
Religions," North American Review, VII (May, 1818), 87.

a steady sale,[78] while a new confidence was reflected in her prefaces. Abandoning the abject apologies with which she had issued her early works, she now simply requested from her readers "a continuance of the same candid indulgence I have so long experienced."[79]

---

78 Most of the American magazines gave Miss Adams's works enthusiastic reviews. A sample would include Port Folio, ser. 3, VIII (July, 1812), 41; General Repository and Review, III (April, 1813), 393; North American Review, VI (May, 1818), 86-91 and XX (April, 1825), 367 (the last by Jared Sparks). Charles Brockden Brown had earlier singled her works out for praise in his Monthly Magazine and American Review, I (September-December, 1799), 446-447, and American Review and Literary Journal, II (January-March, 1802), 38-41. She was generally commended for her accuracy and objectivity, especially in her Dictionary of All Religions, which went through four editions in the United States and one in England.

79 A Dictionary of All Religions (New York, 1817), 4. At her death in 1831 she had the distinction of being the first person buried in the new Mt. Auburn Cemetery in Cambridge. There is no good modern account of this interesting episode and its implications. The biographies of Morse mistake the issue involved and call it plagiarism. This charge was only a side-issue, based on a malicious rumor (started by a Harvard student) that Morse had copied from a manuscript lent him by Miss Adams. She vigorously denied this, though not until the rumor had spread all over New England and New York. The real issues, clouded from the beginning with emotion but recognized on both sides, were 1) Morse's competing with Miss Adams in a field she regarded as her own and with a book from which after years of struggle and poor health she was hoping to win financial security, and 2) Hannah Adams's hurt feelings at Dr. Morse's neglecting to acknowledge her contributions to New England history in the preface to his text. This omission, she maintained, "slighted and injured [her], in her reputation as a writer." (Morse, Appeal, 91.) Morse's 200-page Appeal printed all the documents in the case as well as his rage at his predicament; Hannah Adams summed up her side of the argument clearly and simply in her Narrative. She mentions it only briefly in her posthumous Memoir.

When a frail woman like Hannah Adams could pass unscathed
through the worst perils of authorship, sturdier souls had
little to fear. Maria Edgeworth thought there was little reason for literary ladies to be disturbed by either the "malignant envy of critics" or "the idle remarks of the ignorant
vulgar." After all, were their reputations actually suffering
through their exposure to the public view? Sydney Smith turned
a blast of cold common sense on the shrinking sisterhood. Indeed, "it may be an evil for ladies to be talked of: but we
really think those ladies who are talked of only as Miss Edgeworth, Mrs. Barbauld, and Mrs. Hamilton are talked of, may bear
their misfortunes, with a very great degree of christian patience
. . ."[80]

The timidity with which the women authors faced the public
arose only partly from a distaste, real or affected, for the
limelight. They were also suffering genuine misgivings about
the literary defects of their work. Anxious prefaces repeatedly
tried to fend off criticism by admitting inadequacies in advance
and stressing high motives and good intentions. In presenting
her novel The Gamesters to the world Caroline Warren was

---

[80] Edgeworth, Letters for Literary Ladies (Works, II), 14, 21;
Smith, "Female Education," Port Folio, ser. 3, IV (July,
1810), 110. The Port Folio took Smith's essay from the
Edinburgh Review, XV (January, 1810).

"confident the work would not pass unscorched through the fiery ordeal of criticism. . . ." It was "the production of a youth, whose education has been limited, whose opportunities have been penurious. . . ." Miss Warren herself, however, would be content if her pages "lure one profligate from the arms of dissipation, or snatch from the precipice of ruin, one fair fabric of innocence," and she believed that "the really learned and virtuous" critics "will approve the intention, though a want of merit should oblige them to censure the execution of the work." Sarah Wood was "very sensible" that her "simple style" lacked grace and power. Nevertheless, she reflected with some pleasure that if her book could not win "the praise of the literati, it will not offend the moralist. . . ."[81]

Even Susanna Rowson took out insurance. It was all very well, she wrote in her preface to Mentoria, to please "those partial friends whose kind encouragement prompted me to submit these pages to the inspection of the public"; the reviewers were another matter. "Yet, conscious that I never wrote a line that would convey a wrong idea to the head, or a corrupt wish to the heart, I sit down satisfied with the purity of my intentions, and leave it to the happy envied class of mortals, who have received a liberal education, to write with that taste and elegance which can only be acquired by a thorough knowledge of the

81 The Gamesters, ii-iv; Wood, Julia, ix.

classics."[82]

While the authoress worried over her reception at the hands of the critics, the critics debated what attitude they should assume toward productions of the female pen. It was their responsibility to pass judgment upon her work for the guidance of readers at large. Should they subject it to the same frank analysis as they gave the writings of brother authors? Or did they owe the same chivalry to woman in her professional as in her social capacity? It was a foregone conclusion. Most of the women were writing special kinds of literature in a particular style for a restricted audience. To judge them by the same standard as men would obviously be unfair. To censure the lucubrations of a modest female would be churlish. Chivalry would be the order of the day -- so long at least as the authoress played the part of lady sans reproche to the knights of journalism.

Not every female writer, to be sure, won the complete suspension of judgment granted to Susanna Rowson by a London reviewer of her first book. "The author wishes to inculcate filial piety; and she has executed her design in a number of well-chosen pathetic tales. In such a cause Criticism smooths his brow, and takes off his spectacles, willing to see no fault. She who

---

[82] Mentoria; or the Young Lady's Friend (Philadelphia, 1794), I, iii-v.

would support the cause of piety and virtue cannot err."[83]

But most critics couched what censure was inescapable in terms

of elaborate politeness. The gentleman assigned the task of

reviewing Poetical and Moral Pieces by young Lydia Huntley of

Connecticut for the Analectic Magazine in 1815 was a model of

tact if not of syntax. "With a heart full of tenderness, ben-

evolence and friendship, and a mind purified and warmed by re-

ligion, her effusions all appear to be tinctured with these

virtues; and though not perhaps aspiring to gain . . . lasting

renown, yet we think she has succeeded in weaving . . . 'A

Garland of domestic flowers,' that will win affection, though

it may not command applause."[84] (The reviewer apparently had

---

83 Critical Review (January, 1787), quoted in R. W. G. Vail,
Susanna Haswell Rowson, the Author of Charlotte Temple,
American Antiquarian Society, Proceedings, XLII (1932), 148.

84 Analectic Magazine, V (March, 1815), 262. Writers of higher
caliber of course received more serious treatment. After
pulling their punches in review after review the critics
greeted a new work of Maria Edgeworth's, for instance, with
relief. Here was a writer "whose genius is of that vigorous and healthful constitution as to allow the fair and
ordinary course of criticism to be administered. . . . No
demands on the tenderness of the schoolmaster; -- no puling
appeal to sex or age; -- no deprecation of the rod! Praise
may be awarded -- severe truth may be told -- and the Reviewer be . . . guiltless. . . ." "Miss Edgeworth's Patronage,"
Edinburgh Review, XXII (January, 1814), 417, reprinted in
the Analectic Magazine, IV (July, 1814). Most reviewers felt
apologetic about criticizing even sturdy Miss Edgeworth,
however. In view of her own indifference to literary merit
and her engrossing concern for moral teaching many thought
artistic canons should not be applied at all. See Willard
Phillips's "Miss Edgeworth's Harrington and Ormond," North
American Review, VI (January, 1818), 159, a review which
echoed (and lifted some phrases from) Francis Jeffrey's
article on the same Edgeworth novels in the Edinburgh the
previous summer. (XXVIII, [August, 1817], 392.)

no premonition of the fame and profits that were to accrue to
Miss Huntley when as Mrs. Sigourney she became the household
poet of the next generation.)

American authoresses could present another claim to clem-
ency almost as powerful as a pure heart. Patriotism, it was
hoped, would cover a multitude of sins. As she brought forth
her second novel in 1801 Sarah Wood was sure she could never
compete with "a Moore [sic]" or "a Burney." But she felt her
attempts would be worthwhile if they inspired other American
women "better qualified to instruct and amuse" to contribute
to a native literature. Then "I am sure that no future author
would agree with the Abbe Raynal, 'That America had produced
but few persons of genius' . . . . The following pages," she
concluded proudly, whatever their faults, "are wholly American.
. . . The author has endeavoured to catch the manners of her
native land. . . ."[85]

Sarah Morton, in presenting her first long poem (a romantic Indian tale) to the public in 1790, likewise hoped that
"the attempting a subject wholly American will in some respect
entitle me to the partial eye of the patriot."[86] Mrs. Morton
need not have worried. She was not only a woman but a beautiful and charming one, and incidentally the queen of Boston
society. Furthermore, since poets -- the aristocrats of

---

85 _Dorval_, iv-v.

86 Pendleton and Ellis, _Philenia_, 44-45.

literature -- were rare in America, patriots smarting under a
sense of inferiority to the mother country easily persuaded
themselves that in Philenia they had another Sappho.[87]  Even
her hackneyed Della Cruscan effusions were extravagantly
praised, and when it became known that she had undertaken an
epic commemorating the Revolution, to be dedicated to "the
Citizen-Soldiers, who fought, [and] conquered . . . under the
banners of WASHINGTON and FREEDOM," American bosoms swelled
with pride.  An orator at the Harvard Phi Beta Kappa exercises
in 1797 prophesied that the work "will do honor to the country
that gave it birth, and induce the candid critics of the
English Reviews to appreciate their estimation of cis-Atlantic
genius."  Unhappily, however, epic poetry proved to be beyond
Philenia's slender talents.  When the first installment of the
long-awaited masterwork appeared, the flattering voices were
hushed in disappointment.  Silence spoke louder than words to
sensitive Sarah Morton.  The epic was never finished, and
Philenia symbolized the passing of her vogue by retiring to
country life in the fashionable suburb of Dorchester.[88]

Ardent patriot or no, any woman who took up authorship

---

87 The editors of the Massachusetts Magazine dubbed Mrs. Morton
"the Sappho of America" in 1791.  (Pendleton and Ellis,
Philenia, 52.)  Her fellow-authoresses paid her generous
tributes; see, for example, Foster, Boarding School, 201;
Hannah Mather Crocker, Observations on the Real Rights of
Women (Boston, 1818), 45; Wood, Julia, 81.

88 Pendleton and Ellis, Philenia, 62-63, 67.

under the stern pressure of financial necessity could count
on immediate succor and encouragement. The picture of a lone,
unprotected female speeding pen over paper with one eye on the
wolf at the door was bound to touch popular sensibilities.
Novelists, particularly, found the public "indulgent to the
critical errors of pages composed for its amusement, under
circumstances, not of vanity or choice, but of necessity. . . ."
As the ordinarily sharp-tongued Quarterly Review put it, "In
such cases criticism became but a secondary duty; for his feelings would not be much envied, who would pause to examine the
construction of a sentence, when not the pursuit of fame, but
the fear of distress, evidently dictated the production."[90]

89 Sydney Morgan, quoted in William John Fitzpatrick, The
   Friends, Foes, and Adventures of Lady Morgan (Dublin, 1859),
   85.

90 [John Mitford and William Gifford], "Mary Russell Mitford's
   Poems," Quarterly Review, IV (November, 1810), 514. Even
   the supercilious young Bostonians of the Monthly Anthology
   circle, ordinarily caustic on the subject of female authorship, softened before this plea. Reviewing a novel written
   by a girl of eighteen, "residing in an obscure town, and by
   her needle maintaining her aged parents," Joseph Tuckerman
   held his fire. "We do not recollect any American female,
   except Mrs. Rowson, who has written a novel which can be
   read with any pleasure; and we are not disposed to encourage
   the exertions of females to become known as authors, unless
   convinced that the amusement and instruction which they can
   furnish will extend beyond the circle of their own partial
   friends. Considering however the age at which it was written, and the peculiar embarrassments of the author, the novel before us is deserving of commendation." (Monthly
   Anthology, II [May, 1805], 267-268. The novel in question
   was Emily Hamilton [Worcester, 1803], by one Eliza Vicary.)
   When Mrs. Rowson deserted novels for poetry she did not
   fare so well at the Anthology's hands. "From the respectable manner in which we understand she fulfils the duties of
   life," wrote S. C. Thacher in 1804, "we took up her volume
   with a disposition to be pleased. We have given our approbation to her intentions; but to say, that she possesses in

Woe betide even the needy authoress, however, if she transgressed the code of propriety. The critics might be ready and willing to overlook slips of the female pen, but not slips in female conduct. Any trace of vulgarity was of course most improper. (Frowning over a Minerva Press novel of 1817, the American Monthly Magazine and Critical Review took the author to task for indulging in scenes and allusions "very suitable indeed to the pages of Tom Jones and Roderick Random, but altogether inconsistent with that chasteness of sentiment, and delicacy of language, which ought to character-ize the works of female writers."[91]) Egotism called for stern remonstrance, little piety for shocked rebuke. The worst of-fender, however, was she who intruded into men's most sacred sphere, the realm of politics.

Naturally it was a rare authoress who had the slightest desire to tread on this forbidden ground. Mrs. Sarah Wood skirted it with elaborate care. Caught up by the war hysteria in 1798, Mrs. Wood read with fascinated horror a book which pur-ported to expose an international conspiracy fomented by a society of "Illuminati" in Bavaria to spread the doctrines of

any high degree the qualities of a poet is praise, which, if we would descend to offer, the publick would not endure." I (November, 1804), 612.

91 II (January, 1818), 236; Blakey, Minerva Press, 257.

anarchy, atheism, and free love.[92]  This was clearly fine
material for a novel, but after she had cleverly combined
the themes of distressed womanhood and freethinking villainy
in Julia and the Illuminated Baron she began to have misgivings.
The story, she feared, "may, by some, be considered, a political
work; as I have ever hated female politicians, I think it absolutely necessary to declare it is not; intirely [sic] unacquainted with politics, I should have viewed a revolution of
the greatest part of Europe as it respected them, with uncon-
cern and indifference. . . ."  Yet when a political upheaval
threatened to shake loose religion and morality from their
moorings in society, Sarah Wood felt it was woman's duty to help
sound the alarm.[93]

One or two British authoresses openly flouted the taboo
and took the consequences.  The irrepressible Sydney Morgan
championed the cause of Irish nationalism through a series of
novels and then in 1816 brought down a storm of critical wrath
on her head for a travelogue extolling the Revolutionary reforms

---

92 In view of her interest in the subject it seems likely that
Mrs. Wood had read John Robison's Proofs of a Conspiracy
(Edinburgh, 1797), or perhaps listened to some of the ser-
mons by Federalist clergymen like Jedidiah Morse which
helped spread Robison's lurid tales around her region.
Vernon Stauffer gives an account of this Red Scare, occa-
sioned by the cold war with France, 1798-1800, in New
England and the Bavarian Illuminati (New York, 1918).

93 Julia and the Illuminated Baron, A Novel: Founded on Recent
Facts, Which Have Transpired in the Course of the late Revolution of Moral Principles in France, vii-ix.

in France. Too good a daughter of Erin to miss a chance for a fight, Lady Morgan retorted to her reviewers with gusto, much to the entertainment of the host of readers who refused to take either Sydney or her opinions seriously.[94] Such an experience, however, could be a shattering ordeal for a woman of more sensitive temperament. The barrage of abuse that Anna Laetitia Barbauld received in 1811 for her poem protesting against England's interminable war with France caused her to give up writing altogether, thus ending a distinguished forty-year career.[95]

America's only politically-minded authoress managed to wield a pungent pen in party causes and yet escape public censure. Mrs. Mercy Otis Warren owed this good fortune primarily to the fact that until the very end of her career her partisan writings appeared anonymously. It was daring enough for a lady to take a part in the controversies of Mrs. Warren's day even with this protection; without it she would not have written at all.

Mercy's authorship was of course no secret to her family and friends. Indeed they put the pen in her hand and insisted that she use it. A week after the Boston Tea Party jubilant

---

94 Lionel Stevenson has written an excellent biography of Lady Morgan, The Wild Irish Girl (London, 1936). She was a particular favorite in America.

95 Grace A. Oliver, The Story of the Life of Anna Laetitia Barbauld, with Many of Her Letters (Boston, n.d.).

John Adams was writing James Warren to "Make my compliments to Mrs. Warren, and tell her that I want a poetical genius to describe a late frolic among the sea-nymphs and goddesses." Flattered, Mercy obliged with several pages of heroic couplets celebrating the "late glorious event" in the best Augustan style.[96] A few months previously she had contributed to the cause a satirical drama called The Adulateur, which pictured the struggle of a band of noble Romans (the patriot leaders in thin disguise) against a rapacious tyrant representing Tory Governor Thomas Hutchinson, and the next year she renewed the attack on Tory officialdom in The Group.[97] Her husband and Adams at first circulated these pieces privately in manuscript, but Mercy had so well expressed the feeling of the revolutionary party, at fever pitch during these years just before the war, that her plays were soon published.

Questions of propriety now arose. Was it seemly for a lady to indulge in political satire? Mercy Warren, apprehensive at seeing The Group in print, applied to John Adams for reassurance. Even though "the particular Circumstances of our unhappy time" might justify "a little personal Acrimony . . . in your Sex," she asked him, "must not the female Character

---

96 John Adams to James Warren, December 22, 1773, The Works of John Adams, Charles Francis Adams, ed. (Boston, 1850-1856), IX, 335. The poem is quoted in Alice Brown, Mercy Warren (New York, 1896), 107-109.

97 Moses Coit Tyler, The Literary History of the American Revolution, 1763-1783 (New York, 1897), II, 193-198.

suffer"? Adams, replying, dismissed the question of sex.
"The faithful Historian," he told Mercy, "delineates Characters truly, let the Censure fall where it will. . . ." In
any case, he added gallantly, he knew of no genius, ancient
or modern, which had combined "the keen and severe" with "the
Soft, the Sweet, the amiable and the pure in greater Perfection" than her own.[98]

James Warren also reassured his wife when a few weeks
later Boston rumor, to her distress, identified her as the
author of The Group. "God has given you great abilities;" he
told her, "you have improved them in great Acquirements. . . .
They are all now to be called into action for the good of Mankind, for the good of your friends, for the promotion of
Virtue and Patriotism. Don't let the flutterings of your Heart
interrupt your Health of disturb your repose."[99]

Both men, long accustomed to sharing their public interests
with their wives, had little use for the polite convention which
barred women from this field. On the contrary, Adams wrote
Warren in 1775, "I have ever been convinced that Politicks and
War, have in every Age been influenced, and in many, guided and
controuled by . . . [the] Sex." Yet, he added, even if he

98 Mercy Warren to John Adams, January 30, 1775, Warren-Adams
Letters (Boston, 1917-1925), I, 37; John Adams to Mercy
Warren, March 15, 1775, ibid., 42, 44.

99 James Warren to John Adams, February 20, 1775, ibid., 41;
James Warren to Mercy Warren, April 6, 1775, ibid., 46.

believed it "best for a general Rule that the fair should be
excused from the arduous Cares of War and State," he would certainly regard his wife Abigail and Mercy Warren as exceptions,
"because I have ever ascribed to those Ladies, a Share and
no Small one neither, in the Conduct of our American Affairs."[100]

Twelve years passed before Mercy again entered a political
fight, and by this time the Warrens and the Adamses had parted
company. Adams had been shocked at his old friend's defense
of Shays's Rebellion in 1786, and when James Warren joined the
forces fighting the ratification of the federal constitution
in Massachusetts the following year the breach was complete.
It was just as well John and Abigail did not know that "The
Columbian Patriot" who wrote one of the most vehement pamphlets
against ratification was Madam Mercy Warren. This time Mercy's
secret remained inviolate.[101]

Ever since the Revolution associates of the Warrens had

---

100 Adams to Warren, September 26, 1775, ibid., 115. Busy with
preparations for the first Continental Congress the previous year, Adams had written Warren that they would have to
leave it "to Mrs. Warren, and her friend Mrs. Adams, to
teach our sons the divine science of the politics;' adding
with a smile, "and to be frank, I suspect they understand
it better than we do." June 24, 1774, The Works of John
Adams, IX, 339.

101 The pamphlet was long attributed to Elbridge Gerry, its
real authorship remaining unknown until 1932, when Charles
Warren published a letter from his ancestress "whispering"
the secret to her friend Mrs. Catharine Macaulay Graham
in England. Charles Warren, "Elbridge Gerry, James Warren,
Mercy Warren and the Ratification of the Federal Constitution in Massachusetts," Massachusetts Historical Society
Proceedings, LXIV (Boston, 1932), 143-164. The Warren-
Adams Letters of the 1780's clearly reveal the widening
breach over the issues of the Confederation period.

known that Mercy was working on a history of that conflict,
using the expert inside knowledge she had acquired through
her family connections. It was 1805, however, before the long-
awaited work finally appeared, the title page now proclaiming
the name of its author, "Mrs. Mercy Warren, of Plymouth,
Mass."[102] By this time Mercy was seventy-seven, but even at
her advanced age she felt impelled to account for this venture
into past politics. Her mind, she said frankly, had never
"yielded to the assertion, that all political attentions lay
out of the road of female life." Certainly it was "the more
peculiar province of masculine strength, not only to repel the
bold invader of the rights of his country, . . . but in the
nervous style of manly eloquence, to describe the blood-stained
field. . . ." As she thought of this, her hand had "often
shrunk back from the task." Yet the recollection "that every
domestic enjoyment depends on . . . civil and religious liberty,
that a concern for the welfare of society ought equally to glow
in every human breast" had made her persevere.[103]

---

102 This was actually not Mrs. Warren's first publicly acknowledged work; her Poems, Dramatic and Miscellaneous, including
the Tea Party piece and some other poems of the Revolutionary
period (but not her satirical dramas) had appeared in Boston
in 1790. The Massachusetts Magazine had politely reviewed
the volume, declaring none of the works "destitute of poetical merit" but remarking that "our fair writer's . . . Poems,
which are inscribed to family or friends . . . breathe a
milder note" than her political verses. (II [September,
1790], 559, [November, 1790], 692.)

103 History of the Rise, Progress and Termination of the American Revolution, Interspersed with Biographical, Political

Proud of her literary talent and continually thirsting
for praise, Mrs. Warren must have hoped at last to hear the
thunder of popular applause. The public, however, received
her life work in chilly silence. None of the leading magazines
of the day reviewed it, old friends ignored it, few copies
were sold. Mrs. Judith Sargent Murray, unsuccessfully solicit-
ing subscribers for her friend's book, put her finger on the
trouble in a tactful letter: "very many," she wrote, "urge the
political principles attributed to the otherwise admired
writer, as a reason for withholding their signatures."[104]

Mercy Warren, alas, had written not a bona-fide history

_____

and Moral Observations (Boston, 1805), I, iv.

In her efforts as chronicler of the Revolution Mercy
Warren had both the example and the personal encouragement
of the English woman historian Mrs. Catharine Macaulay
Graham, author of an eight-volume history of England from
the accession of the Stuarts (published between 1763 and
1783) and a radical Whig who ardently sympathized with the
American rebellion. Mrs. Macaulay Graham, a woman of
marked ability and vigor, withstood harsh attacks from
English critics during all her career for her liberal
views, her unseemly presumption in writing, and her second
marriage, at forty-seven, to a stripling of twenty-one.
Her republican convictions naturally proved more accept-
able to Americans, many of whom, like Mercy Warren, so
much respected "the superiority of her Genius" that they
were willing to "draw a veil over the foibles of the Woman."
"The celebrated Mrs. Macaulay" was cordially received when
she traveled in America in 1784 and 1785, and was entertaine
at Mount Vernon and in the homes of other prominent citizens
like the Warrens. Her history was so full of partisan
rancor as to make it nearly worthless as a record. Brown,
Mercy Warren, 58-61; William Prideaux Courtney, "Mrs.
Catharine Macaulay," Dictionary of National Biography.

104 Judith Murray to Mercy Warren, June 1, 1805, Warren-Adams
Letters, II, 346.

but another anti-Federalist tract. Embracing the principles of Jefferson's Republican party "With all the strong passions of a female," as a contemporary put it,[105] she had used her chronicle of the Revolution (extended to 1797) to snipe at the Federalists in general and her old friend John Adams in particular. To launch this sort of history into the arch-Federalist New England of 1805 was inviting disaster. Madam Warren's age, her sex, and her family's prestige restrained critics from open attack; the only alternative was to ignore the book.[106]

This, however, was beyond the endurance of its principal

105 William Bentley, The Diary of William Bentley, D.D. (Salem, 1905-1914), III, 233.

106 John Adams's judgment on the work, though hardly cool, was essentially correct: "Mrs. Warren, it is my opinion, and that of all others of any long experience that I have conversed with, that your History has been written to the taste of the nineteenth century, and accommodated to gratify the passions, prejudices, and feelings of the party who are now predominant. The characters are not such as you esteemed them in the times when they acted. . . ." Adams to Mercy Warren, August 15, 1807, Correspondence between John Adams and Mercy Warren Relating to Her "History of the American Revolution," July-August, 1807, Massachusetts Historical Society, Collections, 5th ser. IV (Boston, 1878), 463. Mrs. Warren's relatives tried to avoid the touchy subject. Her Federalist nephew Harrison Gray Otis jokingly refused to be drawn into a political argument in 1809, adding, "To be serious, my dear Aunt, my respect and affection for you, are so utterly at variance with the political views and party attachments which to my great sorrow and mortification you have been led to embrace; that I have for twenty years, studiously evaded all discussions of the last, lest the former might be brought into jeopardy." Otis to Mercy Warren, February 4, 1809, Warren-Adams Letters, II, 362. Mercy finally decided there must be "a combination to sink into oblivion . . . a late History of the Revolution." To John Adams, August 27, 1807, Correspondence between John Adams and Mercy Warren, 1807, 489.

victim. John Adams's public career had now ended, but back
on his Braintree farm the ex-president smarted from a feeling
that his countrymen had not appreciated his services. Mercy's
barbed words reopened old wounds. Wrathfully Adams sat down
in the summer of 1807 and for six week bombarded Mrs. Warren
with a series of letters protesting her insinuations. "Pride
of talents and much ambition," she had written, "were undoubtedly combined in the character of the president who . . . succeeded general Washington. . . ."[107] Adams angrily fired back where
he knew it would hurt most. "If it was not 'pride,' it was
presumption of 'talent,' in a lady," he told her, "to write a
history with . . . so little impartiality."

Mercy, however, could use this weapon too. It was "wonderful," she rejoined, that Adams "should have lost all sense
of decency and politeness due to the sex, even where there is
no friendship. . . ."[108] Only when both parties had run out
of ammunition did the battle cease, leaving them further es-
tranged than ever. In time, however, tempers cooled; Governor
Elbridge Gerry was eventually able to arrange a reconciliation
which reunited the two old couples in something like their old
cordial friendship. Locks of hair were exchanged in token of
affection, and once more John Adams addressed flattering

---

107 History of the American Revolution, III, 393.

108 Adams to Mercy Warren, July 30, 1807, Correspondence, 382;
     Mercy Warren to Adams, August 7, 1807, Ibid., 422.

compliments to "the historical, philosophical, poetical, and satirical consort of . . . General James Warren of Plymouth." Yet the old enthusiasm was gone. "History," Adams privately maintained to Gerry, "is not the Province of the Ladies."[109]

Mercy Warren was hardly a typical authoress, nor did the public usually regard her in this light. The drama of her authorship was played out in private; the common reader to whom the names of Barbauld, Edgeworth, and More were household words hardly knew that she existed. When at the turn of the quarter century critics paused to take stock of women's literary record, they were thinking rather of the females who had conveyed "virtuous principle" to the public "through the medium of books of amusement."[110]

"Until within a comparatively recent period," observed Alvan Lamson of the North American Review as he turned his attention to the New York edition of Mrs. Barbauld's Works in 1826, "the appearance of a female writer . . . was a rare phenomenon. . . . Our female literature has now swollen to a

---

109 Letters recording Gerry's efforts are printed in the appendix to ibid., 495ff. Adams to Mrs. Warren, July 15, 1814, Works of John Adams, X, 99; Adams to Gerry, April 17, 1813, Warren-Adams Letters, II, 380. The reconciliation took place in 1812.

110 F. W. P. Greenwood, "Hope Leslie," North American Review, XXVI (April, 1828), 410.

large bulk." The ladies had rescued fiction "from the service of corruption and profligacy, . . . converting it into a powerful agent in correcting the moral judgment." They had demonstrated the need for a children's literature and done something to fill it.[111]

Women had indeed sensed a popular demand and found that their special training in morals and conduct and their experience in family living was all the equipment needed to meet it. They had sent new kinds of reading matter into homes all over England and the United States, providing entertainment and instruction as it were to an enlarged family circle. Writing, they were discovering, was a new activity which brought gratifying influence and prestige without disturbing in the least the comfort and security of their accustomed way of life.

By 1825 the English-speaking public had come to think it quite natural for women to be useful and agreeable in literature as they were in life. This settled concept of female authorship, however, had recently received a jolt through one of those unpredictable accidents of women's history, the appearance of a woman whose genius easily overflowed the bounds society set for her sex. The literary wonder of the western world in the second decade of the century was the Swiss-born Madame de Staël, critic, cosmopolite, and conversationist, whose dramatic escape from Napoleon's Europe brought her to public attention in England

---

111 North American Review, XXIII (October, 1826), 368-369.

and America in 1813.[112] British critics now rediscovered her
pioneering study De la Littérature (1800), which had toppled
over the arbitrary rules of classical criticism by demonstrating
how social and political forces had shaped the literature of
every age and nation differently. They hailed the publication
in London of her De l'Allemagne, an analysis of German character and thought which in effect introduced the principles of
romanticism to the rest of Europe.[113]

Writing of this caliber was rare from any hand; from a
woman it was sensational. Editor Francis Jeffrey of the
Edinburgh Review expressed the general amazement in a leading
article quickly reprinted across the Atlantic.

> While other female writers have contented
> themselves, for the most part, with embel-
> lishing or explaining the truths which the
> more robust intellect of the other sex had
> previously established, -- in making
> knowledge more familiar, or virtue more en-
> gaging . . . , -- this distinguished person
> has not only aimed at extending the boundar-
> ies of knowledge, . . . but has uniformly
> applied herself to trace out the operation
> of general causes. . . .

"We are not acquainted, indeed," Jeffrey was frank to admit,
"with any writer who has made such bold and vigorous attempts
to carry the generalizing spirit of true philosophy into the
history of literature and manners. . . ." When Madame de

---

112 Lydia Maria Child, The Biographies of Madame de Staël and
Madame Roland (Boston, 1832), 86.

113 Gustave Lanson, Histoire de la Littérature Française, 19th
edition (Paris, 1912?), 882-885.

Staël's untimely death ended her career in 1817, the voice of the Edinburgh was only one of a chorus mourning the loss of "the most brilliant writer that has appeared in our days. . . . -- and the greatest writer, of a woman, that any time or any country has produced."[114]

By comparison with this exotic Parisian plant the home-grown product looked drab. Madame de Staël, as Lord Byron inelegantly put it in a letter to his publisher, "beats all your natives hollow as an authoress. . . ."[115] Sadly a few critics began to see their favorites for the first time in larger perspective. "Of these writers," wrote Alexander H. Everett in the North American Review, "Miss More has the least femality . . . in her mode of thinking and writing; but her style, though pure and manly, has no grace and little power, and her reach of mind is limited. Though remarkable as a writer, she is quite secondary in the general literary scale. In the works of Miss Edgeworth, however interesting and valuable, we catch not unfrequently a glimpse of the petticoat."[116] The

---

114 "Mad. de Staël -- Sur la Literature [sic]" in Edinburgh Review, XXI (February, 1813), 2-3 and Analectic Magazine (Philadelphia), II (September, 1813), 178-179; [Francis Jeffrey], "Mad. de Staël sur la Revolution Françoise [sic]," Edinburgh Review, XXX (September, 1818), 275. These opinions were many times echoed in both British and American periodicals.

115 To John Murray, January, 1814, quoted in Child, Madame de Staël, 92.

116 "Posthumous Works of Madame de Stael," XIV (January, 1822), 112.

others -- Rowsons, Mortons, Woods -- were not even in the
running.

Pursuing this train of thought led to speculation as to
why women so rarely achieved that "variety of knowledge, flex-
ibility of power, elevation of view, and comprehension of
mind"[117] with which Germaine de Staël had dazzled her readers.
Clearly the role which society expected women to play was not
one which encouraged either the development or the expression
of individual talent. "While men," observed Edward Everett,
"are allowed to be as peculiar, . . . as independent as they
wish, and are prized in proportion to their originality, their
poor wives and daughters are almost as much subjected to the
fashion of time and place in their characters and pursuits, as
in their dress." Furthermore, as Theophilus Parsons pointed
out, little mental effort was likely to be made by a sex from
which little was expected.[118]

These, however, were the solitary reflections of a few
literati. The majority of the reading public enjoyed the
spectacle of a female genius without bothering about its implications. Nor were they so ready as the literati to judge
the lady solely on her literary merits. It was common knowledge

---

117 "De L'Allemagne, par Mad. de Stael" [from the Edinburgh
Review], Analectic Magazine, III (April, 1814), 308.

118 Everett, "Miss Edgeworth," North American Review, XVII
(October, 1823), 387-388; Parsons, "Life and Writings of
Madame de Staël," North American Review, XI (July, 1820),
126.

that Madame de Staël's private life had been stormy and by
Anglo-Saxon standards not above suspicion. In their eyes their
own authors lost no luster by comparison. "While, then," concluded the Philadelphia Analectic Magazine, "we . . . class her
with the most powerful intelligences and eloquent writers of
the age, we find her far less respectable, -- as she must
have found herself, with all her celebrity, far less happy, --
than the Mores, the Edgeworths, and the Hamiltons, of Britain,
whose lives and writings conspire to strengthen the sacred
delicacy of their sex, and to teach the true ends of female
ambition."[119]

119 "Madame de Stael," [an original American article], XII
    (August, 1818), 106.

CONCLUSION

# CONCLUSION

Any study of changing ideas about women, whatever its period, raises certain problems of method and material. Of these the most important is the question of scope. How comprehensive can the historian be? Whose ideas will be discussed? And what women? The reader of the foregoing pages will have noted that the account refers often to "the middle class" or "the upper classes," rarely to the lower ranks in society. Obviously this choice of subject matter calls for justification. The reader may at times have felt, too, that he was forming a better picture of English than American attitudes from a study professing to describe ideas about women in the United States. He may wonder also why the story ends in 1825. Some attempt to throw light on these questions is therefore relevant.

In the absence of a hereditary aristocracy, social standing in America has usually been determined by economic status and hence been gained or lost with greater ease than in stratified societies. This has an important effect on people's thinking, for a man who expects to rise in the social scale will study the attitudes of his superiors and imitate them so far as he is able. This in turn makes it difficult for the historian to define class attitudes in this country with much exactitude.

His task is easiest in the seventeenth century. The first

279

colonists were nearly all middle-class folk, yeomen or arti-
sans, with a scattering of gentry occupying the seats of
spiritual and temporal power. And the rigors of pioneer life
in the early days tended to perpetuate a middle-class citizenry.
With hard work everyone could make a decent living; no one
starved, but few grew rich either. When a Puritan minister,
therefore, discoursed on the duties of the female sex, inculcating the virtues of industry, sobriety, and godliness, we
can be sure that he was speaking to all his people, expressing
values meaningful alike to his own spouse, to the governor's
lady, and to the ordinary goodwife.

Eighteenth-century society was less homogeneous. With the
rise of plantation, land and shipping fortunes, as we have
seen, an upper class came into being. It was this group, stead-
ily augmented by able young men from the middle ranks, which
ran the provincial governments, provided most of the leadership
for the American Revolution, and then directed the affairs of
the nation until the end of the period covered by this study.
Socially this element tended to identify itself with the leisure
class in England; the wealthiest and most fashionable of them
followed English manners and customs with almost slavish fidelity, expecting their women to be as delicately bred as the
best English models. As a whole, however, this indigenous
aristocracy had a strong middle-class tinge. Few of its members were far enough from their origins -- or had money enough --
to forget their old ways entirely.

John Adams, for instance, may (as his enemies charged) have imbibed undemocratic ideas in England, but he and his wife lived to the end of their lives in unassuming simplicity. Visitors to their Massachusetts farm in later years could find the ex-First Lady shelling beans for the family dinner like any housewife.[1] Benjamin Franklin rose from a printer's apprentice to move easily with ministers and kings, but his wife, who had helped him run the shop during their early married life, remained a thoroughly middle-class person, never accepted even by Philadelphia society, and refusing to cross the ocean to share her husband's triumphs. Franklin saw to it that his daughter was brought up in sensible fashion and instructed in housewifely skills, yet he sent her to dancing school and counseled her to read The Ladies Library, a handbook inculcating the attitudes of patrician Englishwomen.[2]

Obviously the lines are difficult to draw. Both the upper and middle classes apparently found the views of the long series of English writers from Lord Halifax to Hannah More congenial, notwithstanding that the books were specifically written for women of the aristocracy. The cabinetmaker's daughter could profit by Mrs. Chapone's rules for the improvement of the mind and probably read her directions for handling

---

1 William Bentley, The Diary of William Bentley, D.D. (Salem, 1905-1914), IV, 556.

2 Carl Van Doren, Benjamin Franklin (New York, 1941), passim; Mary S. Benson, Women in Eighteenth-Century America (New York, 1935), 133.

a large staff of servants with as much interest as the daughter of the merchant prince. The few Americans who tried their hand at the genre toward the end of the century evidently saw nothing inappropriate in the tone of the standard English works, since they pitched theirs at the same social level. Even though the leisure-class life was outside the experience of all but a few Americans, it seems to have set the social standard for the greater part of the reading population.

The non-reading population remains unaccounted for. Closely associated though the middle and upper ranks may have been, they regarded the lower orders of society from across a wide gulf. The laboring-class woman existed in large numbers in England and was not unknown in America even in the seventeenth century. Yet one looks in vain for any recognition of her in the didactic works addressed to the female sex, in the popular literature of the time, in the private letters and memoirs commenting on women's place in the social scheme. The reason is not hard to find: if questioned by a visitor from another planet, any writer of the time would have explained that the condition of the working class was immutably fixed by divine decree[3] (or natural law); it was unnecessary to define it and would be ridiculous to question it.

Toward the end of the period, under stimulus of the

---

3 M. G. Jones discusses this attitude in her Hannah More (Cambridge, 1952), 235-236.

religious revival, the humanitarian conscience of the nineteenth century was beginning to stir. The ladies who busied
themselves in the charitable societies of the early 1800's
were quite unconsciously making the first breach in the old
theory, merely by acknowledging the female poor as a problem.
As we have seen, however, they had no wider goal than to correct the moral and religious errors of these unfortunates,
and their efforts were short-lived. The humanitarian impulse
would gather strength only when infused with the democratic
spirit of the next generation. For the most part the more
privileged groups remained unconcerned, and since the prole-
tarian woman herself was too inarticulate to express her own
views of her situation, this study has largely had to pass her
by.

Fortunately for the historian's purposes, women of the
upper classes were always causing controversy. Every major
economic change altering their way of life forced an adjustment
in ideas about women's place; every shift in the intellectual
climate produced a challenge to accepted theory which in turn
brought about reforms in practice. The development of ideas
on female education illustrates the process.

The American girl of the seventeenth century began in
early childhood to learn from her mother the difficult skills
required to run a household, picking up from her father, also
at home, some knowledge of farming or trade which would enable
her later to give her husband a helping hand at his work. She

needed little formal schooling, just enough to read an occasional devotional work, cookery book, or herbal. Beyond the rudiments she might, if she lived in a trading community, study enough bookkeeping to manage the accounts of a small family business, as Cotton Mather advised.

Custom is slow to change, and to some conservatives this sort of training still seemed good enough even when the empire-wide commerce of the eighteenth century, showering prosperity on the colonies, had relieved women of many former responsibilities. More fashionable people, however, scorned "that vulgar system of education which rounded the little circle of female acquirements within the limits of the sampler and the receipt-book."[4] Instead, they advocated a program tailored to the life of leisure to which everyone could now aspire. The modern young lady would acquire the ornamental accomplishments and feminine graces suitable for ballroom or drawing room, together with such a smattering of the liberal arts as would enable her to enter into polite conversation. The best authorities also enjoined strict training in an artificial code of conduct designed to preserve her delicacy and purity intact in a society which under its veneer could be both coarse and dissolute.

By 1790, however, such a scheme seemed woefully inadequate. Fired with new social ideals, this generation had higher ends

---

4 Hannah More, Strictures on the Modern System of Female Education (The Complete Works of Hannah More [New York, 1835], VI), 55.

in view for women. Criticism of the contemporary system came
from every side: from Americans like Benjamin Rush and Noah
Webster, interested in the theories of Rousseau; from Mary
Wollstonecraft, inspired by the Revolutionary doctrine of the
rights of man; from Mary's arch-foe Hannah More, armed with the
militant faith of the religious revival. All joined in condemning the ornamental education which, they said, had created
an idle, vain, and worldly race unfit for woman's proper duties.

In the hubbub of voices the spokesmen of the religious
revival prevailed; their program largely replaced the old.
These earnest reformers wished to put the leisure of upper-
class women to use: in careful attention to the rearing of
children, in practicing and promoting Christian principles in
home and community, in works of charity. To prepare women to
perform these functions writers like Hannah More recommended,
besides rigorous religious training, the reading of solid works
of history and literature, more for the sake of moral discipline,
however, than for the intellectual content. Accomplishments
would by no means be banned ("Piety maintains no natural war
with elegance," Hannah declared[5]); they would add the finishing
touch appropriate for a lady without monopolizing her time.

Little of this, of course, was education in the modern
sense. That would wait until an industrial society, taking
shape in America after 1825, developed new demands for women's

---

5 Ibid., 46.

services requiring regular schooling like that of men. What
this earlier day called "education" was largely home training:
for the seventeenth century, in the exacting vocation of
housewifery; for the eighteenth, with its leisure-class ideals
for women, in character, deportment, polish, and grace.


With the upper classes consciously aping English practices,
it is little wonder that colonial America turned to English
writings on the subject of women. But social conditions in
the New World by no means duplicated those of the homeland. Did
no distinctive ideas arise during two centuries of separate development? More important, when the Revolution made a conscious
political break with the mother country, did it have no social
counterpart? Should the historian still trace changing American ideas in terms of English writers even after 1776?

One early contrast with English life which has often been
stressed was the more privileged status women enjoyed in America. Certainly they had greater freedom of choice in marrying,
since wives were in short supply, and they probably bore greater economic responsibility. Yet it evidently never occurred
to the colonists to alter their theories about woman's place
because of this. The seventeenth-century maiden, for instance,
surely had little chance of being left a spinster, but she apparently dreaded this fate as much as her English cousins. At

least we find Cotton Mather in 1692 scolding girls who thought it such "a Great Curse to be an Old Maid" that they used "any Hasty Method to get into the Married Row," sometimes even "taking a Bad Husband meerly to avoid the . . . Reproach of having None. . . ."[6]

Mather's book, to be sure, grew out of a local situation; it was part of his campaign to stop the backsliding of his people from the strenuous Puritanism of pioneer days. Nevertheless the arguments he employed in urging the daughters of Zion to abjure worldly for spiritual ornaments were wholly traditional, some of them having survived unchanged since medieval times.

The only other work of this sort produced in colonial America, Benjamin Franklin's Reflections on Courtship and Marriage, was little more original. One suspects that Franklin wrote the pamphlet mostly for fun, as another salable item to run off on his press. The section on courtship is a good copy of the Spectator both in style and content. The sequel on marriage Franklin devoted to humorous aspersions on two extremes in a wife, the slattern and the fussy housekeeper, both evidently pet abominations. His lapse from the sophisticated into the practical was probably not a bad mirror of the colonial state of mind, a combination of trying to live up to European

---

6 Mather, Ornaments for the Daughters of Zion (Cambridge, 1692), 74-75.

standards while relaxing much of the time into simpler ways dictated by American circumstances.

It remained for the post-Revolutionary generation to call these standards into question, though with rather ironic results. At the end of the war, when anti-British feeling ran high, some patriots were in a mood to cut all cultural as well as political ties. "It is high time to awake from this servility," announced Benjamin Rush in 1787, " -- to study our own character -- . . . and to adopt manners in every thing, that shall be accommodated to our state of society and to the forms of our government." The first step was to establish new systems of education suitable for rearing citizens of a republic. The education of young women in particular, Rush felt, "should be conducted upon principles very different . . . from what it was when we were a part of a monarchical empire."[7]

We have already seen how Rush and his fellow-theorists Noah Webster and Enos Hitchcock pressed for a more practical training so that American girls might be helpmates for men with their fortune to make and fit mothers of future citizens. Yet despite all the patriotic fanfare their program was neither very new nor very American. The concept of educational reform as the first step in building a more perfect society itself came from Europe's Enlightenment. Progressive thinkers in England like the Edgeworths were likewise reorienting the

---

7 Rush, Thoughts upon Female Education (Boston, 1787), 19, 5.

upbringing of girls along more practical lines. Of the Americans only Rush advocated any thoroughgoing change, for his
plan omitted the ornamental accomplishments entirely; the
others were content "to shew the necessity of uniting to them,
the knowledge and habits of domestic duties."[8] None of these
writers gave any thought to educating women below the upper
classes; in becoming republicans they had lost none of their
aristocratic prepossessions. Enos Hitchcock and Hannah Foster
in their educational treatises in fictional guise pictured
family life in a "mansion" with "spreading lawns" and "shady
groves" that could have doubled for any English estate, asserting their Americanism chiefly in recommending the reading
of native authors and in urging ladies to rely on their own
taste in dress rather than on British fashions. Noah Webster
may have insisted on American spelling in his "Address to Yung
Ladies," but when he informed female readers that "To be lovely . . . you must be content to be wimen; to be mild, social
and sentimental,"[9] he was speaking the language of Dr. Fordyce
and Dr. Gregory.

These English classics, as we have seen, continued to sell
as briskly in the states as they had in the colonies. Americans
perhaps read them more critically now. Before the Revolution,

---

8 Enos Hitchcock, Memoirs of the Bloomsgrove Family (Boston,
1790), II, 32.

9 Webster, "An Address to Yung Ladies," A Collection of Essays
and Fugitiv Writings (Boston, 1790), 411.

for instance, booksellers had reprinted Gregory's Father's
Legacy verbatim, but in 1792 when the Philadelphia publisher
Mathew Carey was preparing to include this standard work in
his Lady's Pocket Library, one section caught his eye. "A
woman in this country has very little probability of marrying
for love," Dr. Gregory had written. "These observations are
happily inapplicable in America," Carey commented in a foot-
note, "although perfectly just in Great-Britain."[10] Yet in
1800 the Maine belle Eliza Southgate read the same passage in
a discouraged mood and found that the doctor's opinion exactly
coincided with her own.[11]

By the turn of the century Americans had given up their
premature attempt at cultural independence. The nation was
well established; feeling against Britain had died down, and
with it the self-conscious patriotism of the Revolutionary era.
Independence had after all wrought few changes in American society, and in any case the work of the new school of English
moralists like Hannah More was so distinguished as to defy competition. With one exception no one in the United States made
any serious effort to define women's sphere between Hannah
Foster's The Boarding School in 1798 and the end of the period
under study.[12] Evidently Americans could now once again accept

---

10 The Lady's Pocket Library (Philadelphia, 1792), 107.

11 See above, chapter III, pp. 138, 140 and note 33.

12 The exception was a homely tract written in 1818 by Mrs.
Hannah Mather Crocker of Boston, a granddaughter of Cotton

intellectual dependence without resentment and even feel a
certain pride in sharing a common culture, while adopting what
was practical in English thought and ignoring what was not.


Not until after 1825 did the United States stand on its
own feet and speak its own mind.  In the second quarter of the
century the democratic ferment, which had been slowly working
since the Revolution, finally produced the distinctively American society that the patriots had wished for.

What democratic America had in store for women was apparent
as early as 1819, when Emma Willard published her plan for a
new type of female seminary, a state-supported school offering
a standardized course of solid studies.  This would be education in the broad sense, a necessity, Mrs. Willard maintained,
if American women were to discharge their heavy responsibilities
as mothers in a republic.  Such a seminary would also fit girls
to become teachers in the common schools and thus indirectly
raise the educational standards of the whole nation.  Mrs.
Willard failed in her attempt to secure funds from the New York

---

Mather, under the title Observations on the Real Rights of
Women.  A woman of independent mind, Mrs. Crocker admired
the ideas of both Mary Wollstonecraft and Hannah More.  Her
book, written in the Yankee vernacular, was a curious attempt
to amalgamate the two, to prove "in a pleasant manner" that
"though there are appropriate duties peculiar to each sex,
yet the wise Author of nature has endowed the female mind
with equal powers and faculties. . . ." (p. 5).  It seems
to have attracted little attention.

legislature, but she founded her school with private aid and
began to educate the women of the next generation.[13]

Close behind her was Mrs. Sarah J. Hale, who launched the
Ladies' Magazine in Boston in 1828 "with the determined purpose
of making it a work . . . conducive to the improvement and advancement of woman. . . ." Sentiment and seduction found no
place in this periodical, which featured instead improving essays on topics of interest to women, book reviews, and "effusions of female intellect."[14] The elevation of her sex had been
Hannah More's aim also, but in a narrowly religious sense, within the confines of the home. Mrs. Hale had in mind an "enlarged
sphere of female talent and influence,"[15] including teaching
and social work. Hannah More had addressed herself only to the
upper class; Sarah Hale invited everybody to read her magazine,
and when she became editor a few years later of Godey's Lady's
Book, the country took her at her word.

Democratic America had no place for the languishing lady
of the eighteenth century. "Females, who turn their existence
to no good account, contradict the intention of their Creator,"
announced Mrs. Lydia H. Sigourney of Hartford in her Letters to
Young Ladies of 1833. "Publick opinion has not been sufficiently

---

13 Alma Lutz, Emma Willard (Boston, 1929), passim.

14 Ladies' Magazine, IX (December, 1836), 718-719; I (January,
1828), 3.

15 Godey's Lady's Book, XXXIII (November, 1846), 235-236.

distinct, in its reproofs of their aimless life." Mrs. Sigourney had little to say on the subject of manners but much on the virtues of plain living and useful work, advising even the affluent young lady to learn some means of supporting herself in case of necessity.[16] Here was the first handbook for young women with a distinctively American viewpoint. The Letters became a best-seller in the United States and were widely re-printed in Great Britain, where one publisher alone disposed of five thousand copies by 1840.[17]

Mrs. Willard, Mrs. Hale, and Mrs. Sigourney were the pro-gressives of their day, moving in advance of general opinion. Nevertheless, they were setting forth ideas which would become common currency in the next generation. In their lives and in their writings they proclaimed a new standard of female charac-ter. The ideal woman was no longer a delicate ornament to aris-tocratic society, a charming companion for men's leisure hours. The female who passed her time in social gaiety or, if religion taught her an obligation to be useful, in playing lady bountiful, was disappearing from the scene. In her place, as America moved toward democracy, a new ideal was taking shape: a woman who would be an individual rather than merely one of "the fair sex," educated as well as accomplished, with a sense of responsibility for the world she lived in as well as for her own home.

---

16 Letters to Young Ladies (New York, 1839), 233, 87.
17 Gordon S. Haight, Mrs. Sigourney (New Haven, 1930), 56.

# BIBLIOGRAPHY

# BIBLIOGRAPHY

This study is based entirely on printed materials. Among the primary sources the most important are the following: didactic works addressed in whole or in part to women (such as sermons, guides to manners and morals, and popular treatises on education); contemporary novels; contemporary magazines; and personal memoirs. Of the magazines, the literary periodicals proved most useful. With one or two exceptions the feeble ladies' magazines of the day were not consulted for this study, since their stereotyped contents are of small value and have been fully described by Bertha M. Stearns in her excellent series of articles.

The majority of the didactic works cited appeared first in England. For this study of American opinion, however, American editions have ordinarily been used, and these are the ones listed here. Those of English origin are identified in the text and footnotes.

Among the secondary works consulted is a large group of writings on literary history which provided background on the rise of the woman author. The bibliography also includes a list of works on women's history which are significant for this period, with critical comments growing out of the experience of this study. Some of the biographies and a few of the general histories also make important contributions to women's history.

295

PRIMARY SOURCES

I. Didactic Works: Handbooks, Tracts, Sermons, Treatises, etc.

Adams, Hannah, An Abridgement of the History of New-England for the Use of Young Persons. Boston, 1805.

[Adams, John], Sketches of the History, Genius, Disposition, Accomplishments, Employments, Customs, Virtues, and Vices, of the Fair Sex, in All Parts of the World. Gettysburg, 1812.

Aikin, John, Letters from a Father to His Son. Philadelphia, 1796.

Aikin, Lucy, Epistles on Women, Exemplifying Their Character and Condition in Various Ages and Nations. Boston, 1810.

[Allestree, Richard?], The Ladies Calling. 5th impression. Oxford, 1677.

The American Lady's Preceptor. Baltimore, 1811.

The American Spectator, or Matrimonial Preceptor. Boston, 1797. This handbook and the one immediately above consist of essays reprinted chiefly from familiar British writers.

Baldwin, Thomas, A Discourse, Delivered before the Members of the Boston Female Asylum. Boston, 1806.

Bennett, John, Letters to a Young Lady. Philadelphia, 1818.

Bennett, John, Strictures on Female Education. Philadelphia, 1793.

Bentley, William, A Discourse Delivered . . . at the Annual Meeting of the Salem Female Charitable Society. Salem, 1807.

Branagan, Thomas, The Excellency of the Female Character Vindicated. N. Y., 1807.

Brown, Charles Brockden, Alcuin. New Haven, 1935. A facsimile reprint of the first edition, 1798.

Chapone, Hester Mulso, Letters on the Improvement of the Mind, Addressed to a Lady. Boston, 1782.

297

Crocker, Hannah Mather, Observations on the Real Rights of Women, with Their Appropriate Duties, Agreeable to Scripture, Reason and Common Sense. Boston, 1818.

[Crocker, Hannah Mather], A Series of Letters on Free Masonry. By a Lady of Boston. Boston, 1815.

Dana, Daniel, A Discourse Delivered . . . before the Members of the Female Charitable Society of Newburyport. Newburyport, 1804.

Dana, Daniel, A Sermon Delivered before the Gloucester Female Society for Promoting Christian Knowledge. Newburyport, 1815.

Eckley, Joseph, A Discourse, Delivered before the Members of the Boston Female Asylum. Boston, 1802.

Edgeworth, Maria, and Richard Lovell Edgeworth, Practical Education. 2 v. N. Y., 1801.

Emerson, William, A Discourse Delivered before the Members of the Boston Female Asylum. Boston, 1805.

Fordyce, James, Sermons to Young Women. Philadelphia, 1787.

[Foster, Hannah Webster], The Boarding School; or, Lessons of a Preceptress to Her Pupils: . . . Calculated to Improve the Manners and Form the Character of Young Ladies. Boston, 1798.

Gardiner, John S. J., A Sermon, Delivered before the Members of the Boston Female Asylum. Boston, 1809.

Gisborne, Thomas, An Enquiry into the Duties of the Female Sex. London, 1798.

Gregory, John, A Father's Legacy to His Daughters. N. Y., 1775.

Hamilton, Elizabeth, Letters Addressed to the Daughter of a Nobleman, on the Formation of Religious and Moral Principle. 2 v. Salem, 1821.

Hamilton, Elizabeth, The Letters of a Hindoo Rajah. 2 v. Boston, 1819.

Hamilton, Elizabeth, Letters on the Elementary Principles of Education. 2 v. Boston, 1825.

Hamilton, Elizabeth, A Series of Popular Essays, Illustrative of Principles Essentially Connected with the Improvement of the Understanding, the Imagination, and the Heart. 2 v. Boston, 1817.

Hitchcock, Enos, Memoirs of the Bloomsgrove Family. 2 v. Boston, 1790.

Jay, William, Thoughts on Marriage. Boston, 1833.

Knapp, Samuel Lorenzo, Letters of Shahcoolen, A Hindu Philosopher Boston, 1802.

Lathrop, John, A Discourse Delivered before the Members of the Boston Female Asylum. Boston, 1804.

Mather, Cotton, Ornaments for the Daughters of Zion, or the Character and Happiness of a Vertuous Woman: in a Discourse which Directs the Female-Sex how to Express, the Fear of God, in Every Age and State of their Life; and Obtain both Temporal and Eternal Blessedness. Cambridge, 1692.

Morse, Jedidiah, A Sermon . . . before the Managers of the Boston Female Asylum. Boston, 1807.

Morse, Jedidiah, and Elijah Parish, A Compendious History of New England, Designed for Schools and Private Families. Charlestown, 1804.

Murray, Judith Sargent. The Gleaner. 3 v. Boston, 1798.

Nott, Eliphalet, A Discourse Delivered ... . before the Ladies' Society for the Relief of Distressed Women and Children. Albany, 1804.

Parker, Thomas, The Copy of a Letter Written by Mr. Thomas Parker, Pastor of the Church of Newbury in New-England to his Sister, Mrs. Elizabeth Avery, Sometimes of Newbury in the County of Berks, Touching Sundry Opinions by her Professed and Maintained. London, 1650.

Rowson, Susanna Haswell, Mentoria; or the Young Lady's Friend. 2 v. Philadelphia, 1794.

Rush, Benjamin, Thoughts upon Female Education. Boston, 1787.

A Series of Letters on Courtship and Marriage. Springfield, 1796. Includes Benjamin Franklin's Reflections on Court-ship and Marriage (1746).

Stillman, Samuel, A Discourse, Delivered before the Members of the Boston Female Asylum. Boston, 1801.

Taylor, Ann H., Maternal Solicitude for a Daughter's Best Interests. N. Y., 1816.

Taylor, Ann H., Practical Hints to Young Females, on the Duties of a Wife, a Mother, and a Mistress of a Family. Boston, 1816.

Taylor, Ann H., Reciprocal Duties of Parents and Children. Boston, 1825.

Taylor, Isaac, Advice to the Teens. Boston, 1820.

Wadsworth, Benjamin, The Well-Ordered Family: or, Relative Duties. Boston, 1712.

[Warren, Mercy], Observations on the New Constitution, and on the Federal and State Conventions. By a Columbian Patriot. Boston, 1788.

Webster, Noah, A Collection of Essays and Fugitiv Writings. Boston, 1790.

West, Jane, Letters to a Young Lady, in Which the Duties and Character of Women Are Considered. Troy, 1806.

Willard, Samuel, A Compleat Body of Divinity. Boston, 1726.

Wollstonecraft, Mary, A Vindication of the Rights of Woman. London, 1792.

## II. Fiction, Drama, and Poetry, Including Juveniles

Barbauld, Anna Laetitia, and John Aikin, Evenings at Home, or the Juvenile Budget Opened: Consisting of a Variety of Miscellaneous Pieces for the Instruction and Amusement of Young Persons. 2 v. Boston, 1813.

Barbauld, Anna Laetitia, Hymns in Prose for Children. Newburyport, 1813.

Barbauld, Anna Laetitia, and Maria Edgeworth, Lessons for Children. N. Y., 1824.

The British Novelists. Anna Laetitia Barbauld, ed. 50 v.
London, 1810. Mrs. Barbauld's essays on the individual
authors in this series and her general preface in the
first volume on the development of fiction are an expression of the best critical thought of the time.

Bradstreet, Anne, The Works of Anne Bradstreet. John Harvard
Ellis, ed. Charlestown, 1867.

Brown, Charles Brockden, Ormond; or, the Secret Witness.
Philadelphia, 1887.

Brown, William Hill, The Power of Sympathy. 2 v. N. Y.,
1937. A facsimile reprint of the first edition, Boston,
1789.

[Burney, Frances], Evelina. 2nd ed. 3 v. London, 1779.

Edgeworth, Maria, The Parent's Assistant. Philadelphia, 1854.

Edgeworth, Maria, Tales and Novels by Maria Edgeworth. 18 v.
N. Y., 1832-1834.

[Foster, Hannah Webster], The Coquette. Boston, 1833.

The History of Little Goody Two-Shoes. Charles Welsh, ed.
London, 1881. A facsimile reprint of the 3rd edition,
London, 1766.

Morgan, Sydney Owenson, lady, The O'Briens and the O'Flahertys;
a National Tale. 4 v. Philadelphia, 1828.

Morgan, Sydney Owenson, lady, Woman; or, Ida of Athens. 2 v.
Philadelphia, 1809.

Reeve, Clara, The Progress of Romance. N. Y. 1930. A facsimile reprint of the Colchester, 1785 edition. This is a
commentary on the history of English fiction.

Richardson, Samuel, The Works of Samuel Richardson. 12 v.
London, 1883.

Rowson, Susanna Haswell, Charlotte Temple. N. Y., 1905.

Rowson, Susanna Haswell, Charlotte's Daughter. Boston, 1828.
With a memoir of Mrs. Rowson by Samuel L. Knapp.

Rush, Rebecca, Kelroy. Philadelphia, 1812.

Tenney, Tabitha, Female Quixotism: Exhibited in the Romantic Opinions and Extravagant Adventures of Dorcasina Sheldon. 3 v. Boston, 1841.

Thayer, Caroline Matilda, The Gamesters; or Ruins of Innocence. Boston, 1828.

Trimmer, Sarah, The Robins; or, Fabulous Histories, Designed for the Instruction of Children, Respecting Their Treatment of Animals. Boston, 1822.

Trumbull, John, The Poetical Works of John Trumbull. 2 v. Hartford, 1820.

Tyler, Royall, The Contrast. Boston, 1920.

[Warren, Mercy], The Group. Boston, 1775.

Warren, Mercy, Poems, Dramatic and Miscellaneous. Boston, 1790.

[Wood, Sarah], Derval; or the Speculator. Portsmouth, 1801.

[Wood, Sarah], Ferdinand and Elmira: A Russian Story. Baltimore, 1804.

[Wood, Sarah], Julia and the Illuminated Baron, A Novel: Founded on Recent Facts, Which Have Transpired in the Course of the Late Revolution of Moral Principles in France. Portsmouth, 1800.


III. Magazines

American Monthly Magazine and Critical Review (New York), 1817-1819.

American Review and Literary Journal (New York), 1801-1802.

Analectic Magazine (Philadelphia), 1813-1820.

Boston Magazine, 1805-1806.

Boston Weekly Magazine, 1802-1805.

Edinburgh Review, 1802-1830.

Emerald (Boston), 1806-1808.

General Repository and Review (Cambridge), 1812-1813.

Lady's Magazine and Repository of Entertaining Knowledge
(Philadelphia), 1792-1793.

Literary Gazette: or, Journal of Criticism, Science, and the
Arts (Philadelphia), 1821.

Literary Magazine and American Register (Philadelphia), 1803-
1807.

Massachusetts Magazine (Boston), 1789-1796.

Monthly Anthology (Boston), 1803-1811.

Monthly Magazine and American Review (New York), 1799-1800.

New York Mirror, 1823-1830.

North American Review (Boston), 1815-1830.

Port Folio (Philadelphia), 1801-1827.

Portico (Baltimore), 1816-1818.

Quarterly Review (London), 1809-1830.

United States Literary Gazette (Boston), 1826.

United States Review and Literary Gazette (Boston), 1826-1827.

Universal Asylum and Columbian Magazine (Philadelphia), 1786-
1792.

Western Monthly Review (Cincinnati), 1827-1830.

Western Review and Miscellaneous Magazine (Lexington), 1819-
1821.


IV. Travelers' Accounts

Candler, Isaac, A Summary View of America.   London, 1824.

Cobbett, William, A Year's Residence in the United States of America. London, 1819.

Davis, John, Travels of Four Years and a Half in the United States of America during 1798, 1799, 1800, 1801, and 1802. N. Y., 1909.

Duncan, John M., Travels through Part of the United States and Canada in 1818 and 1819. 2 v. Glasgow, 1823.

Dwight, Timothy, Travels in New-England and New-York. 4 v. New Haven, 1821.

Fearon, Henry B., A Narrative of a Journey of Five Thousand Miles through the Eastern and Western States of America. London, 1818.

Hall, Francis, Travels in Canada, and the United States, in 1816 and 1817. 2nd ed. London, 1819.

Hodgson, Adam, Letters from North America. 2 v. London, 1824.

Paulding, James Kirke, Letters from the South. 2 v. N. Y., 1817.

Paulding, James Kirke, A Sketch of Old England. 2 v. N. Y., 1822.

Poletika, Petr Ivanovitch, A Sketch of the Internal Condition of the United States of America, and of Their Political Relations with Europe. Baltimore, 1826.

Tudor, William, Letters on the Eastern States. N. Y., 1820.

Vigne, Godfrey T., Six Months in America. 2 v. London, 1832.

Wright, Frances, Views of Society and Manners in America, N. Y., 1821.

## V. Memoirs, Letters, Diaries, and Collected and Miscellaneous Works

Adams, Abigail, Letters of Mrs. Adams. Charles Francis Adams, ed. 2 v. Boston, 1840.

Adams, Abigail, and John Adams, Familiar Letters of John Adams and His Wife, Abigail Adams, During the Revolution. Charles Francis Adams, ed. N. Y., 1876.

Adams, Hannah, An Alphabetical Compendium of the Various Sects Which Have Appeared in the World from the Beginning of the Christian AEra to the Present Day. Boston, 1784.

Adams, Hannah, A Dictionary of All Religions. N. Y., 1817.

Adams, Hannah, A Memoir of Miss Hannah Adams, Written by Herself. Boston, 1832.

Adams, Hannah, A Narrative of the Controversy between the Rev. Jedidiah Morse, D.D. and the Author. Boston, 1814.

Adams, John, The Works of John Adams. Charles Francis Adams, ed. 10 v. Boston, 1850-1856.

Adams, John, and Mercy Warren, Correspondence between John Adams and Mercy Warren Relating to Her "History of the American Revolution," July-August, 1807. Massachusetts Historical Society Collections, 5th ser. Vol. IV. Boston, 1878.

The Articulate Sisters, Passages from Journals and Letters of the Daughters of President Josiah Quincy of Harvard University. M. A. DeWolfe Howe, ed. Cambridge, 1946.

Barbauld, Anna Laetitia, The Works of Anna Laetitia Barbauld, with a Memoir by Lucy Aikin. 3 v. Boston, 1826.

Barbauld, Anna Laetitia, The Works of Anna Laetitia Barbauld, with a Memoir by Lucy Aikin. 2 v. N. Y., 1826. The contents of these two editions differ, despite their identical titles and dates.

Benger, Elizabeth Ogilvy, Memoirs of the Late Mrs. Elizabeth Hamilton. 2 v. London, 1818.

Bentley, William, The Diary of William Bentley, D.D. 4 v. Salem, 1905-1914.

Bowne, Eliza Southgate, A Girl's Life Eighty Years Ago, Selections from the Letters of Eliza Southgate Bowne. N. Y., 1887.

Channing, William Ellery, and Lucy Aikin, Correspondence of William Ellery Channing, D.D., and Lucy Aikin, from 1826 to 1842. Anna Laetitia Le Breton, ed. Boston, 1874.

Chapone, Hester Mulso, The Works of Mrs. Chapone. 4 v. Boston, 1809.

Child, Lydia Maria, The Biographies of Madame de Staël, and Madame Roland. Boston, 1832.

Child, Lydia Maria, Letters from New York. 2nd ser. N. Y., 1845. Contains her reminiscences of Hannah Adams.

Chronicles of a Pioneer School from 1792 to 1833, Being the History of Miss Sarah Pierce and Her Litchfield School. Emily Noyes Vanderpoel, comp., Elizabeth C. Barney Buel, ed. Cambridge, 1903.

D'Arblay, Frances Burney, Diary & Letters of Madame D'Arblay. Charlotte Barrett, ed. 6 v. London, 1904.

Dunlap, William, The Life of Charles Brockden Brown. 2 v. Philadelphia, 1815. Volume I contains the second part of Brown's Alcuin.

Dwight, Elizabeth A., Memorials of Mary Wilder White, A Century Ago in New England. Mary Wilder Tileston, ed. Boston, 1903.

Edgeworth, Maria, The Works of Maria Edgeworth. 12 v. Boston, 1824.

Elwood, Anne Katharine Curteis, Memoirs of the Literary Ladies of England. 2 v. London, 1843.

Fisher, Josephine, "The Journal of Esther Burr," New England Quarterly, III (April, 1930), 297-315.

Franklin, Benjamin, The Works of Benjamin Franklin. Jared Sparks, ed. 10 v. Boston, 1838.

Franklin, Benjamin, The Writings of Benjamin Franklin. Albert H. Smyth, ed. 10 v. N. Y., 1905-1907. Franklin's Dogood Papers are in vol. II,

Gilbert, Ann Taylor, Autobiography and Other Memorials of Mrs. Gilbert. Josiah Gilbert, ed. London, 1878.

Godwin, William, Memoirs of the Author of A Vindication of the Rights of Woman. London, 1798.

Grant, Anne MacVicar, Memoir and Correspondence of Mrs. Grant of Laggan. J. P. Grant, ed. 3 v. 2nd ed. London, 1845.

Hunt, Leigh, Men, Women, and Books; a Selection of Sketches, Essays, and Critical Memoirs from His Uncollected Writings. 2 v. N. Y., 1847.

Jefferson, Thomas, Thomas Jefferson and Education in a Republic. Charles Flinn Arrowood, ed. N. Y., 1930.

Journal of the Proceedings of the Anthology Society. M. A. De Wolfe Howe, ed. Boston, 1910.

Le Breton, Anna Laetitia Aikin, Memories of Seventy Years by One of a Literary Family. Mrs. Herbert Martin, ed. London, 1884.

More, Hannah, The Complete Works of Hannah More. 7 v. N. Y., 1835.

Morgan, Sydney Owenson, lady, The Book of the Boudoir. 2 v. N. Y., 1829.

Morse, Jedidiah, An Appeal to the Public, on the Controversy Respecting the Revolution in Harvard College, and the Events Which Have Followed It; Occasioned by the Use Which Has Been Made of Certain Complaints and Accusations of Miss Hannah Adams against the Author. Charlestown, 1814.

Morton, Sarah Wentworth, My Mind and Its Thoughts. Boston, 1823.

Radcliffe, Ann, Gaston de Blondeville. 4 v. London, 1826. Volume I of this novel contains Thomas Noon Talfourd's valuable "Memoir of the Life and Writings of Mrs. Radcliffe," still the best biography.

Ramsay, David, Memoirs of the Life of Martha Laurens Ramsay. 2nd ed. Charlestown, 1812.

Roberts, William, Memoirs of the Life and Correspondence of Mrs. Hannah More. 2 v. N. Y., 1835.

Rowlandson, Mary, The Soveraignty & Goodness of God, together with the Faithfulness of His Promises Displayed, Being a Narrative of the Captivity and Restauration of Mrs. Mary Rowlandson. Boston, 1937. A facsimile reprint of the 2nd edition, Cambridge, 1682.

Taylor, Jane, The Writings of Jane Taylor. 5 v. Boston, 1832.

Trimmer, Sarah, Some Account of the Life and Writings of Mrs. Trimmer. London, 1825.

Walpole, Horace, The Letters of Horace Walpole. Peter Cunningham, ed. 9 v. London, 1891.

Walpole, Horace, The Yale Edition of Horace Walpole's Correspondence. W. S. Lewis et al., ed. 16 v. New Haven, 1937-1951.

Warren, Mercy, History of the Rise, Progress and Termination of the American Revolution. Interspersed with Biographical, Political and Moral Observations. 3 v. Boston, 1805.

Warren, James, John Adams, Mercy Warren and others, Warren-Adams Letters. 2 v. Boston, 1917-1925.

Winthrop, John, The History of New England from 1630 to 1649. James Savage, ed. 2 v. Boston, 1826.

## SECONDARY WORKS

## I. General History

Adams, Charles Francis, Three Episodes of Massachusetts History. 2 v. Boston, 1894.

Adamson, John W., A Short History of Education. Cambridge, 1930.

Barnard, H. C., A Short History of English Education from 1760 to 1944. London, 1947.

Bayne-Powell, Rosamond, Eighteenth Century London Life. London, 1937.

Bayne-Powell, Rosamond, The English Child in the Eighteenth Century. London, 1939.

Bryson, Gladys, Man and Society: the Scottish Inquiry of the Eighteenth Century. Princeton, 1945. An examination of the Scottish school of moral philosophy, several of whose members were considered authorities on female education.

Channing, Edward, History of the United States. 6 v. N. Y.,
1905-1925.

Cleveland, Catharine C., The Great Revival in the West, 1797-
1805. Chicago, 1916.

Craig, Hardin, "A Contribution to the Theory of the English
Renaissance," Philological Quarterly, VII (October, 1928),
321-333.

Fox, Dixon Ryan, "The Protestant Counter-Reformation in America,"
New York History, XVI (January, 1935), 19-35.

George, M. Dorothy, London Life in the XVIIIth Century. London,
1925.

Good, Harry G., Benjamin Rush and His Services to American Education. Berne, Ind., 1918.

Greene, Evarts B., "A Puritan Counter-Reformation," American
Antiquarian Society Proceedings, n.s., XLII (April, 1932),
17-46.

Grylls, Rosalie Glynn, William Godwin and His World. London,
1953. A sympathetic but detached modern evaluation of
Godwin and his circle, rich in historical background. Includes the best recent account of Mary Wollstonecraft.

Haraszti, Zoltan, John Adams and the Prophets of Progress.
Cambridge, 1952.

Hazen, Charles Downer, Contemporary American Opinion of the
French Revolution. Baltimore, 1897.

Jones, Howard Mumford, America and French Culture, 1750-1848.
Chapel Hill, 1927.

Keller, Charles Roy, The Second Great Awakening in Connecticut.
New Haven, 1942.

Koch, G. Adolf, Republican Religion. N. Y., 1933.

Lecky, William Edward Hartpole, A History of England in the
Eighteenth Century. 8 v. N. Y., 1878-1890.

Link, Eugene Perry, Democratic-Republican Societies, 1790-
1800. N. Y., 1942.

McMaster, John B., A History of the People of the United States.
7 v. N. Y., 1913.

Morgan, Edmund S., The Puritan Family. Boston, 1944.

Morison, Samuel Eliot, Builders of the Bay Colony. Boston, 1930.

Morison, Samuel Eliot, The Puritan Pronaos. N. Y., 1936.

Mott, Frank Luther, A History of American Magazines. 3 v. Cambridge, 1930-1938.

Owst, G. R., Literature and Pulpit in Medieval England. Cambridge, 1933.

Quinlan, Maurice J., Victorian Prelude. N. Y., 1941. An illuminating study of the effect of the eighteenth-century religious revival on English life and manners.

Rourke, Constance, The Roots of American Culture. N. Y., 1942.

Schlesinger, Arthur M., Learning How to Behave. N. Y., 1946.

Somervell, D. C., English Thought in the Nineteenth Century. N. Y., 1940.

Stauffer, Vernon, New England and the Bavarian Illuminati. N. Y., 1918.

Thrupp, Sylvia, The Merchant Class of Medieval London. Chicago, 1948.

Warren, Charles, "Elbridge Gerry, James Warren, Mercy Warren and the Ratification of the Federal Constitution in Massachusetts," Massachusetts Historical Society Proceedings, LXIV (Boston, 1932), 143-164.

Whiteley, J. H., Wesley's England, a Survey of XVIIIth Century Social and Cultural Conditions. London, 1938.

Wright, Louis B., Middle-Class Culture in Elizabethan England. Chapel Hill, 1935. A rich mine of material on the reading matter of England's rising middle class from about 1550 to 1650, throwing light on the cultural milieu out of which America's first settlers came.

## II. Literary History

Baker, Ernest A., The History of the English Novel. 10 v. London, 1938-1950.

Barry, Florence V., A Century of Children's Books. N. Y., 1923.

Baugh, Albert C., Tucker Brooke, Samuel C. Chew, Kemp Malone, and George Sherburn, A Literary History of England. Albert C. Baugh, ed. N. Y., 1948.

Blakey, Dorothy, The Minerva Press, 1790-1820. London, 1939. A fine scholarly study of the popular book trade and its practices during this period.

Boas, Frederick S., From Richardson to Pinero. London, 1936.

Bolton, C. K., "Circulating Libraries in Boston, 1765-1865," Colonial Society of Massachusetts Publications, XI (Boston, 1910), 196-20%.

Brown, Herbert R., "Elements of Sensibility in The Massachusetts Magazine," American Literature, I (November, 1929), 286-296.

Brown, Herbert R., "Richardson and Sterne in the Massachusetts Magazine," New England Quarterly, V (January, 1932), 65-82.

Brown, Herbert R., "Sensibility in Eighteenth-Century American Drama," American Literature, IV (March, 1932), 47-60.

Brown, Herbert R., The Sentimental Novel in America, 1789-1860. Durham, 1940. Both scholarly and entertaining, but somewhat weak in historical background. In this respect the book compares poorly with its English counterpart, Tompkins' Popular Novel in England (see below).

Cambridge History of English Literature. 15 v. Cambridge, 1932.

Collins, Arthur S., Authorship in the Days of Johnson, 1726-1780. London, 1927. Good well-rounded social history.

Collins, Arthur S., The Profession of Letters, 1780-1832. London, 1929.

Cowie, Alexander, The Rise of the American Novel. N. Y., 1948.

Cruse, Amy, The Englishman and his Books in the Early Nineteenth Century. N. Y., 1930.

Cruse, Amy, The Shaping of English Literature and the Readers' Share in the Development of Its Forms. N. Y., 1927.

Downs, Brian W., Richardson. London, 1928.

Ernle, Rowland Edmund Prothero, baron, The Light Reading of our Ancestors. N. Y., 1927. An excellent short survey of the rise of the novel, written with an eye to the underlying social and intellectual causes.

Gregory, Allene, The French Revolution and the English Novel. N. Y., 1915.

Heidler, Joseph Bunn, The History, from 1700 to 1800, of English Criticism of Prose Fiction (University of Illinois Studies in Language and Literature, XIII, no. 2). Urbana, 1928.

Kiefer, Monica, American Children through Their Books. Philadelphia, 1948.

Lanson, Gustave, Histoire de la Littérature Française. 19th ed. Paris, n.d.

Loshe, Lillie D., The Early American Novel. N. Y., 1907.

Lovett, Robert M., and Helen S. Hughes, The History of the Novel in England. Boston, 1932.

McDowell, Tremaine, "Sensibility in the Eighteenth Century American Novel," Studies in Philology, XXIV (July, 1927), 383-402.

Orians, G. Harrison, "Censure of Fiction in American Romances and Magazines, 1789-1810," PMLA, LII (March, 1937), 195-214.

Raddin, George G., An Early New York Library of Fiction. N. Y., 1940.

Smith, Bernard, Forces in American Criticism. N. Y., 1939.

Stephen, Leslie, English Literature and Society in the Eighteenth Century. London, 1904.

Taylor, John Tinnon, Early Opposition to the English Novel, The Popular Reaction from 1760-1830. N. Y., 1943.

Tinker, Chauncey Brewster, The Salon and English Letters. N. Y., 1915.

Tompkins, J. M. S., The Popular Novel in England, 1770-1800.
London, 1932. Both analytical and descriptive, this study
covers all aspects of the subject, including the rise of
the woman author and her professional problems, and women's
life as revealed in the novels.

Tyler, Moses Coit, The Literary History of the American Revolution, 1763-1783. 2 v. N. Y., 1897.

Woolf, Virginia, The Common Reader. 2 v. in 1. N. Y., 1948.

Wright, C. H. C., The Background of Modern French Literature.
Boston, 1926.

## III. Women's History

Abram, A., English Life and Manners in the Later Middle Ages.
London, 1913. The author's chapter on the position of
women contains a useful short survey of woman's legal
status under the common law and exceptions commonly made
to it in practice.

Benson, Mary Sumner, Women in Eighteenth-Century America, A
Study of Opinion and Social Usage. N. Y., 1935. An ex-
haustive catalogue of 18th century ideas without much
pattern or analysis.

Blanchard, Rae, "Richard Steele and the Status of Women,"
Studies in Philology, XXVI (July, 1929), 325-355. Contains
a clear and thorough survey of ideas about women's character, mind, education, and role in society which were current in the England of Steele's day.

Blease, W. Lyon, The Emancipation of English Women. London,
1913. Suffragist history.

Calhoun, Arthur W., A Social History of the American Family.
3 v. Cleveland, 1918.

Camden, Carroll, The Elizabethan Woman. Houston, 1952. A
curious piece of antiquarian history: a wealth of contemporary material served up helter-skelter in a sumptuous
format. Camden's discussion of ideas about women adds
nothing to that of Louis B. Wright in his Middle-Class
Culture in Elizabethan England.

Clark, Alice, The Working Life of Women in the Seventeenth Century. London, 1919. A study of the effects of rising capitalism on women's life in the 17th century: a major work in women's history, combining the approaches of economics and sociology.

Clark, David Lee, Brockden Brown and the Rights of Women. Austin, Tex., 1922.

Cometti, Elizabeth, "Women in the American Revolution," New England Quarterly, XX (September, 1947), 329-346.

Dexter, Elisabeth Anthony, Career Women of America, 1776-1840. Francestown, N. H., 1950. Mrs. Dexter is at her best in describing the activities of women in business. Her accounts of women in the professions are superficial and, because they take no account of historical change during the period, misleading.

Dexter, Elisabeth Anthony, Colonial Women of Affairs. 2nd ed. Boston, 1931. In this earlier book Mrs. Dexter turned fresh light on women's life in colonial times by showing how many were able to carry on "careers" in business and other fields within the home. A useful supplement to Alice Clark's study of the English side of this phenomenon in her Working Life of Women in the Seventeenth Century.

Earle, Alice Morse, Child Life in Colonial Days. N. Y., 1899. Mrs. Earle's books, now over 50 years old, are still valuable because they grew out of a close familiarity with the life and literature of her period both in England and America. She wrote for the general reader but treated her material with respect.

Earle, Alice Morse, Colonial Dames and Good Wives. Boston, 1895.

Earle, Alice Morse, Colonial Days in Old New York. N. Y., 1896.

Earle, Alice Morse, Customs and Fashions in Old New England. N. Y., 1894.

Earle, Alice Morse, Home Life in Colonial Days. N. Y., 1898.

Gardiner, Dorothy, English Girlhood at School. London, 1929. A comprehensive survey of women's education in England from the middle ages to the end of the 18th century, including all classes of the population.

Hemlow, Joyce, "Fanny Burney and the Courtesy Books," PMLA, LXV (September, 1950), 732-761.

Hentsch, Alice A., De la Littérature Didactique du Moyen Age S'Addressant Spécialement aux Femmes. Cahors, 1903. Excellent individual summaries and critical analyses of this literature: the writings of the church fathers, of the courtly love school, and of the moral preachment school of the later middle ages.

Hornbeak, Katherine G., Richardson's Family Letters and the Domestic Conduct Books (Smith College Studies in Modern Languages, XIX). Northampton, 1938.

Horner, Joyce M., The English Women Novelists and their Connection with the Feminist Movement (1688-1797) (Smith College Studies in Modern Languages, XI). Northampton, 1930.

Howard, George Elliott, A History of Matrimonial Institutions. 3 v. Chicago, 1904.

Humphreys, A. R., "The 'Rights of Woman' in the Age of Reason," Modern Language Review, XLI (July, 1946), 256-269. A sound brief survey of feminist ideas from Plato to the 18th century Enlightenment.

The Legacy of the Middle Ages. C. G. Crump and E. F. Jacob, eds. Oxford, 1926. Contains Eileen Power's classic essay on "The Position of Women," written with a broad view stimulating to the worker in women's history in any era.

MacCarthy, B. G., The Later Women Novelists, 1744-1818. Oxford, 1948. First-rate literary history. Viewpoint somewhat feminist but relatively unemotional.

MacCarthy, B. G., Women Writers, Their Contribution to the English Novel 1621-1744. Cork, 1945.

O'Malley, I. B., Women in Subjection, A Study of the Lives of Englishwomen before 1832. London, 1933. An ardent feminist surveys the lives of Englishwomen of all classes during the century before the rise of the woman's rights movement. Despite its bias this is an impressive book, thoroughly researched and written with fire.

Phillips, Jane Hake, "Addison and Steele and the Women of their Time" (unpublished undergraduate honors thesis, Smith College, 1938). In the Smith College Library.

Powell, Chilton Latham, English Domestic Relations, 1487-1653.
N. Y., 1917. A sound study of concepts of marriage as
revealed in the law, conduct books, theological writings,
etc.

Power, Eileen, Medieval English Nunneries. Cambridge, 1922.
Eileen Power's largest work, interesting to the historian
of women in any period for her emphasis on the monastic
life as a profession for unmarried upper-class women in
the middle ages.

Power, Eileen, Medieval People. 2nd ed. London, 1925.
Sketches of representative medieval characters, including
two women: a prioress and the wife of a well-to-do merchant
of Paris.

Reynolds, Myra, The Learned Lady in England, 1650-1760. Boston,
1920. This scholarly study deals both with individual
learned women and with popular attitudes toward "the learned
lady."

Smith, Frank, "The Authorship of 'An Occasional Letter of the
Female Sex'," American Literature, II (November, 1930),
277-280.

Spruill, Julia Cherry, Women's Life and Work in the Southern
Colonies. Chapel Hill, 1938. Social history at its best.

Stearns, Bertha M., "Before Godey's," American Literature, II
(November, 1930), 248-255.

Stearns, Bertha M., "Early English Periodicals for Ladies,"
PMLA, XLVIII (March, 1933), 38-60. Covers the period 1700-
1760.

Stearns, Bertha M., "Early New England Magazines for Ladies,"
New England Quarterly, II (July, 1929), 420-457.

Stearns, Bertha M., "Early New York Magazines for Ladies,"
New York History, XIV (January, 1933), 32-41.

Stearns, Bertha M., "Early Philadelphia Magazines for Ladies,"
Pennsylvania Magazine of History and Biography, LXIV
(October, 1940), 479-491.

Stearns, Bertha M., "Early Western Magazines for Ladies,"
Mississippi Valley Historical Review, XVIII (December, 1931),
319-330.

Utter, Robert P., and Gwendolyn B. Needham, Pamela's Daughters.
N. Y., 1936.

Violette, Augusta Genevieve, Economic Feminism in American Literature Prior to 1848 (University of Maine Studies, 2nd ser., no. 2). Orono, 1925.

Whitmore, Clara H., Women's Work in English Fiction, from the Restoration to the Mid-Victorian Period. N. Y., 1910.

Woody, Thomas, A History of Women's Education in the United States. N. Y., 1929.

Woolf, Virginia, A Room of One's Own. N. Y., 1929. Virginia Woolf's own brand of feminism: an explanation of why women writers appeared so late on the scene.

Wright, Louis B., "The Reading of Renaissance Englishwomen," Studies in Philology, XXVIII (October, 1931), 139-156.

Wright, Thomas, Womankind in Western Europe from the Earliest Times to the Seventeenth Century. London, 1869.

## IV. Biography

Ainger, Alfred, Lectures and Essays. 2 v. London, 1905. Volume I contains an essay on Mrs. Barbauld.

Brailsford, Henry Noel, Shelley, Godwin, and their Circle. N. Y. 1913.

Brightfield, Myron F., John Wilson Croker. Berkeley, 1940.

Brown, Alice, Mercy Warren. N. Y., 1896.

Campbell, Helen, Anne Bradstreet and her Time. Boston, 1891.

Chapman, Clayton Harding, "Benjamin Colman's Daughters," New England Quarterly, XXVI (June, 1953), 169-192.

Clark, David Lee, Charles Brockden Brown, Pioneer Voice of America. Durham, 1952.

Clarke, Isabel C., Maria Edgeworth, her Family and Friends. London, 1949.

Cole, Charles C., Jr., "Brockden Brown and the Jefferson Administration," Pennsylvania Magazine of History and Biography, LXXII (July, 1948), 253-263.

Compayré, Gabriel, Jean Jacques Rousseau and Education from Nature. N. Y., 1907.

Copinger, W. A., On the Authorship of the First Hundred Numbers of the "Edinburgh Review." Manchester, 1895.

Edgeworth, Maria, The Life and Letters of Maria Edgeworth. Augustus J. C. Hare, ed. 2 v. Boston, 1895.

Ellis, Grace A., Memoirs, Letters, and a Selection from the Poems and Prose Writings of Anna Laetitia Barbauld. 2.v. Boston, 1874.

Ellis, Grace A., The Story of the Life of Anna Laetitia Barbauld, with Many of her Letters. Boston, n.d.

Ellis, Harold Milton, Joseph Dennie and his Circle (University of Texas Studies in English, no. 3). Austin, 1915.

Field, Vena B., Constantia, A Study of the Life and Works of Judith Sargent Murray (University of Maine Studies, 2nd ser., no. 17). Orono, 1931.

Fitzpatrick, William John, The Friends, Foes, and Adventures of Lady Morgan. Dublin, 1859.

Hilbish, Florence, Charlotte Smith. Philadelphia, 1941.

Jones, M. G., Hannah More. Cambridge, 1952. A distinguished biography which recreates Hannah More as her contemporaries saw her.

McIntyre, Clara Frances, Ann Radcliffe in Relation to her Time. New Haven, 1920. This study fails to live up to the promise in its title.

McKee, William, Elizabeth Inchbald. Washington, D.C., 1935.

Menzies-Wilson, J., and Helen Lloyd, Amelia, The Tale of a Plain Friend. Oxford, 1937.

Morse, James King, Jedidiah Morse, A Champion of New England Orthodoxy. N. Y., 1939.

Nason, Elias, A Memoir of Mrs. Susanna Rowson. Albany, 1870.

Paul, C. Kegan, William Godwin: His Friends and Contemporaries. 2 v. Boston, 1876.

Paterson, Alice, The Edgeworths, A Study of Later Eighteenth Century Education. London, 1914.

Pendleton, Emily, and Harold Milton Ellis, Philenia, The Life and Works of Sarah Wentworth Morton, 1759-1846 (University of Maine Studies, XXXIV no. 4, 2nd ser. no. 20). Orono, 1931.

Platt, Harrison Gray, Jr., "Astraea and Celadon: An Untouched Portrait of Aphra Behn," PMLA, XLIX (June, 1934), 544-559.

Ravenel, Harriott Horry, Eliza Pinckney. N. Y., 1909.

Sackville-West, V., Aphra Behn, The Incomparable Astraea. London, 1937.

Schlesinger, Elizabeth Bancroft, "Cotton Mather and his Children," William and Mary Quarterly, 3rd ser. X (April, 1953), 181-189.

Shine, Hill, and Helen Chadwick Shine, The Quarterly Review under Gifford, Identification of Contributors, 1809-1824. Chapel Hill, 1949.

Shurter, R. L., "Mrs. Hannah Webster Foster and the Early American Novel," American Literature, IV (November, 1932), 306-308.

Slade, Bertha Coolidge, Maria Edgeworth, 1767-1849, A Bibliographical Tribute. London, 1937.

Sprague, William B., The Life of Jedidiah Morse, D.D. N. Y., 1874.

Stearns, Bertha M., "A Speculation Concerning Charles Brockden Brown," Pennsylvania Magazine of History and Biography, LIX (April, 1935), 99-105.

Stevenson, Lionel, The Wild Irish Girl, The Life of Sydney Owenson, Lady Morgan (1776-1859). London, 1936.

Thomson, C. Linklater, Jane Austen, A Survey. London, 1929.

Vail, R. G. W., Susanna Haswell Rowson, the Author of Charlotte Temple (American Antiquarian Society Proceedings, XLII). Worcester, 1932.

Van Doren, Carl, Benjamin Franklin. N. Y., 1941.

Warfel, Harry R., Charles Brockden Brown, American Gothic Novelist. Gainesville, Fla., 1949.

Warfel, Harry R., Noah Webster, Schoolmaster to America. N. Y., 1936.

Whicher, George Frisbie, The Life and Romances of Mrs. Eliza Haywood.  N. Y., 1915.

Wilson, Mona, Jane Austen and Some of her Contemporaries. London, 1938.

INDEX